PUNCHES ON THE PAGE

PUNCHES ON THE PAGE

A BOXING ANTHOLOGY

David Rayvern Allen

MAINSTREAM
PUBLISHING

EDINBURGH AND LONDON

First published in Great Britain in 1998 by
MAINSTREAM PUBLISHING COMPANY (EDINBURGH) LTD
7 Albany Street
Edinburgh EH1 3UG

This edition 1998

ISBN 1 85158 987 2

A catalogue record for this book is available from the British Library

Typeset in Van Dijck MT and Giovanni Book
Printed and bound in Great Britain by Butler and Tanner Ltd, Frome

Contents

Introduction

David Rayvern Allen

The boxer is a hero. A hero because he moves in an area where few dare to go. We need him as, vicariously, we fight through him, although not as a symbol of virility. This intangible relationship is never admitted openly and seldom secretly, even to ourselves. But the boxer it is who allows a safe glimpse beneath the veneer of civilisation and who among us manages to be civilised all the time? Back to primitive life in the playgrounds of our youth we go where everything seemed attainable through physical firepower until reality struck – hard.

In our arena seat those rationalisations recede as the pre-fight rituals take place. The M.C.'s magniloquence engages our emotions – regardless. Thought is suspended and pretence can begin. But not in the ring. There, dreams wait for the end of the contest.

Like no other sport boxing is personal. Save synthetic leather there is nothing between two bodies striving to batter each other into submission. Cricket has chest-protectors, football has ankle-guards, motor-racing has crash helmets and boxing has – well, bare flesh. Cauliflower ears, squashed nose, bruised cheeks, cut eyes, split lips; oh yes, boxing is personal all right, deeply personal – intimate, in fact.

Once the paraphernalia has been removed and the bell has been rung the crowd's roar builds to a crescendo. Pent-up feeling is released and cheers and cat-calls compete in tandem. The powerful ring-lights emphasise the isolation of the fighters. Boxing is not a team game and the spectators are quickly redundant – they continue to shout, but are not heard. Soon in an evenly matched contest, the shouts become sporadic and the dominant sounds are of the squeaking of soles on resin, the plops of padded gloves on skin and the gasps and heavy breathing of extreme effort. Punctuation is provided occasionally by the referee and regularly by the timekeeper. The seconds flap and cajole every three minutes oblivious of the curvaceous round-number carriers who are chasséing around the ring raising the libido of the male audience. The boxers' concentration and energy are reserved for one another. This is, essentially, a private engagement and everyone else takes the role of bystanders at a stranger's funeral.

That impressionistic picture is mostly unchanging and instantly recognisable to all fight fans whether or not they have thought about it in those terms. The scenario is, of course, equally conspicuous to all those who are not fight fans and have thought about it in entirely antipathetical terms.

To them the very notion of enjoying a boxing match is abhorrent. Any society that has access to the benefits of culture should not, they maintain, need to pander to basic instincts. And beside the high moral view, the pro-abolitionists voice pragmatic concerns; the threat to life itself and of permanent brain damage and the elements of corruption within the sport allowing mercenary operators to control boxers ill-equipped to cope.

No sensible person would deny the validity of a lot of the endlessly debated arguments surrounding boxing and its future existence. The most hardened fight *aficionado* is, at times, ambivalent about their sport and harboured doubts are more likely to be triggered amid the hothouse atmosphere of a one-sided contest that has been allowed to continue too long, than by cold polemic in the realms of the media. Many would say that some progress has already been made with the likelihood of financial chicanery being exposed and with the investment in better medical supervision before, during and after fights. And if, in an ideal world, both the deceit and the death could not happen, that is not to demur regarding the need for further improvements all round. But despite the soul searching, raw combat will always exist, not just because it cannot be suppressed but because it is an integral part of human nature.

The fact that many fight-watchers identify so strongly with this part of their disposition has nothing to do with sadistic blood lust nor the acquiring of courage by osmosis. Rather it is an expression of affinity for gladiatorial tussle. And the boxers themselves, in spite of our ifs and buts and their biffs and butts, positively want the experience of pitting their skill and strength against that of an opponent. Aware of the risks, they are consenting adults boldly taking part in an activity that is on the edge. In an age where so much of life is in the middle, who are we to try and stop them?

Why it seems unavoidable to lead any reflection on boxing with some kind of vindication I am not quite sure. Asked that very question a recent writer took refuge in humour: 'Boxing is as old a game as the oldest game' he replied, 'and over the years someone has always ended up flat on their back'. It is tempting to add that, if indeed fighting is as natural as sex, generally boxers do not perform as often – that is, in the ring.

Men have fought with their fists in competition since becoming bipeds. The ancient Olympics in Greece included bouts from the outset and the Ionian Homer relates in *The Iliad* of a fight following the chariot race at the funeral games of Patroclus during the last year of the siege of Troy. Four or five centuries later the Athenians Socrates and Plato in the *Dialogues* found in boxing a universal reference and so did the Roman Virgil in the *Aeneid* during the period when BC approached AD. Disproving the theory that they never came back, the old champion Entellus returns to see off the young challenger Dares.

The sport has always engaged the intellectual and particularly the literary mind. Sir Arthur Conan Doyle no less, formerly a gymnasium boxer and a frequenter of the National Sporting Club, nearly accepted an invitation to referee the Jack Johnson–Jim Jeffries world heavyweight clash. Wisely perhaps he preferred to bask in kudos from his historical romance *Rodney Stone* which focused on the English Prize Ring of a hundred years earlier. Other *literateurs* who have found boxing an inspiration to their pen spring readily to mind: Victor Hugo; Ernest Hemingway; O. Henry; Irwin Shaw; Paul Gallico; Arnold Bennett and John Masefield.

None of these names provide pieces for this anthology and perhaps their absence is explained by most of them choosing boxing as a catalyst for fiction rather than as a basis of reality. The concentration on the pages that follows is firmly first-hand, either autobiographical, biographical or with ringside report. Authenticity has been a guiding factor and nothing gives a closer impression of towering events in boxing's history than to read the actual words of the practitioners, John L. Sullivan, James J. Corbett, Gene Tunney, Willie Pep, Rocky Graziano, Jake La Motta and Max Schmeling or the deliberations of the professional observers, Jimmy Cannon, Frank G. Menke, A.J. Liebling, Jack Birtley, George Whiting, Harry Mullan, Reg Gutteridge and Bob Mee. Oh yes, and who would be without the spellbinding George Bernard Shaw adding his mordant wit to boxing's rich republic of letters?

In some cases with those inside the ropes literary help has been at hand, but it is *their* thoughts and *their* expressions that we hear. In all cases with those outside the ropes the descriptions have such vividity as to make us feel we had been present.

The action in these articles and extracts conveniently covers most of this century and a little of the last – a hundred years of epic combat; modern boxing in its widest historical sense, from the dying days of old-fashioned pugilism to the early days of new-fashioned pyrotechnics which provide an ostentatious overture to many recent promotions.

Not long ago on an American TV station, a self-confessed sceptic and coward said that he was exploring the world of boxing to try and find where intelligence ends and courage begins, though he did not expect to find an answer. He could not perhaps realise that courage can only begin where intelligence exists.

Throughout this book are to be found remarkable feats by remarkable people who, in the pursuit of what they do best, have given their lives and ours another dimension. It was that outstanding sports journalist Hugh McIlvanney who once wrote that 'for some of us boxing, with all its thousand ambiguities, offers in its best moments a thrill as pure and basic as a heartbeat'.

An imperishable line to cling on to as the stories unfold.

David Rayvern Allen
Chorleywood, 1998

A Visit with John L. Sullivan

Nellie Bly

John L. Sullivan is generally considered to be the last of the old pugilists and the first of the modern champions. Bridging what, in fact, was an overlapping division between the bare-knuckles of the prize-ring and the 'fair-sized, best quality new gloves' prescribed by John Sholto Douglas, Marquess of Queensberry, his boast was that he could lick anyone in the world.

Certainly the sporting folk of Boston, Massachusetts, entertained no doubts about the ability of the local lad. In August 1887 they presented Sullivan with a glittering belt containing no less than 397 diamonds that were configured to spell out his name, emblematic of his standing at the pinnacle of the fight game.

The oppressive heat and humidity of mid-summer Mississippi was not the ideal time to stage the last bare-knuckle championship fight in the USA. Despite the temperature, or perhaps because of it, Sullivan took 75 rounds to batter Jake Kilrain into submission at Richburg on 8 July 1889. In the course of the bout Kilrain was off his feet 48 times.

At his training headquarters six weeks before, Sullivan had given an interview to Nellie Bly, who was shortly to gain fame herself when she circled the globe in over a week less than it had supposedly taken Phileas Fogg, the hero of Jules Verne's romance Around the World in Eighty Days.

Bly, whose real name was Elizabeth Cochrane, had adopted the nom de plume *from the title of a Stephen Foster song. She was a star feature writer for the* New York World.

If John L. Sullivan isn't able to whip any pugilist in the world I would like to see the man who is. I went to Belfast, NY, to see him last week and I was surprised. Why? Well, I will tell you.

I have often thought that the sparring instinct is inborn in everything – except women and flowers, of course. I have seen funny little spring roosters, without one feather's sprout to crow about, fight like real men. And then the boys! Isn't it funny how proud they are of their muscle, and how quiet the boy is who hasn't any? Almost as soon as a boy learns to walk he learns to jump into a position of defence and double up his fists.

We reached Belfast about half past seven in the morning and were the only passengers for that place. Mr William Muldoon's house, where Mr Sullivan is training, is in the prettiest part of the town and only a short distance from the hotel. Fearing that Mr Sullivan would go out for a walk and that I would miss him, I went immediately to the Muldoon cottage.

One would never imagine from the surroundings that a prize-fighter was being trained there. The house is a very pretty little two-storey building, surrounded by the smoothest and greenest of green lawns, which helps to intensify the spotless whiteness of the cottage. A wide verandah surrounds the three sides of the cottage, and the easy chairs and hammocks give it a most enticing look of comfort. Large maple trees shade the house from the glare of the sun.

I rang the bell, and when a coloured man came in answer I sent my letter of introduction to Mr Muldoon. A handsome young man, whose broad shoulders were neatly fitted with a grey corduroy coat, came into the room, holding a light grey cap in his hand. His face was youthful, his eyes blue, his expression pleasing, his smile brought two dimples to punctuate his rosy cheeks, his bearing was easy and most graceful, and this was the champion wrestler and athlete, William Muldoon.

'We have just returned from our two-mile walk,' he said, when I told him I had come to see Mr Sullivan, 'and Mr Sullivan is just being rubbed down. If you will excuse me one moment I will tell him.'

In a few moments Mr Muldoon returned, followed by a man whom I would never have taken for the great and only Sullivan. He was a tall man, with enormous shoulders, and wore dark trousers, a light cheviot coat and vest and slippers. In his hand he held a light cloth cap. He paused almost as he entered the room in a half-bashful way, and twisted his cap in a very boyish but not ungraceful manner.

'Miss Bly, Mr Sullivan,' said Mr Muldoon, and I looked into the great fighter's dark, bright eyes as he bent his broad shoulders before me.

'Mr Sullivan, I would like to shake hands with you,' I said, and he took my hand with a firm, hearty grasp, and with a hand that felt small and soft. Mr Muldoon excused himself, and I was left to interview the great John L.

'I came here to learn all about you, Mr Sullivan, so will you please begin by telling me at what time you get up in the morning,' I said.

'Well, I get up about six o'clock and get rubbed down,' he began, in a matter-of-fact way. 'Then Muldoon and I walk and run a mile or a mile and a half away and then back. Just as soon as we get in I am given a showerbath, and after being thoroughly rubbed down again I put on an entire fresh outfit.'

'What kind of clothing do you wear for your walk? Heavy?' I asked.

'Yes, I wear a heavy sweater and a suit of heavy corduroy buttoned tightly. I also wear gloves. After my walk I put on a fresh sweater, so that I won't take cold.'

'What's a sweater?' I asked.

'I'll show you,' he said with a smile and, excusing himself, he went out. In a moment he returned with a garment in his hand. It was a very heavy knit garment, with long sleeves and a standing collar. It was all in one piece and, I imagine, weighed several pounds. 'Well, what do you wear a sweater for, and why do you take such violent walks?' I asked, my curiosity being satisfied as to the strange 'sweater'.

'I wear a sweater to make me warm, and I walk to reduce my fat and to harden my muscles. Last Friday I lost six pounds and last Saturday I lost six and a half pounds. When I came here I weighed 237 pounds, and now I weigh 218. Before I leave here I will weigh only 195 pounds.'

'Do you take a cold showerbath when your walk is finished?'

'No, never, I don't believe in cold water. It chills the blood. I always have my showerbath of a medium temperature.'

'How are you rubbed down, then, as you term it?'

'I have two men give me a brisk rubbing with their hands. Then they rub me down with a mixture of ammonia, camphor and alcohol.'

'What do you eat?'

'I eat nothing fattening. I have oatmeal for breakfast and meat and bread for dinner, and cold meat and stale bread for supper. I eat no sweets or potatoes. I used to smoke all the day, but since I came here I haven't seen a cigar. Occasionally, Mr Muldoon gives me a glass of ale, but it doesn't average one a day.'

'Then training is not very pleasant work?'

'It's the worst thing going. A fellow would rather fight twelve dozen times than train once, but it's got to be done,' and he leaned back in the easy chair with an air of weariness. 'After breakfast I rest awhile,' he continued, 'and then putting on our heaviest clothes again we start out at 10.30 for our 12-mile run and walk, which we do in two hours. We generally go across the fields to Mr Muldoon's farm because it is all uphill work and makes us warm. When we get back I am rubbed down again and at one we have dinner. In the afternoon we wrestle, punch a bag, throw football, swing Indian clubs and dumbbells, practise the chest movement and such things until suppertime. It's all right to be here when the sun is out, but after dark it's the dreariest place I ever struck. I wouldn't live here if they gave me the whole country.'

The 'Champion Rest', the name by which Mr Muldoon's home is known, is surrounded by two graveyards, a church, the priest's home and a little cottage occupied by two old maids.

'I couldn't sleep after five o'clock this morning on account of Mr Muldoon's cow. It kept up a hymn all the morning and the birds joined in the chorus. It's no use to try to sleep here after daybreak. The noise would knock out anything.'

'Do you like prize-fighting?' I asked Mr Sullivan, after he had laid his complaint about the 'singing cow' before Mrs Muldoon.

'I don't,' he replied. 'Of course I did once, or rather I was fond of travelling about and the excitement of the crowds, but this is my last fight.'

'Why?'

'Well, I am tired and I want to settle down. I am getting old,' and he leaned back wearily.

'What is your age?'

'I was born the 15th of October, 1858. I began prize-fighting when I was only 19 years old. How did I start? Well, I had a match with a prize man who had never been downed, and I was the winner. This got me lots of notice, so I went through the country giving exhibitions. I have made plenty of money in my day, but I have been a fool and today I have nothing. It came easy and went easy. I have provided well for my father and mother, and they are in comfortable circumstances.'

'What will you do if you stop fighting?'

'If I win this fight I will travel for a year giving sparring exhibitions, and then I will settle down. I have always wanted to run a hotel in New York, and if I am successful I think I shall spend the rest of my life as an hotel proprietor.'

'How much money have you made during your career as a prize-fighter?'

'I have made $500,000 or $600,000 in boxing. I made $125,000 from 26 September 1883 to 26 May 1884, when I travelled through the country offering $1,000 to anyone I couldn't knock out in four rounds, which takes 12 minutes.'

'How do you dress when you go in a prize-ring?'

'I wear knee breeches, stockings and shoes, and no shirt.'

'Why no shirt?'

'Because a man perspires so freely that if he wears a shirt he is liable to chill, and a chill is always fatal in a prize-ring. I took a chill when I fought with Mitchell, but it didn't last long.'

'What kind of shoes do you wear?'

'Regular spike shoes. They have three big spikes to prevent slipping.'

'How will you fight Kilrain, with or without gloves?'

'I will fight Kilrain according to the London prize-ring rules. That's without gloves and allows wrestling and throwing a man down. We get a rest every 30 seconds. Under the Marquess of Queensberry rules we wear gloves, anything under 11 ounces. They give us three minutes to a round under the Queensberry, and when the three minutes are up you have to rest whether you could whip your man the next instant or not.'

'Your hands look very soft and small for a fighter.'

'Do they?' and he held one out to me for inspection. 'My friends tell me they look like hams,' and he laughed. 'I wear number nine gloves.'

I examined his hand, he watching me with an amused expression. It looks a small hand to bear the record of so many 'knockout' elbows. The fingers were straight and shapely. The closely trimmed nails were a lovely oval and pink. The only apparent difference was the great thickness through.

'Feel my arm,' he said, with a bright smile, as he doubled it up. I tried to feel the muscle, but it was like a rock. With both my hands I tried to span it, but I couldn't. Meanwhile the great fellow sat there watching me with a most boyish expression of amusement.

'By the time I am ready to fight there won't be any fat on my hands or face. They will be as hard as a bone. Do I harden them? Certainly. If I didn't I would have pieces knocked off of me. I have a mixture of rock salt and white wine and vinegar and several other ingredients which I wash my hands and face with.'

'Do you hit a man on the face and neck and anywhere you can?' I asked.

'Certainly, any place above the belt that I get a chance,' and he smiled.

'Don't you hate to hit a man so?'

'I don't think about it,' still smiling.

'When you see that you have hurt him don't you feel sorry?'

'I never feel sorry until the fight is over.'

'How do you feel when you get hit very hard?'

The dark, bright eyes glanced at me lazily and the deep, deep voice said with feeling: 'I only want a chance to hit back.'

'Did you ever see a man killed in the ring?'

'No, I never did, and I only knew of one fellow who died in the ring, and that was Walker, who died at Philadelphia from neglect after the fight was over.'

Although I had my breakfast before reaching Mr Muldoon's cottage I accepted his proposal to break bread with him and his guests. At a nearer view the dining-room did not lose any of its prettiness and the daintiness of everything – the artistic surroundings, the noiseless and efficient coloured waiter, the open windows on both sides, giving pretty views of green lawns and shady trees; the canary birds swelling their yellow throats occasionally with sweet little thrills, the green parrot climbing up its brass cage and talking about 'crackers', the white table linen and beautiful dishes, down to the large bunch of fragrant lilacs and another of beautifully shaped and coloured wild flowers, separated by a slipper filled with velvety pansies – was all entirely foreign to any idea I had ever conceived of prize-fighters and their surroundings.

Yes, and they were all perfectly at ease and happy. At one end of the table sat Mrs Muldoon and facing her was Mr Muldoon. Next to Mrs Muldoon sat my companion, then came myself, and next Mr Sullivan. On the opposite side were the assistant trainers, Mr Barnitt, a well-bred, scholarly looking man, and Mr Cleary, a smooth-faced, mischievous man who doesn't look much past boyhood. Mr Sullivan's brother, who is anxious to knock out somebody, sat opposite Mr Sullivan. And the wild flowers which graced the table were gathered by these great, strong men while taking their morning walk through the country.

About a mile from Champion Rest, his town home, is Mr Muldoon's beautiful farm of 70 acres, which is well stocked with fine cattle. In the rear of Champion Rest are the barn and the training quarters. On the first floor are three stalls, fitted out after the latest improved method, where Mr Muldoon keeps his favourite horses. Everything is as clean and pleasant as in a dwellinghouse.

In the next room, suspended from the ceiling, is a rugby football, which Mr Sullivan pounds regularly every day in a manner which foretells hard times for Kilrain's head. The big football with which they play ball daily is also kept here. It is enormous and so heavy that when Mr Muldoon dropped it into my arms I almost toppled over. Upstairs the floor is covered with a white wrestling pad, where the two champions wrestle every afternoon. In one corner is a collection of dumbbells, from medium weight to the heaviest, and several sizes of Indian clubs. Fastened to one side of the wall is a chest expander, which also comes in for daily use.

Downstairs is Champion Muldoon's den. Everything about it, as about the barn, is of a hardwood finish. There is no plaster nor paper anywhere. In one corner of the den is a glass case, where hang a fur-lined overcoat and several other garments. Along the case is suspended a gold-headed cane. In the centre of the room is a writing table, with everything ready for use. Along one side of the hall is a rattan lounger, at the foot of which is spread a yellow fur rug. The floor is neatly carpeted, and several rocking chairs prove that the den is for comfort.

The walls are covered with photographs of well-known people and among them several of Modjeska, with whom Mr Muldoon at one time travelled. There are also a number of photographs of Mr Muldoon in positions assumed in posing as Greek statues. On a corner table are albums filled with photographs of prominent athletes, and scrapbooks containing hundreds of notices of Champion Muldoon's favourite authors – Bryant, Longfellow and, I believe, Shakespeare.

'I don't make any money by this,' said Mr Muldoon, in speaking about turning his home into training quarters, 'but I was anxious to see Mr Sullivan do justice to himself in this coming fight. It was a case of a fallen giant, so I thought to get him away from all bad influences and to get him in good trim. This is the healthiest place in the country and one of the most difficult to reach – two desirable things. On the way here we had a special car, but there were more people in our car than in any other. When we go to New Orleans we will keep our car locked and none but Mr Sullivan's backers and representatives of the press will be admitted. Mr Sullivan is the most obedient man I ever saw. He hasn't asked for a drink or a smoke since he came here and takes what I allow him without a murmur. It is a pleasure to train him.'

'Does Mr Sullivan never get angry?' I asked.

'If you would hear him and Mr Barnitt sometimes, you would think they were going to eat one another,' said Mrs Muldoon.

'When he gets angry he runs over the fields until his good humour returns,' said Mr Barnitt, while Mr Muldoon said that Mr Sullivan was as docile as a lamb. They all spoke in praise of his strong will power and his childlike obedience.

'You are the first woman who ever interviewed me,' said Mr Sullivan in the afternoon, 'and I have given you more than I ever gave any reporter in my life. They generally manufacture things and credit them to me, although some are mighty good fellows.'

'When reporters act all right we will give them all they want,' said Mr Muldoon. 'The other day a fresh reporter came here, and he thought because he was going to interview prize-fighters he would have to be tough, so he said, "Where's old Sullivan?" That queered him. We wouldn't give him a line.'

'Yes, he came up to me first and said, "Where's old Sullivan?"' said Mr Sullivan. 'And I told him, "In the barn." And he soon got put out of there for his toughness.'

At suppertime Mr Cleary had a great story to tell about his Irish bird trap. He had caught one robin, which Mrs Muldoon released, and another had left his tail behind him. Then Mr Barnitt and Mr Sullivan's brother told how they had put some bird feathers in the cage to cheat the bird trapper.

And then the carriage came to take us to the train, and after I bade them all goodbye I shook hands with John L. Sullivan and wished him success in the coming fight, and I believe he will have it, too, don't you?

New York World
26 May 1889

Sullivan v Corbett

James J. Corbett

Date: 7 September 1892
Place: New Orleans, USA
Event: The first heavyweight title fight with gloves under the Queensberry rules

Sullivan weighed just over 15 stones. Corbett just under 13 stones. At 26, Corbett had a seven-year advantage in age. The purse was $25,000, plus a $20,000 stake.

'Gentleman Jim' Corbett was an original. One of the builders of modern boxing technique, he scientifically employed subterfuge and tactics as a primary weapon. Articulate and with polished manners, he was also something of an iconoclast – liking not to conform. The boxing fraternity therefore tended to regard him with some suspicion, perhaps feeling patronised, but in the world outside the sweaty gymnasiums and the unfumigated offices of the promoters, Corbett gained respect and appreciation.

This account of the fight is from The Roar of the Crowd, Corbett's life story told in his own words with literary assistance from Robert Gordon Anderson.

I started in to do some light training in the Southern Athletic Club and all the time thousands of people were in and out watching me. There were also large audiences at the other club watching Sullivan, and after seeing both of us, the bettors decided that instead of three to one on Sullivan the odds should go up to four to one. This increase was due, I think, to our difference in weights.

If I had ever relied much on others' opinions I wouldn't have had much confidence or strength left for the fight. Even my old friend from California, Tom Williams, who had backed me heavily in the Choynski fight, and had also seen me fight my 61 rounds with Peter Jackson, blew into New Orleans and bet, so someone was kind enough to tell me, $5,000 on Sullivan. Not because I was hurt at all, but simply because I liked Williams, I wrote him a letter the day before the fight. In it I said: 'Tom, I understand you are betting on Sullivan. I'm not mad, but I wish you would switch your bet and put it on me. I'm in splendid condition. You saw me fight Choynski and Jackson. You know I can go the distance; and no man who has lived the life that Sullivan has lived can beat me in a finish fight.' A few years later, when I was going abroad, I happened to run into Tom Williams on the steamer. We were talking over old times and got down to this fight. 'Do you remember the letter you wrote me,' he said, 'before your fight with Sullivan, telling me to bet on you?'

'Yes,' I replied, and somehow managed not to grin.

'Well,' continued Williams, 'after I received your letter I went out and bet a thousand more on Sullivan!'

I had also written to my father and figured he would receive the letter a day or two before the fight – which he did. I told him in what good condition I was, and prophesied that by taking my time and being careful I would win the fight between the twentieth and twenty-fifth round; and my dear old dad wore that letter out after the fight, just as he did the telegram after the Kilrain battle.

The excitement in New Orleans was intense from the start, as this was the first heavyweight championship fight ever arranged to be fought under the protection of the police. All other fights up to this time had been under London prize-ring rules and with bare knuckles, and, being against the law, had been pulled off in private.

Just before we left New York for New Orleans, I had told Brady to see how much money he could dig up to bet on me. He took all the money his wife had and what he could skirmish up himself, and it amounted to $3,000 – we had used up so much for training expenses; but that morning I gave it to Brady and said, 'You take this 900 and the 3,000 you have, and go down and put it on me.'

'Jim,' he said, 'I'll bet my 3,000, but you had better keep your money. If we should lose the fight, that's all we'd have, and we'll have to ride the brakes out of town.'

So after thinking it over, I took his advice and kept my 900, Brady going downtown to bet the 3,000 – four to one.

In a couple of hours he came back, all excitement, and exclaimed: 'They're betting five to one on Sullivan!'

'That's great!' I replied. 'Did you put the money up?'

'No,' he answered, looking a little sheepish. Then he added, 'Don't you think, Jim, we'd better keep it in case you get licked?'

I got angry at this.

'You fool!' I blurted out. 'You were willing to take four to one, but now when it's five to one you get cold feet. Sullivan and I are just the same as when it was three to one: we haven't changed any.'

Then, pushing out of the door, I gave him this parting message: 'Don't you come back here unless that 3,000 is on!'

I had noticed that the strain was beginning to tell on my trainers, and even Delaney. With all his coolness, he was trying to hum little songs to himself to make me feel he was happy and wasn't thinking about the fight at all. And others were whistling too loud and too often. All their actions, I could see, were so unnatural and unlike them. They were all doing it for the effect on me, and, if I do say it myself, I think I was the only one in the whole crowd that really felt normal.

To lead up to the climax, the club had arranged bouts between famous fighters to be fought on successive nights before the heavyweight battle – Monday night, George Dixon fought Jack Skelly for the featherweight championship of the world; on Tuesday, the wonderful lightweight Jack McAuliffe defended his lightweight title against Billy Meyers of Streator, Illinois; on Wednesday night, John L. Sullivan was to defend his title.

McAuliffe gave Meyers an awful beating on Tuesday night, and it suddenly occurred to me that it would be a grand idea to have the last meal before I fought Sullivan with poor Billy Meyers. This did not strike me as ominous, for I was never superstitious – in fact, often defied and flew in the face of superstition purposely. This annoyed my companions considerably sometimes, so now when I suggested that I go out with the loser, Billy Meyers, there was a terrible uproar. 'Why, he's a Jonah!' they said.

They begged and pleaded with me, but I insisted on going and dragged them all out there with me!

Meyers came down into the dining-room and met us. I knew him very well and liked him very much. He had a big black eye and a cracked lip, and I started to 'kid' him about these marks of his battle. 'You may look worse than I do when Sullivan gets through with you tonight,' he retorted.

'No, Billy,' I replied. 'Sullivan won't have to hit me as many times as McAuliffe did you to lick me. If it's done, it will be done with one punch!'

So we talked and joked with each other, and finally, about nine o'clock, we started for the Olympic Club.

Now the following incident comes back to me as I write these words, 33 years afterwards.

As I was starting to put on a light summer suit, with a straw hat and a little bamboo cane to match, Delaney exclaimed, 'You're not going to the fight that way, are you?'

'Certainly, Mr Delaney,' I replied, examining myself in the mirror, as I thought I looked grand.

It was too much for him. He wanted me to go to the arena like the usual short-haired, big-sweatered type of pug with a scowl that would scare people, and here I looked like a dude that a good man could break in two. For a moment he couldn't say anything; simply looked his disgust.

'What difference does it make how I'm dressed going up?' I continued, as I gave a little extra twist to my tie. 'I don't expect to fight in these clothes.'

The streets of the city were black with people, and as our carriage was working through, all I could hear from every side was the murmur: 'Sullivan, Sullivan, Sullivan!' Not once did I hear the name 'Corbett'; it was all Sullivan in the air.

We reached the club and I stepped out. As I walked in at the door, right ahead of me hurried my old friend, Mose Guntz, from San Francisco, the one who gave Jack Dempsey a thousand dollars to second. After that incident we had become great friends, and have been such ever since.

He turned around at my hail and started to speak cheerfully, but when he saw my get-up he looked kind of embarrassed and strange and, although he didn't say anything about my trimmings, I knew what effect they had on him, also that it wouldn't be but a couple of minutes before someone would tell Sullivan that Corbett came to the club with a cane in his hand and a straw hat on, like a dude! I could picture the look on Sullivan's face when he heard this news.

When I reached my dressing-room, one of the club managers came in and announced, 'Sullivan wants to toss up for the corners.'

'Let him take any corner he likes,' I answered as I started to get ready. 'He's going in the ring first anyway.'

Word immediately came back that I was to go in the ring first. However, the question was settled by Brady's going down to Sullivan's dressing-room and tossing a coin.

Now the only reason for my insisting that Sullivan enter ahead of me was the wonderful ovation I knew Sullivan would receive. Just then I felt quite calm and I didn't want anything to excite me in any way, and it was possible his great reception might. But Brady had won the toss and finally it was announced that Sullivan was in the ring.

My seconds and I started down the aisle. The seats were banked circus fashion and only a few of the audience could see us, but I could see the ring and Sullivan was not in it. The managers had lied to me. So I stopped.

Now Sullivan thought I was in the ring, because I had started and enough time had elapsed for me to get there. As I stopped and turned back I met Sullivan, for the first time since I had boxed with him in San Francisco at my benefit. I looked him in the eye and said, 'You're the champion and I'm the short end. You're going in that ring first, if we stand here all night!'

This enraged Sullivan, who was always aggressive in manner anyway. He gave a roar like a wounded lion, strode down the aisle and bounded into the ring. Never before or since have I heard an ovation equal to that given him as he came through the ropes.

I said a little prayer to myself: 'I hope to God I am as cool in the ring as I am now,' and then, as the cheers subsided, skipped into the ring, receiving the usual reception that any fellow would get from an audience, which meant about as much as, 'Well, anyway he showed up!'

When I entered the ring I noticed that the floor was of turf instead of boards, on which I had always trained and fought. My shoes were of the solid sort used nowadays and I wondered how my feet would hold on turf. As soon as I entered the ring I started dancing around, and found that my feet would hold pretty well – in fact, much better than I had expected – so I was considerably relieved.

There was a reason, you see, for these jumping-jack antics that night, but I wish someone would tell me why present-day fighters do the same thing. They have been training on boards, and are fighting on boards, and using the same shoes and everything, so there is no reason for the practice unless to cover up nervousness. But it has been followed generally by fighters ever since that night. It is funny how customs and habits go down from generation to generation.

Meanwhile, Sullivan sat in his corner trying to catch my eye, his clenched fists on his knees, elbows out, and his head thrust forward in an ugly fashion. He had a wicked eye.

Now, as I had always done before, I was trying to convince him that he was the last person or thing in the world I was thinking about. I was bowing to people I didn't even see, smiling at entire strangers, waving my hand and talking to my seconds, laughing all the time.

Finally the referee, whose name was John Duffy, called us up to the centre of the ring for our final instructions. We walked up, Sullivan with his arms still folded, looking right at my eyes – not in them, for I never met his stare – and rising and falling on his toes without a pause. I waited for the referee, my gaze on him, and you could have heard a pin drop in the place. You wouldn't think 10,000 people could be so quiet. At last the referee got down to 'hitting in clinches'.

'When I tell you to break,' he told us, 'I want you to drop your arms.'

Immediately I grasped the referee by the shoulder – mind you, all for the effect on Sullivan – and sneered, 'That's very well for you to say, "Drop your arms when I say break!" But suppose this fellow' – even then I didn't look at Sullivan, just jerked my thumb at him – 'takes a punch at me when I drop my arms?'

'If he does that, he'll lose the fight; and you'll lose, too, if you try it,' Duffy answered.

'Then what about clinching like this?' I asked, and took hold of the referee and put my elbow up under his chin, pushing his head back, and repeated, 'What if he does this?'

'That's a foul, of course,' he answered. 'The one that does it will be cautioned once. If he tries it a second time, he loses the fight.'

'All right,' I said, as gruffly as I could, 'that's all I wanted to know.'

Then, for the first time since entering the ring, I looked Sullivan square in the eye and very aggressively, too. He stopped his rising and falling on his toes and stood staring at me as if he were petrified, so surprised was he at this sudden change in my attitude, and I saw at once it had the effect I intended: I had him guessing!

In a very cocksure manner I jerked the towel from my shoulders, turned my back on him and ripped out, 'Let her go!'

This piece of business had its effect not only on Sullivan, but also on the audience, for they cheered me louder then than they had when I entered the ring. They must have come to the conclusion, 'Why, this fellow thinks he can whip Sullivan. We'll see a fight!'

'Time' was called, and the first round was on.

Now, I knew that the most dangerous thing I could do was to let Sullivan work me into a corner when I was a little tired or dazed, so I made up my mind that I would let him do this while I was still fresh. Then I could find out what he intended doing when he got me there. In a fight, you know, when a man has you where he wants you, he is going to deliver the best goods he has.

From the beginning of the round Sullivan was aggressive – wanted to eat me up right away. He came straight for me and I backed and backed, finally into a corner. While I was there I observed him setting himself for a right-hand swing, first slapping himself on the thigh with his left hand – sort of a trick to balance himself for a terrific swing with his right. But before he let the blow go, just at the right instant, I side-stepped out of the corner and was back in the middle of the ring again, Sullivan hot after me.

I allowed him to back me into all four corners, and he thought he was engineering all this, that it was his own work that he was cornering me. But I had learned what I wanted to know – just where to put my head to escape his blow if he should get me cornered and perhaps dazed. He had shown his hand to me.

In the second round he was still backing me around the ring. I hadn't even struck at him yet, and the audience on my right hissed me for running away and began to call me 'Sprinter'. Now I could see at a glance that Sullivan was not quite near enough to hit me, so suddenly I turned my side to him, waved both hands to the audience and called out, 'Wait a while! You'll see a fight.'

That made an awful 'sucker' out of Sullivan, as the gallery birds say, and it was quite unexpected. And since he didn't know that I knew he couldn't reach me when I pulled this stunt, he was the more chagrined. So he dashed right at me, angry as a bull, but immediately I was away again. At the end of the round I went to my corner and said to Brady and Delaney, 'Why, I can whip this fellow slugging!'

At this there was panic in my corner, all of them starting to whine and pleading with me.

'You said you were going to take your time,' they said. 'What are you going to take any chances for?'

'All right,' I replied, to comfort them, 'but I'll take one good punch at him this round, anyway.'

So far Sullivan hadn't reached me with anything but glancing blows, and it was my intention, when the third round started, to hit him my first punch, and I felt that it must be a good one! If my first punch didn't hurt him, he was going to lose all respect for my hitting ability.

So, with my mind thoroughly made up, I allowed him to back me once more into a corner. But although this time I didn't intend to slip out, by my actions I indicated that I was going to, just as I had before. As we stood there, fiddling, he crowding almost on top of me, I glanced, as I had always done before, first to the left, then to the right, as if looking for some way to get out of this corner. He following my eye and thinking I wanted to make a getaway, determined that he wouldn't let me out this time!

For once he failed to slap himself on the thigh with his left hand, but he had his right hand all ready for the swing as he was gradually crawling up on me. Then, just as he finally set himself to let go a vicious right I beat him to it and loosed a left hand for his face with all the power I had behind it. His head went back and I followed it with a couple of other punches and slugged him back over the ring and into his corner. When the round was over his nose was broken.

At once there was pandemonium in the audience! All over the house, men stood on their chairs, coats off, swinging them in the air. You could have heard the cheers clear to the Mississippi River!

But the uproar only made Sullivan the more determined. He came out of his corner in the fourth like a roaring lion, with an uglier scowl than ever, and bleeding considerably at the nose. I felt sure now that I would beat him, so made up my mind, though it would take a little longer, I would play safe.

From that time on I started doing things the audience were seeing for the first time, judging from the way they talked about the fight afterwards. I would work a left-hand on the nose, then a hook to the stomach, a hook up on the jaw again – a great variety of blows, in fact, using all the time such quick side-stepping and footwork that the audience seemed to be delighted and a little bewildered, as was also Mr Sullivan. That is, bewildered, for I don't think he was delighted.

In the twelfth round we clinched, and with the referee's order, 'Break away', I dropped my arms, when Sullivan let go a terrific right-hand swing from which I just barely got away; as it was it just grazed the top of my head. Some in the audience began to shout 'Foul!' but I smiled and shook my head, to tell him, 'I don't want it that way.'

So the next eight rounds continued much in the fashion of toreador and the bull, Sullivan making his mad rushes and flailing away with his arms, rarely landing on me, but as determined as ever. Meanwhile I was using all the tricks in my boxing repertoire, which was an entirely new one for that day and an assortment that impressed the audience. Then I noticed that he was beginning to puff and was slowing down a little.

When we came up for the twenty-first round it looked as if the fight would last ten or 15 rounds longer. Right away I went up to him, feinted with my left and hit him with a left-hand hook alongside the jaw pretty hard, and I saw his eyes roll. Quicker than it takes to tell it, I saw that I had then the same chance that I had had in the fight with Peter Jackson, but had failed to take – the same chance that was Firpo's when Dempsey stood helpless before him, and which he also failed to take.

This time I did not let it slip. Summoning all the reserve force I had left I let my guns go, right and left, with all the dynamite Nature had given me, and Sullivan stood dazed and rocking. So I set myself for an instant, put just a little more in a right and hit alongside the jaw. And he fell helpless on the ground, on his stomach, and rolled over on his back! The referee, his seconds, and mine picked him up and put him in his corner; and the audience went wild.

As Sullivan struck the floor, the few people who were for me jumped up and yelled, but the mass of that vast audience were still as death; just clenched their hands, hoping their champion would rise. When the last count ended and it was over beyond doubt, then came an uproar like Niagara tumbling over the cliffs, followed by the greatest shower you ever saw, of hats, coats, canes, belts, flowers and buttonholes, everything, falling on me and my seconds and all over the floor of the ring. I have often thought what a business I could have started down in Baxter Street with such an assorted stock!

So the roar of the crowd went on. I should have felt proud and dazed, but the only thing I could think of, right after the knockout, was Sullivan lying there on the floor. I was actually disgusted with the crowd, and it left a lasting impression on me. It struck me as sad to see all those thousands who had given him such a wonderful ovation when he entered the ring turning it to me now that he was down and out.

In justice to the man who had reigned so long as champion of the world, I think it is only fair to say that I was not fighting the Sullivan I had seen and admired in San Francisco at the Paddy Ryan bout, then 26 and in the pink of condition; but a man who had not been careful of his habits and who had enjoyed too much the good fellowship and popularity the championship brings.

I got him when he was slipping; and that goes for all the champions down the line.

The Roar of the Crowd
Curtis Publishing Co.
1924

Great International Contest: Fitzsimmons v Corbett

The Sportsman

The epic confrontation between 'Britisher' Bob Fitzsimmons and Californian James J. Corbett lies now in the land of virtual reality. Memories cannot even pretend to go back that far. For undeterred columnists, however, for whom virtual is as right as real, 100 years is as an instant. Whenever the latest Anglo-aspirant steps tentatively across the Atlantic in search of the elusive heavyweight pot of gold, he carries the weight of the Cornishman's punch to the solar plexus on his back. The citation and any comparison is brief, but it is enough. What happened in Carson City set the yardstick.

Considerable enmity existed between the two boxers. The original match in 1895 had fallen through for compounded reasons; Corbett then announced his retirement and placed his champion's mantle on the shoulder of Irishman Peter Maher who had been beaten by Fitzsimmons; Fitzsimmons responded by beating Maher again, this time under two minutes, and began calling himself 'champion of the world' and then at every opportunity letting it be known that fear was the reason for Corbett's retirement. And so it went on with the press seizing every opportunity to fuel the animosity. More than once, when the men met in the street or in a hotel, they were prevented with difficulty from coming to blows. Eventually, Corbett announced his return to the ring for the sole purpose of giving a good thrashing to 'the upstart farrier', as he called Fitzsimmons, who by now had had to take out American citizenship in order to gain official recognition as a challenger.

There were further delays surrounding the sanctioning of the fight and the search for a suitable venue but, at last, amid considerable excitement in both countries, battle commenced at a specially constructed arena in the silver-line centre of Nevada, the only state that would permit the contest.

In London, a huge crowd gathered in teeming rain outside the offices of The Sportsman *in Fleet Street to await the result. The next day the paper devoted several pages to the fight and its background from various sources. Extracts, including a round by round description, surface here for perhaps the first time since a century ago.*

Yesterday morning James J. Corbett rose from his couch in the glory of an unbeaten pugilist. By one o'clock in the afternoon, American time, he had joined the ranks of the defeated. It was Corbett's boast that he had never received a black eye nor a knock-down blow, and that the fighter was not living who could claim to have drawn a drop of blood from him. All that is changed now, for Corbett was beaten yesterday by a man his inferior in everything but pluck and hard hitting. Two years ago Corbett decided to retire from the ring. He talked to the writer of these notes of the pitchers that had gone too often to the well, and he expressed his determination to abandon the game of fisticuffs with his honours thick upon him. The hot-headed, impetuous Californian, however, was a victim to jealousy, and his dog-in-the-manger policy finally brought him to grief. Corbett has gone by the board, whipped by a man who first saw daylight in Merrie England. Yesterday's battle, which has been the chief talk in boxing circles for weeks past, found a long-armed, level-headed, punishing hitter in Fitzsimmons opposed to a quick and 'scientific' boxer in the person of Corbett. The Californian had an advantage of fully a stone in weight and over an inch in height but Corbett was bowed by the tremendous power in the blows of his rival.

The struggle lasted less than 54 minutes, and at the finish Fitzsimmons struck his most deadly blow. Two minutes previously it was either man's fight on points, but reading between the lines one can see what a protracted battle must have ensued to give Corbett the victory. He fought to wear his man down, as in his contest with Peter Jackson. His blows, however, failed in their effect on the Cornishman, and all along Fitzsimmons possessed a hit which never belonged to his rival. The Britisher waited for his opportunity. It was a contest for endurance, and he could not lose so long as he was not down ten seconds. The opening came in the fourteenth round, when Corbett, leaving himself exposed, received a blow in the wind that brought him down. We are told that he quickly recovered, but it was too late, for the fatal ten seconds had expired. From the way the affair ended Corbett cannot be satisfied, and a challenge for a second trial will surely come from the loser. Meanwhile we can comfort ourselves that the championship of the world has been won once more by an English-born man.

REUTER'S SPECIAL SERVICE

Carson, Nevada, 17 March

Jim Corbett and Bob Fitzsimmons met here this morning, before a big attendance, to box to a finish for $10,000 a side and a purse of $15,000.

The weather was beautifully clear and in every way favourable for the fight. The town is full of sporting men from all parts of the country. The eastern contingent is smaller than was expected, owing to the great distance, but there is a very large representation from San Francisco.

The weather bureau predicted sunshine, but the combatants agreed that if it should prove cloudy the battle should be postponed, the object being to secure a good kinetoscope record of every movement and incident throughout the contest. To this arrangement great importance was attached, as copyright in the production will be secured in the United States, the United Kingdom, France, Germany, Russia and Canada.

The probable attendance was estimated beforehand at something under 5,000. The betting was comparatively light.

Corbett won the toss for choice of corners. He chose buff as the colour of his gloves, while Fitzsimmons selected green. The odds as the hour for the contest approached ranged from 100 to 70 to 65 in favour of Corbett.

The vast arena rapidly filled with eager spectators.

Great excitement was caused by a representative of John L. Sullivan challenging the winner of the contest. Loud cheers were given for Sullivan, who said he thought there was one more fight left in him and that he meant business. The representatives of Goddard and Sharkey also announced that they had deposited money for a fight with the winner.

At ten minutes past 11, Carson time, which is eight hours earlier than that of London, about 4,000 persons had assembled at the ringside, and the arrival of another heavily laden special train was momentarily expected.

Both pugilists on entering their dressing-rooms were heartily cheered.

The attendance was swollen by a considerable crowd who presently arrived from the last special train, and by ten minutes to 12 all were present at the ringside. Among the spectators were a number of women.

Corbett and Fitzsimmons entered the ring a few minutes before 12, and immediately stripped. Fitzsimmons looked light, but was a perfect bunch of muscles. Corbett looked easily 15 pounds heavier, and his skin, as well as that of Fitzsimmons, shone like polished mahogany.

THE CONTEST

Fitzsimmons refused to shake hands with his opponent. Time was called at seven minutes past 12. The following is a detailed description of the fight.

Round 1

Sparring for an opening Fitzsimmons forced Corbett to his corner. He tried a left swing, which Jim ducked cleverly. Jim meanwhile was smiling, but Fitzsimmons was very aggressive. He landed lightly on Corbett's neck. Jim feinted, and delivered a left hook on his opponent's stomach, following this up with a left hook on Fitzsimmons's jaw. The men clinched, but no damage was done in the break-away. Corbett next landed a right swing on his antagonist's ribs. A second clinch resulted in no damage. On the break-away Fitz landed heavily with his left on Jim's head, and Corbett landed hard with his right on Fitz's short ribs. Another clinch followed, and Fitz landed heavily with his right hand on Corbett's head. Jim laughed and landed again with his right on Fitz's ribs, when the gong ended the round.

Round 2

Corbett advanced to the centre and clinched, but no damage resulted in the break-away. More clinching followed. Corbett was very cautious, and kept a keen look-out for the slightest opening. He landed two stiff left swings on his opponent's head. The fighting now became very rapid, both being extremely lively on their feet. Jim landed hard with his left in a half-round jab on Fitz's stomach, and followed with another on the same place. He was jabbing Fitz hard with his right and left on the body when the bell rang.

Round 3

Corbett started with his right and got in with a hard left hook on the body. Fitzsimmons became savage, and tried with his left and right at Corbett's head, but did very little damage. Corbett landed another left jab on the body, following it up with a right short on the ribs. Jim clinched and landed with his right hard over the heart. Fitz mixed it up, and put the heel of his glove in Corbett's face. In the clinch Jim kept his right working like a piston rod on Fitzsimmons's body. They clinched and Fitz roughed it in the break-away. As the gong sounded Fitz seemed anxious to continue, but Corbett, laughing, stuck his right glove in his opponent's face and they retired to their corners.

Round 4

Corbett rushing in landed his left again on Fitzsimmons's body. The latter was short with his counter, and Fitzsimmons followed with a stiff left on Jim's stomach, and they clinched. Fitz roughed it again. They were now fighting at a terrific rate and making a magnificent contest. Fitz rushed and Jim met him with a stiff right-hand short blow on the stomach. Fitz was now doing a good deal of rushing and hitting, and roughing it in the break-aways. It looked long odds on Corbett making a cleverer fight of it. He was playing systematically with his right and left on the body. An exchange of lefts at the head followed, and time was called.

Round 5

Corbett landed with his left on Fitz's jaw. Immediately again Jim's left went on his opponent's jaw. The blows dealt by Fitzsimmons had plenty of steam behind them, but were not as frequent as Corbett's. They clinched and exchanged compliments with one arm loose. Corbett led with a very slow left and Fitz landed with his left on Jim's neck. The latter threw a stiff half-round blow with his left on his antagonist's nose, drawing first blood. Jim landed another stiff right on the body, then left on the chin. This round ended in favour of Corbett.

Round 6

The men clinched and Fitzsimmons tried to wrestle Corbett down. There were loud cries of 'Oh! Oh!'. Corbett landed lightly with a left jab on the face,

Fitzsimmons countering on the jaw. Corbett uppercut Fitz fiercely with his right hand and had him going. Fitzsimmons was now literally covered with blood, but was fighting like a demon. Corbett was beginning now to show signs of the fast work. Fitzsimmons was down on one knee and took the time to the limit, but he was full of fight on getting up again. Corbett, however, was simply slaughtering him with his uppercuts. At the same time Jim's leads were wild and he missed many well-intentioned blows. When time was called Fitzsimmons looked very much the worse for wear and Corbett was puffing a lot.

Round 7

Corbett now forced the exchanges. He missed a left swing at the head, but uppercut Fitz hard on the face. Fitzsimmons was bleeding again, but fighting hard. Both men were now looking for a knockout blow. Jim landed a light left on Fitz's now sore mouth. Fitzsimmons missed right and left swings; then tried another left swing, which Corbett ducked. Jim countered with a heavy right over the heart. Corbett now looked very tired, and Fitzsimmons was bleeding freely. He nevertheless looked as strong as his opponent.

Round 8

Fitz now forced the fighting. An exchange of blows did very little damage. Fitz missed a left swing and was lifted off his feet by a straight left jab from Corbett on the mouth. Fitzsimmons did all the forcing in this round. He tried a right-hand cross, but Corbett ducked. Fitz landed with his left on Corbett's face, and Jim countered with his right on the body. The combatants sparred for wind. Fitz tried his hard right at Corbett's head, but was countered heavily on the jaw with a good left from Corbett. Fitzsimmons had the worst of this round.

Round 9

This bout began with some long-range sparring. Both men were still very active on their feet. Fitzsimmons landed below the belt and was cautioned by the referee. Corbett delivered a stiff left on his opponent's wind. Fitzsimmons rushed Corbett, but did very little damage. Jim was jabbing, clinching, and uppercutting with his right. In the break-away Fitz landed very hard with a left-hand swing on Jim's jaw and tried a right cross, but Jim was inside. Fitzsimmons again tried a right cross, but was short. He was now, however, landing more frequently than Corbett.

Round 10

Fitzsimmons was now spitting blood. He tried a hard left swing at Corbett's head and came back with a stiff left and right on Corbett's head and body. At this stage he appeared to be very much cooler and stronger than Corbett. The latter stopped a left swing with a straight left on the mouth. Fitzsimmons meanwhile was bleeding profusely, but forced Corbett back, being apparently the stronger man. They mixed it up, and honours were about even, both fighting hard. Fitzsimmons caught Corbett round the neck and dragged him to the ropes, when time was called.

Round 11

Corbett landed a light left on Fitz's mouth. His blows lacked force, but he was still fighting very cautiously. A clinch followed. Corbett landed with his right on the ribs and was countered with a left jab on the chin. Fitzsimmons was now receiving many of Corbett's left jabs, but he looked as strong as a bear. Corbett missed a half-round hook on the jaw, and Fitz landed a hard left straight on Corbett's face. They clinched and Fitz crossed with his right. They mixed it and Fitz had decidedly the better of the roughing. He fought Corbett to his corner and had him weak as the gong sounded.

Round 12

Corbett rushed in; he missed with his left and was countered on the face. It was evident that Fitzsimmons was now bent on rushing it, and Corbett kept away. Fitz got the worst of it in the dash. There was more clinching, and Corbett landed with his left on his opponent's nose, following with a half-round at the body. Corbett forced Fitz to the ropes and smashed hard on his short ribs. It was now Corbett who was forcing. He landed one or two rights and lefts on the 'Britisher's' face. He again delivered with his left on Fitz's face and followed with a right on the body. He then tried for a knockout with an uppercut with his right, but it was too short. The round ended in favour of Corbett.

Round 13

Fitzsimmons landed a right short on Corbett's ribs, and a left on the jaw. Jim next found Fitz with a good left. Fitz rushed Jim over to his corner, but did little damage. Corbett jabbed Bob lightly on the head and again on the body. Corbett at this stage was sparring beautifully and ducking some very dangerous blows. Fitz landed with his left straight and hard on Jim's face. He then tried a hard right swing but did no good. Jim's glove was in Fitz's face when time was called. It was anybody's fight at the end of this round.

Round 14 and last

Corbett led but was baulked. He then landed a left jab on Fitz's head. Fitz countered with a crushing swing on Corbett's neck and had Corbett going back for a few moments. Fitz then landed a terrible left-hand jab on Corbett's stomach and Corbett went to his knees with a frightful look of agony on his face. The timekeeper called ten seconds, but Corbett came to his feet, rushed to Fitzsimmons and endeavoured to strike.

A terrible uproar ensued, but the referee decided that Fitzsimmons had won. The blow that did the business landed over Corbett's heart and he collapsed.

The concluding round lasted just one minute and 45 seconds.

REMARKS

The arena in which the fight took place is situated in the centre of the race track, about a third of a mile from the main street of Carson City. The structure was entirely composed of undressed timber, and the men fought practically in the open air. The spectators numbered about 5,000, the price charged for seats ranging from $5 to $40. The ring was raised about four feet above the level of the floor.

William Muldoon, a New York wrestler, was the official timekeeper. Louis Houseman, of Chicago, held the watch for the 'American'; while James Colville performed a like office for Corbett. George Stiler, of Chicago, was referee. Five-ounce gloves were used. Corbett, who won the toss yesterday evening, chose the south-east corner, with his back to the sun. Both men had a little army of seconds, selected from the trainers who helped them to reach a condition of physical perfection.

Corbett's fighting garb consisted of short trunks and white shoes, and a red, white and blue belt, with green trimmings. He, however, laid his belt aside just before time was called. Fitzsimmons wore black shoes, green silk tights, and a red, white and blue belt, having in its centre the American eagle with its wings spread. Fitzsimmons, however, also took off his belt as soon as the time for the fight arrived.

Fitzsimmons kissed his wife as he entered the ring. Corbett was received with louder applause than his opponent. Fitzsimmons's face was expressionless, but Corbett looked very vicious. Clinches were frequent throughout the fight and, owing to the interpretation of the rules, both were extremely careful on break-aways. The pictures of the two almost naked men, their muscles straining and gleaming in the brilliant sunlight, was like one from ancient Athenean games.

The partisans of the combatants yelled frantically at the fall of each blow. Corbett's friends were in the majority, but Fitzsimmons, too, had plenty of supporters, who were as wildly enthusiastic as those of the Californian.

For the first five rounds the battle continued without much advantage on either side. Corbett landed oftener than his opponent, but when Fitzsimmons got in his terrible right on the head or body he counted heavily. In the fifth round Fitzsimmons was on his knees, and stayed there eight seconds. His trainer rushed frantically around outside the ropes, yelling, 'Get up, Bob! Get up quick!' and Fitzsimmons, though covered in blood from his forehead to his waist, came to his feet. When the round ended Corbett's partisans yelled that all was over, but after a minute's rest the red-headed fighter came to the mark apparently as fresh as ever. The combat continued with alternating gains until the close, as above described.

CORBETT IN A RAGE

Robert Fitzsimmons, who is a British-born, naturalised American, is both middle and heavyweight world's champion pugilist, having gained the heavyweight honours by defeating James J. Corbett, whose only consolation will be his share of the receipts of the kinetoscope reproductions of the fight. Fitzsimmons, besides his share of these, will receive a purse of $15,000 and the stakes of $10,000 a side. The event has proved a great financial success to theatrical and other ventures.

It was in the fourteenth round that Fitzsimmons delivered a left-hand blow over the heart. Corbett staggered and Fitzsimmons then struck him with his right on the jaw. Jim sank down, clinging to the ropes. His face was contorted with pain and he was unable to breathe. He tried in vain to rise, sinking back each time in agony, with his hands over his heart. Fitz stood over his fallen rival, waiting to administer the finishing blow if Jim should get up, but that caution proved unnecessary.

Corbett presently revived, and learning that he had lost the fight, he became frantic, broke away from his seconds, and rushed about hunting for Fitzsimmons, striking blindly right and left. It was a pitiful exhibition of impotent rage. Finally his seconds carried him by force from the ring. Fitzsimmons showed his joy by dancing about in a frantic manner, while Mrs Fitzsimmons, in her box close to the ring, laughed and cried alternately. The crowd then escorted the winner to his quarters, the fight having lasted 54 minutes.

The Sportsman
18 March 1897

Jack Johnson v Jim Jeffries

Jack London

The anathematical racist publicity surrounding the matching of James J. Jeffries with Jack Johnson is as astonishing to today's uninitiated reader as it would be for a reader at the time to be astonished.

Much of the responsibility for the bigoted ballyhoo lies with Jack London, pseudonym of John Griffith Chaney, American novelist and short story writer. He it was who started a crusade in the New York Herald to persuade the former undefeated world heavyweight champion Jeffries to return from a six-year retirement. Along with much other barely hidden bile, he wrote: '[He] must emerge from his alfalfa farm and remove the golden smile from Johnson's face. Jeff, it's up to you!'

Johnson had upset white sensibilities, or rather the lack of them, by becoming the first black man to hold the heavyweight crown – and this at a time when black boxers were only tolerated if they were beaten. What made it worse was that it did not seem as if Johnson could be beaten. He was an exceptionally skilful defensive boxer with a devastating counter-punch and paraded many of the fistic sleights and aptitude for arrogant repartee later practised by Muhammad Ali; added to which – 'could it be even worser?', a phrase used deliberately by London to deride syntax-seekers – Johnson had a penchant for white women (unforgivable in those days) whom he ditched as soon as he had had his wicked way. Which is where Jim Jeffries was tempted to come in, not, of course, as a substitute for the women, or even as an avenging angel, but rather by a purse for $40,000 and the aforesaid literary hobo (so-called from his days journeying on freight trains and as a member of Kelly's industrial army – a protest troop of the unemployed).

The blend of socialism and caucasian superiority which London had created for himself came from public library reading of the popularised versions of the works of Darwin, Marx and Nietzche. His writing reflects his life as a restless adventurer and tends to be uneven and, at times, repetitive, rather in the manner of a revivalist preacher hammering home edicts from the gospel. Fundamental though, to the marketing of any revival, is a goodly ration of passion and impact and it is to be found here, which not only is London's salvation but more than rescues the piece from its questionable provenance. He absolutely compels the reader to join him on the white-knuckle roller-coaster ride.

Reno, Nevada, 5 July 1910 – Once again has Johnson sent down to defeat the chosen representative of the white race and this time the greatest of them.

And as of old, it was play for Johnson. From the opening round to the closing round he never ceased his witty sallies, his exchanges of repartee with his opponent's seconds and with the audience. And, for that matter, Johnson had a funny thing or two to say to Jeffries in every round.

The golden smile was as much in evidence as ever and neither did it freeze on his face nor did it vanish. It came and went throughout the fight, spontaneously, naturally.

It was not a great battle after all, save in its setting and significance. Little Tommy Burns, down in far-off Australia, put up a faster, quicker, livelier battle than did Jeffries. The fight today was great only in its significance. In itself it wasn't great. The issue, after the fiddling of the opening rounds, was never in doubt. In the fiddling of those first rounds the honours lay with Johnson, and for the rounds after the seventh or eighth it was more Johnson, while for the closing rounds it was all Johnson.

Johnson played as usual. With his opponent not strong in attack, Johnson, blocking and defending in masterly fashion, could afford to play. And he played and fought a white man, in the white man's country, before a white man's audience. And the audience was a Jeffries audience.

When Jeffries sent in that awful rip of his the audience would madly applaud, believing it had gone home to Johnson's stomach, and Johnson, deftly interposing his elbow, would smile in irony at the audience, play-acting, making believe he thought the applause was for him – and never believing it at all.

The greatest fight of the century was a monologue delivered to 20,000 spectators by a smiling Negro who was never in doubt and who was never serious for more than a moment at a time.

As a fighter Johnson did not show himself a wonder. He did not have to. Never once was he extended. There was no need. Jeffries could not make him extend. Jeffries never had him in trouble once. No blow Jeffries ever landed hurt his dusky opponent. Johnson came out of the fight practically undamaged. The blood on his lip was from a recent cut received in the course of training and which Jeffries managed to reopen.

Jeffries failed to lead and land. The quickness he brought into the fight quickly evaporated, and while Jeffries was dead game to the end, he was not so badly punished. What he failed to bring into the ring with him was his stamina, which he lost somewhere in the last seven years. Jeffries failed to come back. That's the whole story. His old-time vim and endurance was not there. Something has happened to him. He lost in retirement outside of the ring the stamina that the ring itself never robbed him of. As I have said, Jeffries was not badly damaged. Every day boys take worse lacings in boxing bouts than Jeffries took today.

Jeffries today disposed of one question. He could not come back. Johnson, in turn, answered another question. He has not the yellow streak. But he only answered that question today. The ferocity of the hairy-chested caveman and grizzly giant did not intimidate the cool-headed Negro. Many thousands in the audience expected the intimidation, and were correspondingly disappointed. Johnson was not scared, let it be said here, and beyond the shadow of any doubt, not for an instant was Johnson scared. Not for a second did he show the flicker of fear that the Goliath against him might eat him up.

But the question of the yellow streak is not answered for all time. Just as Johnson has never been extended, so has he never shown the yellow streak. Just as any man may rise up, heaven alone knows where, who will extend Johnson, just so may that man bring out the yellow streak; and then again he may not. So far the burden of proof all rests on the conclusion that Johnson has no yellow streak.

And now to the battle and how it began! All praise to Tex Rickard, the gamest of sports, who pulled off the fight after countless difficulties and who, cool, calm and quick with nervous aliveness, handled the vast crowd splendidly in his arena and wound up by refereeing the fight.

Twenty thousand filled the great arena and waited patiently under the cloud-flecked, wide Nevada sky. Of the many women present some elected to sit in the screened boxes far back from the ring, for all the world like old-time Spanish ladies at the theatre. But more, many more women, sat close to the ringside beside their husbands or brothers. They were the wiser by far.

Merely to enumerate the celebrities at the ringside would be to write a sporting directory of America – at least a directory of the 400 sportsmen, and of many more hundreds of near 400s. At four minutes to two Billy Jordan cleared the ring amid cheers and stood alone, the focal point of 20,000 pairs of eyes, until the great William Muldoon climbed through the ropes to call ringing cheers from the 20,000 throats for the state of Nevada, the people of Nevada and the governor of Nevada.

Beginning with Tex Rickard, ovation after ovation was given to all the great ones, not forgetting Bob Fitzsimmons, whom Billy Jordan introduced as 'the greatest warrior of them all'. And so they came, great one after great one, ceaselessly, endlessly. Until they were swept away before the greatest of them all, the two men who were about to do battle.

It was half past two when Johnson entered. He came first, happy and smiling, greeting friends and acquaintances here and there and everywhere in the audience, cool as ice, waving his hand in salute, smiling, smiling, ever smiling with eyes as well as with lips, never missing a name nor a face, placid, plastic, nerveless, with never a signal of hesitancy or timidity. Yet he was keyed up, keenly observant of all that was going on, ever hearing much of the confused babble of the tongues about him – hearing, aye, and understanding, too.

There is nothing bearish or primitive about this man Johnson. He is alive and quivering, every nerve fibre in his body, and brain. Withal that it is hidden so artfully or naturally under that poise of facetious calm of his. He is a marvel of sensitiveness, sensibility and perceptiveness. He has the perfect mechanism of mind and body. His mind works like chain lightning and his body obeys with equal swiftness.

But the great madness of applause went up when Jeffries entered the ring two minutes later. A quick, superficial comparison between him and the Negro would have led to a feeling of pity for the latter. For Jeff was all that has been said of him. When he stripped and his mighty body could be seen covered with mats of hair, all the primordial adjectives ever applied to him received their vindication. Nor did his face belie him. No facial emotion played on that face, no whims of the moment, no flutterings of a lighthearted temperament.

Dark and sombre and ominous was that face, solid and stolid and expressionless, with eyes that smouldered and looked savage. The man of iron, grim with determination, sat down in his corner. And the carefree Negro smiled and smiled. And that's the story of the fight. The man of iron, the grizzly giant, was grim and serious. The man of summer temperament smiled and smiled. That is the story of the whole fight. It is the story of the fight by rounds.

At the opening of the first round they did not shake hands. Knowing the two men for what they are, it can be safely postulated that this neglect was due to Jeffries or to the prompting from Jeffries' corner. But it is not good that two boxers should not shake hands before a bout. I would suggest to those protagonists of a perishing game, if they wish to preserve the game, that they make the most of these little amenities that by custom grace their sport and give it the veneer of civilisation.

Both men went to work in that first round very easily. Johnson smiling, of course; Jeffries grim and determined. Johnson landed the first blow, a light one, and Jeffries in the clinches gave a faint indication of his forthcoming tactics by roughing it, by crowding the Negro around and by slightly bearing his weight upon him. It was a very easy round, with nothing of moment. Each was merely feeling the other out and both were exceedingly careful. At the conclusion of the round, Johnson tapped Jeffries playfully on the shoulder, smiled good-naturedly and went to his corner. Jeffries, in the first, showed flashes of catlike quickness.

Round two – Jeffries advanced with a momentary assumption of famous crouch, to meet the broadly smiling Johnson. Jeffries is really human and good-natured. He proved it right here. So friendly was that smile of Johnson's, so irresistibly catching, that Jeffries, despite himself, smiled back. But Jeffries' smiles were doomed to be very few in this fight.

And right here began a repetition of what took place down in Australia when Burns fought Johnson. Each time Burns said something harsh to Johnson in the hope of making him lose his temper, Johnson responded by giving the white man a lacing. And so today. Of course, Jeffries did not talk to Johnson to amount to anything, but Corbett, in his corner, did it for Jeffries. And each time Corbett cried something in particular, Johnson promptly administered a lacing to Jeffries.

It began in the second round. Corbett, in line with his plan of irritating the Negro, called out loudly: 'He wants to fight a little, Jim.'

'You bet I do,' Johnson retorted, and with that he landed Jeffries a stinger with his right uppercut.

Both men were tensely careful, Jeffries trying to crowd and put his weight on in the clinches, Johnson striving more and more than the other to break out of the clinches. And at the end of this round, in his corner Johnson was laughing gleefully. Certainly Jeffries showed no signs of boring in, as had been promised by his enthusiastic supporters.

It was the same story in the third round, at the conclusion of which the irrepressible Negro was guilty of waving his hands to friends in the audience.

In this fourth round Jeffries showed up better, rushing and crowding and striking with more vim than hitherto shown. This seemed to have been caused by a sally of Johnson's, and Jeffries went at him in an angry sort of way. Promptly Jeffries rushed, and even before they came together Johnson cried out: 'Don't rush me, Jim. You hear what I'm telling you?'

No sign there of being intimidated by Jeffries' first dynamic display of ferocity. All he managed to do was to reopen the training cut in Johnson's lip and to make Johnson playful. It was most anybody's round and it was certainly more Jeffries' than any preceding one.

Round five brought Jeffries advancing with his crouch. The blood from Johnson's lip had turned his smile to a gory one, but still he smiled, and to balance things off he opened Jeffries' lip until it bled more profusely than his own. From then until the end of the fight, Jeffries' face was never free from blood, a steady stream, later flowing from his right nostril, added to by an open cut on his left cheek. Corbett's running fire of irritation served but to make Johnson smile the merrier, and to wink at him across Jeffries' shoulder in the clinches.

So far, no problems have been solved, no questions answered. The yellow streak had not appeared. Neither had Jeffries bored in, ripping awfully, nor put it over Johnson in the clinches. Yet one thing had been shown. Jeffries was not as fast as he had been. There was a shade of diminution in his speed.

Johnson signalised the opening of the sixth round by landing stinging blows to the face in one, two, three order. Johnson's quickness was startling. In response to an irritating remark from Corbett, Johnson replied suavely, 'Too much on hand right now,' and at the same instant he tore into Jeffries. It was Johnson's first real aggressive rush. It lasted but a second or two, but it was fierce and dandy. And at its conclusion it was manifest that Jeff's right eye was closing fast. The round ended with Johnson fighting and smiling strong, and with Jeff's nose, lip and cheek bleeding and his eye closed. Johnson's round by a smile all the way through.

The seventh round was a mild one, opening with Jeff grim and silent and with Johnson leading and forcing. Both were careful and nothing happened, save that once they exchanged blows right niftily. So far Jeff's roughing and crowding and bearing in of weight had amounted to nothing; also he was doing less and less of it.

'It only takes one or two, Jeff,' Corbett encouraged his principal in the eighth round. Promptly Johnson landed two stingers. After a pause he landed another. 'See that?' he chirruped sweetly to Corbett in the corner. Jeff perceptibly showed signs of slowing down in this round, rushing and crowding less than ever. Jeff's slowing down was not due to the punishment he had received, but to poorness of condition. He was flying the first signals of fatigue. He was advertising, faintly, it is true, that he had not come back.

The ninth round was introduced by a suggestion from Corbett, heroically carrying out the policy that was bringing his principal to destruction. 'Make the big stiff fight,' was Corbett's suggestion.

'That's right. That's what they all say,' was Johnson's answer, delivered with a true Chesterfield grace across his adversary's shoulder. In the previous rounds Johnson had not wreaked much damage with the forecasted cut, the right uppercut.

In this round he demonstrated indubitably that he could drive the left hand in a way that was surprising. Be it remembered that it had long been denied that he had any sort of punch in that left of his. Incidentally, in this round, it led all the others, and he landed a blow near Jeffries' heart that must have been discouraging.

The tenth round showed Johnson with his unexpected left, as quick as ever, and Jeffries going slower and slower. The conclusion of the first ten rounds may be summed up as follows.

The fight was all in favour of Johnson, who had shown no yellow, who had shown condition, who had shown undiminished speed, who had not used his right uppercut much, who had developed a savage left, who had held his own in the clinches, who had gotten the best of the infighting and all the outfighting, who was unhurt, and who was smiling all the way.

Jeff was in bad shape: he was tired, slower than ever, his rushes had been futile, and the sports who had placed their money against him were jubilant.

There were men who proclaimed they saw the end. I refused to see this end, for I had picked Jeff to win, and I was hoping hugely – for what I did not know, but for something to happen, for anything that would turn the tide of battle. And yet I could not hide myself from the truth, that Jeff slowed down.

The eleventh round looked better for Jeff. Stung by a remark of Corbett's, Johnson rushed and provoked one grand rally from Jeff. It was faster fighting and more continuous than at any time in the preceding ten rounds, culminating in a fierce rally in which Jeff landed hard.

Round 12 found Johnson, if anything, quicker and more aggressive than ever. 'Thought you were going to have me wild?' Johnson queried sweetly of Corbett. As usual every remark of Corbett's brought more punishment to Jeffries. And by the end of this round the second of the two great questions was definitely answered. Jeff had not come back.

The thirteenth round was the beginning of the end. Beginning slowly enough, but stung by Corbett, Johnson put it all over him in the mouth fighting, and all over Jeff in the outfighting and the infighting. From defence to attack and back again and back and forth Johnson flashed like the amazing fight mechanism he is. Jeff was silent and sick, while as the round progressed Corbett was noticeably silent.

A few entertained the fond hope that Jeff would recuperate, but it was futile; there was no comeback in him. He was a fading, heartsick, heartbroken man.

'Talk to him, Corbett,' Jeff's friends appealed in the fourteenth round, but Corbett could not talk. He had long since seen the end. And yet through this round Johnson went in for one of his characteristic loafing spells. He took it easy and played with the big gladiator, cool as a cucumber, smiling broadly as ever, and yet, as careful as ever. 'Right on the hip,' he grinned out once as Jeff in a desperate dying flurry managed to land a wild punch in that vicinity.

Corbett, likewise desperate, ventured a last sally. 'Why don't you do something?' he cried to the loafing, laughing Johnson. 'Too clever, too clever, like you,' was the reply.

Round fifteen and the end. It was pitiful. There happened to Jeff the bitterness that he had so often made others taste, but which for the first time, perforce, he was made to taste himself.

He who had never been knocked down was knocked down repeatedly. He who had never been knocked out was knocked out. Never mind the technical decision. Jeff was knocked out and through the ropes by the punch he never believed Johnson possessed – by the left and not by the right. As he lay across the lower rope while the seconds were tolled off, a cry that had in it tears and abject broken pride went up from many of the spectators.

'Don't let the Negro knock him out! Don't let the Negro knock him out!' was the oft repeated cry.

There was little more to be said. Jeff did not come back. Johnson did not show the yellow streak. And it was Johnson's fight all the way through. Jeff was not the old Jeff at all.

Even so, it is to be doubted if this old Jeff could have put away this amazing Negro from Texas, this black man with the unfailing smile, this king of fighters and monologists.

Corbett and Berger and the others were right. They wanted Jeff to do more boxing and fighting in his training. Nevertheless, lacking the comeback, as he so patently did, this preliminary boxing and fighting would have profited him nothing. On the other hand, it would have saved his camp much of the money with which it backed him.

It was a slow fight. Faster, better fights may be seen every day of the year in any of the small clubs in the land. It is true these men were heavyweights, yet for heavyweights it was a slow fight. It must be granted that plucky Tommy Burns put up a faster fight with Johnson a year and a half ago. Yet the American fight followers had to see this fight of today in order to appreciate what Burns did against this coloured wonder.

Johnson is a wonder. No one understands him, this man who smiles. Well, the story of the fight is the story of a smile. If ever a man won by nothing more fatiguing than a smile, Johnson won today.

And where now is the champion who will make Johnson extend himself, who will glaze those bright eyes, remove that smile and silence the golden repartee?

New York World – Telegram and Sun
1910

Joe Beckett v Georges Carpentier

George Bernard Shaw

Carpentier was George Bernard Shaw's dream fighter. Or he thought he was – thinking and dreaming though cerebral partners more often taking tangential routes.

But whatever the mental stimuli, Shaw, having seated himself at the Holborn Stadium on 4 December 1919 to report for The Nation *on the European heavyweight battle between Joe Beckett the British challenger and Georges Carpentier the French holder, must have postulated that the realms of fiction and reality were indeed one and the same.*

Nearly 40 years before, as a then struggling novelist and would-be amateur boxing champion, Shaw was undergoing lessons in self-defence at Professor Ned Donnelly's Gymnasium off the Haymarket in London. At the same time, he was penning Cashel Byron's Profession, *the story of a scientific boxer who conquers his slugging rival to become champion. There were many apparent similarities, between the Shavian fantasy and the existing 'Pride of Paris', emphasised no doubt by his opponent's background in the boxing booths of the fairground, but, as Benny Green points out in his splendid analysis of 'Shaw's Champions', it was not an exact model.*

Strangely, in view of the intellectual disdain in which the sport is supposed to have been held, there was another novelist present at Holborn that night. Providing copy for The New Statesman *was Arnold Bennett, who in the not too distant past had resided in Paris for eight years. Bennett's major works form an important link between the English novel and the mainstream of European Realism – another contiguity.*

Both Bennett and Shaw found arguments to support the noble art, in the former's case not least, because he had been 'deeply interested'. As for Shaw, he thought he would not go to watch boxing again, not for a long time anyway, unless Carpentier was 'one of the performers'.

If you were not at the Great Fight, and are at all curious about it, imagine 4,000 people packed by night into a roofed enclosure with a gallery round it. I had better not call it a building, because that word has architectural associations; and this enclosure has none. It is fearfully ugly, and calls itself a stadium, probably to provide modern poets with a rhyme for radium. The 4,000 people are all smoking as hard as they can; and the atmosphere, which will be described in the morrow's papers as electric, is in fact, murky, stifling and fumesome. In the midst is a scaffold, or place of execution, 24 feet square, fenced by ropes, and glared down upon so intolerably by arc lights that some of the spectators wear improvised brown paper hat brims to shield their eyes. On the scaffold is a mild man, apparently a churchwarden, but really a referee, patiently watching two hard-working Britons earning a precarious livelihood by boxing for the amusement of the 4,000. They are tired, and have not the smallest amount of animosity to give a bitter sweet to their exertions; but they are most earnest and industrious; and one feels, in spite of the sportive alacrity which they keep up like a ballet dancer's smile, and their attempts to give a little extra value when the arc lights are increased to cinematograph the last round or two, that they are thinking of their little ones at home. One of them presently gets a tooth, real or artificial, loosened. His second extracts it with his fingers; his opponent apologetically shakes hands; and they return to the common toil, the nightly toil. It seems indelicate to stare at them; and I proceed to study the audience.

Like all sporting audiences it consists mostly of persons who manifestly cannot afford the price of admission. My seat has cost more than ten times what I have paid to hear *Parsifal* at Bayreuth or Beethoven's Ninth Symphony at a very special performance at the Grand Opera in Paris. Certainly there are people here who can spare ten guineas or 25 easily enough; honourables and right honourables, explorers, sporting stockbrokers, eminent professional men, plutocrats of all sorts, men with an artistic interest in the display like Robert Loraine, Granville Barker, Maurice Baring, Arnold Bennett and myself. But the prevalent impression is the usual one of a majority of men who have sacrificed a month's wages to be present, and hope to retrieve it by bets on the result. Here and there is a lady. Not any particular sort of lady or no lady; just an ordinary lady. The one who happens to be sitting by me is one next to whom I might find myself in the stalls of any theatre, or in church. The girl at the end of the next row would be perfectly in place in any West End drawing-room. My lady neighbour watches the weary breadwinners on the scaffold, and tries to feel excited when they seek rest by leaning their heads affectionately on one another's shoulders, and giving one another perfunctory thumps on the ribs and on the nape of the neck to persuade the audience that they are 'mixing it', and dealing out terrible 'kidney punches' (this is modern infighting, which seems to me simply despicable). But I fancy she is trying to stifle a suspicion that she had better have stayed at home and spent the price of her ticket on a new hat. As for me, nothing would have induced me to stay in the place four minutes had I not been waiting for the not very far off undivine event towards which the sporting section of creation had moved.

Everything comes to an end at last, even the minor items in a boxing programme. The boxers retired, presumably to their ain firesides; and the scaffold was occupied by men unknown to me; for I belong to an older generation. One of these philanthropists earned my gratitude by adjuring the audience, if it loved the champions, to refrain from smoking; after which the atmosphere cleared until it was no thicker than an average fog. Suddenly a figure from the past – from my past – was announced and appeared. It was Jack Angle, no longer a trim, clean-shaven young amateur athlete, but a *père noble* in white moustaches, exactly like Colonel Damas in *The Lady of Lyons*. I found myself saying involuntarily 'Thank Heaven! here at last is somebody who knows something about boxing'. I looked round for his contemporaries, Chinnery, Douglas, Michel, Frost-Smith, and the rest; but if they are alive and were present I could not identify them. He instructed us politely but authoritatively how to behave ourselves.

Then the cheering began, rather localised, because from most of the seats little could be seen except the platform. Even the Prince of Wales had had some difficulty in procuring silence for his brief speech when he entered; and several people believed for some time that it had been made by Carpentier. As it happened I was near the gangway by which the champions came in, and therefore saw at once that the cheering was for Mr Joseph Beckett, who was approaching in an unpretentious dressing-gown. Mr Beckett, though the descriptive reporters insisted on making him play Orson to his opponent's Valentine, is by no means ill-looking. His features are not Grecian; but he can be described exactly as a very sensible looking man; and I may say at once that he behaved all through, and has behaved since, more sensibly than most men could in a very trying situation. I liked Mr Beckett very well, and did not change my opinion later on, as some of his backers did. He mounted the scaffold, and went to his corner. A burst of louder cheering made me look round again to the gangway; and this time I was startled by a most amazing apparition; nothing less than Charles XII, 'the madman of the North', striding along the gangway in a Japanese silk dressing-gown as gallantly as if he had not been killed almost exactly 201 years before. I have seldom received so vivid an impression; and I knew at once that this could hardly be Charles, he must be either Carpentier or the devil. Genius could not be more unmistakable. Being in that line myself I was under no illusion as to genius being invincible. I knew that Mr Beckett might turn out to be Peter the Great, and that Charles might be going to his Poltava; but genius is genius all the same, in victory or defeat. The effect of the audience on the two men was very noticeable. Beckett, too sensible to be nervous, put up with the crowd of people staring at him as a discomfort that was all in the day's work. Carpentier rose at the crowd, and would have had it 40,000 instead of four if he could. He was at home with it; he dominated it; he picked out his friends and kissed hands to them in his debonair way quite naturally, without swank or mock modesty, as one born to move assemblies.

The descriptive reporters began to scribble their tale of a frail French stripling and a massive British Colossus. Utter nonsense. The physical omens were all against the Briton. Beckett, who was trained, if anything, a little too fine, has a compact figure, a boxlike chest, stout, stumpy arms useful only for punching, and a thickish neck too short to take his head far out of harm's way. Carpentier, long and lithe, has a terrible pair of arms, very long, with the forearms heavy just where the weight should be. He has a long chest, a long reach, a long flexible neck, and, last but not least, a long head. Nobody who knew the ABC of boxing could doubt for a moment that unless Beckett could wear him down and outstay him, and stand a good deal during the process, he could not win at the physical odds against him except by a lucky knockout.

When the men stood up, another curious asset of Carpentier's raised the extraordinary question whether he had not been taught to box by a lady. Some years ago Miss Diana Watts, a lady athlete who believed that she had discovered the secret of ancient Greek gymnastics, reproduced with her own person the pose and action of the Discobolus and the archer in the Heracles pediment in the British Museum, both of which had been up to that time considered physically impossible. Her book on the subject, with its interesting photographs, is still extant. Her method was to move and balance the body on the ball of the foot without using the heel, and to combine this with a certain technique of the diaphragm. Now the moment 'time' was called, and Carpentier on his feet in the ring, it was apparent that he had this technique. He was like a man on springs; and the springs were not in his heels but the balls of his feet. His diaphragm *tenue* was perfect. Whether his lady instructor was Miss Diana Watts or Dame Nature, she has turned out a complete Greek athlete. This really very remarkable and gymnastically important phenomenon has been overlooked, partly because it has not been understood, but partly also because the change in Carpentier's face when he sets to work is so startling that the spectators see nothing else. The unmistakable Greek line digs a trench across his forehead at once; his colour changes to a stony grey; he looks 10,000 years old; his eyes see through stone walls; and his expression of intense concentration will frighten everyone in the hall except his opponent, who is far too busy to attend to such curiosities.

There was no fight. There was only a superb exhibition spar, with Beckett as what used to be called a chopping block. For a few moments he wisely stuck close to his man; but Mr Angle gave the order (I did not hear it, but was told of it) to break away; and Beckett then let the Frenchman get clear and faced him for outfighting. From that moment he was lost. Carpentier simply did the classic thing: the long shot with the left; the lead-off and getaway. The measurement of distance – and such a distance! – was exact to an inch, the speed dazzling, the impact like the kick of a thoroughbred horse. Beckett, except for one amazed lionlike shake of his head, took it like a stone wall; but he was helpless: he had not time to move a finger before Carpentier was back out of his reach. He was utterly outspeeded. Three times Carpentier did this, each hit more brilliant if possible than the last. Beckett was for a moment dazed by the astonishing success of the attack: and in that moment Carpentier sent in a splendidly clean and finished right to the jaw. It is not often that perfect luck attends perfect style in this world; but Carpentier seemed able to command even luck. The blow found that mysterious spot that is in all our jaws, and that is so seldom found by the fist. There was no mistaking the droop with which Beckett went prone to the boards. In an old-fashioned fight he would have been carried by his seconds to his corner and brought up to the scratch in half a minute quite well able to go on. Under modern rules he had to lie unhelped; and at the end of ten seconds Carpentier was declared the winner.

Carpentier had made the spar so intensely interesting that the 74 seconds it had occupied seemed like ten; and I could hardly believe that four had elapsed between the moment when Beckett dropped to the boards and the jubilant spring into the air with which Carpentier announced that the decision had been given in his favour. He was as unaffected in his delight as he had been in his nervousness before 'Time' was called, when he had asked his bottle holder for a mouthful of water and confessed to a dry mouth. The usual orgy followed. Pugilists are a sentimental, feminine species, much given to kissing and crying. Carpentier was hoisted up to be chaired, dragged down to be kissed, hung out by the heels from the scaffold to be fondled by a lady, and in every possible way given reason to envy Beckett. Beckett's seconds, by the way, so far forgot themselves as to leave their man lying uncared for on the floor after he was counted out until Carpentier, indignant at their neglect, rushed across the ring and carried Beckett to his corner. I suggest to the masters of ceremonies at these contests, whoever they may be, that this had better not occur again. It is true that the decision was so sudden and sensational that a little distraction was excusable; but if Carpentier, who had the best reason to be carried away by his feelings, could remember, those whose duty it was could very well have done so if they had been properly instructed in their duties.

Now for the seamy side of the affair, the betting side. As I pushed my way through the crowd in Holborn, I could see by the way my news was received that every poor dupe of the sporting papers had put his shillings or pence or even his quid or two on Beckett. Never had a betting ramp been more thoroughly organised. When the war was over nobody knew whether military service had spoiled Carpentier for boxing purposes or left him as good as ever. If he were as good, or better, then clearly oceans of money could be made at a risk no greater than any gambler will take, by persuading the public that his sun has set and that the Carpentier who knocked out Wells in 73 seconds was a back number. Accordingly, the situation was taken in hand in the usual fashion. A British pugilist of something less than commanding eminence was sent to France and pitted against Carpentier, who gave a poor display and obtained the decision with difficulty. Here was proof positive of his decadence. Then the press got to work. Beckett, progressing rapidly from victory to victory, was extolled as invulnerable and invincible. Carpentier's reputation was discounted until hardly a shred of it remained. His two youthful defeats were retold. The public was reminded that he had obtained a decision against Gunboat Smith only on an unintentional foul by that gentleman; and ring reporters solemnly declared their conviction that but for this accident Carpentier could not have lasted another round. I was informed on the strength of private information from 'the French colony' (whatever that may be) that Carpentier had sold the fight, and that it was arranged that Beckett would win. Then came a clump of boxing articles, each giving a dozen reasons to show that nothing but a miracle could prevent Beckett from wiping the floor with the obsolete and exhausted Frenchman. I do not know how high the odds were piled at last; but on the morning of the fight every ringstruck sportsman who knew nothing about boxing (and not one in a hundred of the people who read about boxing, or for that matter, who write about it, knows anything worth knowing) had his bet on Beckett. Most of these poor devils do not know even now how completely they were humbugged. They blame Beckett.

Beckett is not to blame. What happened to him happened to Sayers 66 years ago when he was beaten for the first and only time by Nat Langham. Langham taught Donnelly, who taught Mr Angle's and my generation the long shot with the left and getaway of which Carpentier gave such a brilliant demonstration; and it beat even the invincible Sayers. Langham could not knock him out, because the knockout, though effective for ten seconds, does not last for 30; and Langham had to keep hitting Sayers' eyes until they were closed, and poor Tom, blinded, had to weep over his solitary defeat. But Sayers' most famous achievements came later; and there is no reason in the world why Beckett should not be as successful as ever in spite of his having shared Sayers' fate. When he described his defeat as a million-to-one chance, he exaggerated the odds against a knockout; but the knockout is always a matter of luck; and Beckett has probably taken dozens of clouts on the jaw as heavy, if not so artistic, as Carpentier's, without turning a hair.

As to the brutality of the affair, Beckett was chatting to his friends over the ropes without a mark on his face, and with £3,000 in his pocket, before they stopped kissing Carpentier. There are many industrial pursuits more painful and much more dangerous than boxing. The knockout is probably the most effective anaesthetic known to science; that is why it is so conclusive. Many women would let Carpentier knock them about for 20 rounds for a pension of £150 a year. The valid objection is the old puritan objection: it is not the pain to the pugilist, but the pleasure to the spectator that matters. To the genuine connoisseur it is simply distressing to see a boxer hurt beyond the harmless point up to which every reasonably hardy sportsman is prepared to smart for the sake of the game. Mr Angle's expression of concern as he contemplated Beckett on the boards was a study, though he knew that Beckett was fast asleep. But unquestionably many of the spectators believe that they are witnessing acts of cruelty, and pay for admission for their sake, not understanding boxing in the least. Also, the contests, like all contests, act as a propaganda of pugnacity and competition. Sometimes the demoralising effect is visible and immediate. I have seen men assault their neighbours after witnessing a rough and tumble fight for some time. But the effect of a highly skilled display such as Carpentier gave overawes the spectators. It often reduces them to absolute silence. It fascinates the connoisseurs, and frightens the novices and the riff-raff. The question of the suppression of prize-fighting is, therefore, not a simple one. The commercial exploitation of prize-fighting is bad like the commercial exploitation of everything else; for in pugilism as in other things 'honour sinks where commerce long prevails'; and though such atrocities as the poisoning of Heenan and the rest of the blackguardism which compelled the authorities to make short work of the old prize-ring in the 1860s are now hardly possible, yet Mr Cochran and other entrepreneurs of the ring must bear in mind that they can secure toleration only by being on their very best behaviour. The belief that pugnacity and the competitive spirit are the secrets of England's greatness may give way at any moment to the equally plausible theory that they are the causes of her decline.

The world now waits breathless for the meeting between Carpentier and Mr

Dempsey. The general sentiment on the night of the fourth was undoubtedly 'May I be there to see it'. I know nothing of Mr Dempsey's quality as a boxer; but if he can play at lightning long-shorts with an instinctive command of the duck and counter, and on occasion side-step a boxer who, as the cinematograph proves, has a dangerous habit of leading from off his toes without stepping in, with the certainty of falling heavily on his nose if his adversary takes in the situation and gets out of the way in time, Charles XII may find his Poltava yet.

Such are the impressions of one who has not for 35 years past dreamt of attending a boxing exhibition. If I be asked why I have abstained for so long, I reply that any intelligent person who frequents such exhibitions will soon be convinced that the English are congenitally incapable of the art of boxing. When you have seen a hundred contests between 200 Britons, and have concluded that every single one of the 200 must be the very worst boxer in the world, and his admirers the most abject gulls that ever tipped their way, like Mr Toots, into pugilistic society, you are driven to the conclusion that you would be happier at home, or even in a theatre or concert room. The truth is, of course, that boxing such as Carpentier's demands qualities which their possessors will not waste on so trivial and unamiable a pursuit in such rude company. It was worth Carpentier's while to escape from the slavery of the coal pit and win £5,000 in 74 seconds with his fists. It would not have been worth his while if he had been Charles XII. Thus the prize-fighters are either geniuses like Carpentier, too few and far between to keep up one's interest in exhibitions, or else poor fellows whose boxing is simply not worth looking at except by gulls who know no better. And so I doubt whether I shall go again for another 35 years except when Carpentier is one of the performers.

The Nation
December 1919

Dempsey v Firpo

Frank G. Menke

William Harrison Dempsey started boxing as 'Young' Dempsey, then became the third in the fight game to be known as 'Jack' Dempsey. Sub-editors in search of a caption referred to him as 'The Manassa Mauler' or simply 'Champ' and for posterity, according to boxing historian Nat Fleischer, he was 'a champion among champions'.

His opponents did not care what he was called, they had enough trouble trying to keep away from his frenzied non-stop two-fisted attacks. It must have been rather like tackling an army assault course and finding all the obstacles arriving at once. In between capturing the world heavyweight title with a savage three-round disposal of the giant Kansas cowboy Jess Willard and this meeting four years later with another giant, from the pampas of Argentina, Luis Firpo, Dempsey had made four successful defences, among them the first million-dollar gate in ring history, when he finished Carpentier in four rounds.

Apart from having stature in common, Willard and Firpo shared the dubious distinction of being knocked down seven times in the first round of their fights with Dempsey. Willard also earned an unbefitting bonus by having his cheekbone broken in seven places – Firpo was more than happy to forego that particular privilege – he preferred to save his cheek for his manager when asking why he got the fight in the first place. Even so, at one point boxing history very nearly came to be rewritten.

Frank G. Menke was known for his encyclopaedic knowledge of boxing and as a highly competent ghost writer – handily placed in this case for there could so easily have been one in the ring. In describing a dramatic encounter from a distance of two decades, he risked perjury for his prose style, though the hyperbole relays the excitement in an exceptional way.

Never in the history of American pugilism was there staged a battle so sensational as the Jack Dempsey—Luis Firpo affair in New York on the night of 14 September 1923.

From the moment that the first gong banged until the Argentine warrior lay a crumpled heap upon the canvas – total time: 3 minutes, 57 seconds – there was action so rapid, so cyclonic that the eye could not follow, nor the brain record the exact details.

It was not a boxing match – not a civilised fistic encounter. Two wild men were tossed into the same ring, each with an intent to murder the other – or be murdered in his failure. And 85,000 persons, imbibing the spirit of madness, arose to their feet, and 85,000 voices howled and shrieked in a delirium that made a din which rivalled a thousand Niagaras.

Its like in ring battling had never been seen before – and never will be known again. The story is the epic of ringdom – the fight of all the ages.

With the clang of the first gong, Dempsey fairly catapulted from his corner to meet a huge, hairy giant from the pampas of South America; rushed, crouched, swirled upward and swung a terrific left-hand punch to his foeman's jaw.

It was short – by two inches.

As Dempsey steadied, to try again, Firpo's powerful right hand whistled through the night and struck Dempsey full and solid upon the point of the chin. Every ounce of the South American's gigantic body was concentrated in that blow – one of the hardest ever landed in ring annals.

The knees of the world champion buckled under him; a world champion pitched forward. He was toppling, face forward, to dethronement. One punch – the first of the night – seemed to have sent him to his doom!

If Firpo had been six inches farther away at that very fraction of a second, Dempsey probably would have crumpled into the resin dust, either to rise no more, or, in rising, to be met by a fusillade of blows which probably would have crushed the consciousness from him.

But as Dempsey pitched forward, Firpo was so close that the champion fell against the body of the giant. Instinct made him grab – and hold. Desperately, wildly, Firpo tried to shake off Dempsey. Before he could achieve his purpose, the brief rest saved Dempsey.

Strength and a little power came back to Dempsey's legs; the floodgates of reserve energy opened, revived him, refreshed him – refreshed and revived, however, only the body of him, because Dempsey afterwards said he remembered nothing about that first round after he had been hit with that first pile-driver blow.

He had been hit and hurt by the rushing, tearing, lunging form before him. And that form must be destroyed. Such was the prompting of savage instinct. Everything that Dempsey had learned in years of boxing was forgotten; his clear reasoning power, his coolness and calmness were gone. There was nothing left but the fighting fury which made him known as the Tiger Man of the prize-ring.

Urged on only by a wild and blazing rage, the champion ripped and tore into the giant and, as he did so, he put into his blows every bit of killing power which he could summon. He was relentless, merciless, forgetful of the ethics of the fighting game; a cruel monster, determined that the man before him must be hammered and pounded into absolute helplessness.

Dempsey, loose from the first clinch, rushed at Firpo, both hands working with the power and speed of a locomotive piston rod. A left hand landed with mighty force upon the chin of Firpo. The Argentinian went down in a heap – perhaps 30 seconds after the round had started.

The official proceeded to drone the count. He had reached 'nine' when Firpo started to rise. Then he stopped counting – when he should have gone on, for

Firpo was not in a boxing position and should have been counted out then and there. It was at least 13 full seconds before Firpo was back in fighting pose.

Another flurry of blows met Firpo – and again he toppled. He arose, dealt a right-hander to Dempsey's chin and was rewarded with a right to his own, which floored him again. Once more Firpo arose, but Dempsey hurled himself at the huge Argentinian. Even as Dempsey whirled through the air, Firpo steadied on wobbling legs, swung his world-famous right and again caught Dempsey on the rim of the jaw! Dempsey's body quivered, his legs buckled, he stumbled forward, his hands went to the floor.

As the referee raced over, expecting to begin the count, Dempsey pulled himself together, straightened up, lunged at Firpo and caught him on the jaw with a punch that didn't travel more than eight inches. Firpo dropped almost upon the spot where Dempsey, a few seconds before, had been sprawled.

Again Firpo beat the count and rushed at Dempsey. The champion backed to the ropes, more because he was jockeying to get a newer shot at Firpo's jaw than because of fear of the South American's charge.

Then something happened which forms one of the most astonishing chapters in the entire annals of the prize-ring. A world's champion, a challenger, a referee were in the ring one second. A second later only two figures were visible. The king of kings of the fistic realms suddenly disappeared as though a trap door had opened and swallowed him.

Over 85,000 persons saw the fight – and perhaps 85,000 different accounts have been given as to how Dempsey went out of the ring – and how he got back. Of the 85,000, perhaps no more than 50 persons in the first row of the ringside press seats actually saw what happened. My seat was in the first row – alongside Jim Corbett. My view was wholly unobstructed.

This is what I saw.

Dempsey was backed to the ropes with Firpo crowding with the left side of his body. Firpo's right arm was free. Six times in succession he hit Dempsey on the chin or head without a return, because Dempsey was in such a position that his arms were practically handcuffed.

Realising his peril, Dempsey decided to slide out of the trap. Bending his head low towards his own right arm, he attempted to move along the ropes until he was clear of Firpo.

At the exact moment that Dempsey's head was below the upper strand, and at the exact fraction of a second that his right foot was off the floor, Firpo hit the champion on the chin with a right. The middle of Dempsey's body was up against the middle strand of the ropes at that very second.

The result was this.

Dempsey's legs shot off the ground, and his head shot backwards. A world champion spun around much as does the piece of wood one uses in playing tiddlywinks. And in a head-first backward dive, Jack Dempsey, ruler of the fistic world, went into the press row – while 85,000 persons looked on in hushed amazement.

Much has been written about how reporters saved Dempsey in his fall – and how they helped him back into the ring. The real truth is that the reporters handicapped, more than helped, Dempsey in his ring re-entry.

When 194 pounds of humanity came hurtling through the air directly at their heads, those reporters did only the natural thing. They pushed up their hands to protect themselves; they summoned all the power they could to keep Dempsey from falling upon them and breaking their necks. Their thought was to save themselves – not to aid Dempsey, who suddenly had become a 194-pound menace to their existence.

Dempsey landed among the group. Squirming, twisting, lunging with arms, kicking with legs, he strove to get himself steered in the right direction so that he could climb back through the ropes. In one of his wild lurches, his fist hit Kid McPartland, one of the judges, in the eye – and blackened it for ten days.

It is true that reportorial hands shoved Dempsey as he climbed back through the ropes. But they weren't hands of friendship. The men who pushed him did so because they wanted to be sure Dempsey didn't kick them in the face or body. They were passing Dempsey back and forth, because they wanted none of him floundering on their heads and frail necks.

Never did a man look more bewildered, more 'all gone' than Dempsey, back in the ring just as the referee counted 'nine', flat-footed, legs spread wide for balance, against the ropes. His hands were helpless at his sides. His eyes showed no brain light. His whole body slumped.

This was Firpo's second golden opportunity for world conquest – and for the second and final time it slipped from him.

Had Firpo closed in on Dempsey and thrown every ounce of his titanic power into one punch, Dempsey would have gone down – and his reign would have ended. But Firpo, not sure whether Dempsey was faking, decided to take no chances. He went in cautiously. Precious seconds flew onward into eternity. He finally decided to strike. He swung – and missed – because Dempsey instinctively ducked, as energy came back to him.

The action of Firpo galvanised Dempsey into a new attack. He went forward – revived by some mysterious force. The arms that had been helpless suddenly began whirling through the air. He drove Firpo back – back – and back with his furious charge and, under the avalanche of leather, Firpo crumpled again to the floor. As Dempsey tore into him, Firpo braced and fought back. Toe-to-toe the two men stood, no quarter asked – none given.

The bell banged – the round had passed into official history. But Dempsey never heard it. As Firpo turned to go to his corner the champion's foggy brain construed the act as a new retreat. He went racing after the Wild Bull of the Pampas, showering blows on head, neck and shoulders.

Firpo whirled, a look of surprise on his face – then one of insane rage. He closed in and began slugging viciously, until the referee was able, by locking their arms, to stop the sluggery and tell Dempsey the round was over.

It was a round without dramatic equal in the annals of boxing. Firpo had been down five times; Dempsey had staggered once, was down on his hands later, and out of the ring upon another occasion.

Perhaps a hundred blows had been swung – and about 90 had landed, each with force and power enough to batter any other giant into an hour of unconsciousness. But these were supermen that night.

When the referee finally had stopped the after-bell battling, Dempsey stood in mid-ring. He didn't know the location of his own corner. Jack Kearns, his manager, leaped through the ropes, grabbed Dempsey by the arms, hauled him to his chair, flopped him down, picked up a bucket of ice water and hit Dempsey with its contents. The shock revived Dempsey – brought him back to consciousness for the first time since he was hit with that pile-driver smash in the first round.

There was wild confusion in Dempsey's corner because Kearns could not find the smelling salts. They were in the pocket of his shirt. He had forgotten he had placed them there. Kearns was roaring condemnation at Jerry (The Greek) Luvadis, the trainer, and Jerry was trying to grab at Kearns's pocket to get the salts because Kearns was shouting so loudly he couldn't hear Jerry. Kearns hit Jerry in the nose. Jerry grabbed the bottle from Kearns's pocket. Kearns poked the fumes under Dempsey's nose.

The buzzer announced ten seconds before the bell. Kearns leaned over, yelled at Dempsey.

'Quit taking chances – cover – cover! He's a murderer!'

'What round?' asked Dempsey.

'Second,' answered Kearns – and the bell rang.

Dempsey came out – cautiously. This time Firpo did the rushing. Dempsey, a keen fighter once again now that his mental faculties were restored, crouched, weaved, feinted, and Firpo lashed out with his right. Dempsey had miscalculated Firpo's nearness, and the blow, a murderous drive, crashed into Dempsey's body, under the heart.

Dempsey sagged back. Firpo 'cocked' his right and started to let it go, when, like the flight of a meteor, Dempsey's short left crashed against Firpo's jaw. The South American staggered and fell to the floor with a sickening crash. It seemed that this must be the end. But it wasn't. At 'eight' Firpo was up – and Dempsey was upon him.

Scorning a defence, Dempsey pumped lefts into Firpo's face and body with the precision of drumbeats. Firpo, in desperation, swung a right, missed, and the momentum carried him close to Dempsey. The champion's short left caught Firpo on the point of the jaw. As he started to fall, Dempsey put all he had into a lifting right hook – and Firpo, in falling, went down as if driven by some terrific explosive force.

For six seconds he lay there inert, seemingly lifeless. Blood streamed from his nose and mouth. His eyes were open – but glazed. At 'eight' he made a feeble attempt to rise, lifted himself a few inches – and then toppled back.

'Ten,' droned the referee and Dempsey was still the world's champion.

The Sporting News
27 January 1944

Give Him to the Angels: Harry Greb

James R. Fair

Harry Greb was one of boxing's imperishables; in essence, a ring-master with the heart of a prize-fighter. Absolutely ruthless at close quarters, he literally swept all before him with a torrent of punches from which there was no escape. 'The Human Windmill' with the graveyard eyes – a sort of time and motion in reverse – was also adept at using every trick that was not in the book: 'Prize-fighting ain't the noblest of arts, and I ain't its noblest artist' was his famous quote.

Greb was world middleweight champion for three years from 1923, but had many battles and successes against heavier opponents. He averaged 22 bouts a year and during 1919 incredibly doubled his average. In his career, Greb fought 299 times winning 264 and drawing 12 – a magnificent record. He died in Atlantic City in 1926 when he was under anaesthetic after surgery to his nose following a car accident.

This extract from James R. Fair's biography of Greb paints a vivid picture.

There couldn't have been a better title for the story of Harry Greb than *Never Call Retreat*. Actually, it isn't true to say he never retreated. No fighter with a brain in his head or with a view to keeping one there would refuse to when the milling called for it. But when Greb retreated it wasn't one of those marathons that Field Marshal Erwin Rommel described as 'strategic' after scramming all the way from the gates of Alexandria clear across the African desert to Tunisia, a mere 1,400 miles. When Greb retreated it was orderly and for one purpose: so that, having backed up, the momentum on the forward march would catapult him into more devastating action. But since, in a recent novel, someone else has come up with the title that fitted Greb so well, *Give Him to the Angels* will have to do.

He has been up there with the angels for nearly 20 years now. No matter how many times they may have encased his fists in boxing gloves and sent him to the post against their toughest angels – and there are plenty up there who tangled with him down here – I would vouch for his comportment if – well, there are many ifs, not the least important of which is the referee. He just didn't like referees, especially the ones who called him for such extracurricular activities as sticking his thumb into an opponent's eye. To him, fighting was so much necessary nonsense anyhow, like getting drunk, so why put a third man in the ring to see that the boys behaved?

Sometimes that third man didn't do so well. He did so badly the night Greb slashed Mickey Walker to pieces in their middleweight championship clash that twice he had to pick himself up off the floor. Not only that, but he was recuperating on the ropes a considerable part of that 15 rounds of mayhem that still has an older generation gasping and holding on to their seats.

While no one saw the blows or the shoves that twice dropped Eddie Purdy that night nearly a quarter of a century ago, it is significant that in his corner between rounds Greb expressed the thought that Purdy was favouring Walker in the clinches.

'That meddlesome cop,' he snorted, 'had better keep his hands off me.'

Hot water was what he was in most of the time, but the heat agreed with him. He was forever being barred from boxing in one state or another because of rough-house tactics the very thought of which would chill a commando's spine.

He was in court for one thing or another, sometimes hailed there by his manager.

At least once a wailing chorus girl waited for him at the altar and the next day she wailed for publication. Greb's rebuttal squared everything as far as he was concerned: 'I didn't think splits took me that serious.'

When he took off in his car, a rakish speedwagon reputedly given him by a famous Pittsburgh lady, the betting was 75 to 25, with Greb on the long end, that he would upset it, injuring everybody but himself. For once, however, he let his backers down. He wound up in Pittsburgh's West Penn Hospital with enough internal injuries, compound fractures and lacerations to kill a mule (animal), but not enough even to slow down the kind of mule he was. While Pittsburgh newspapers were posting death watches and news services were sending out advance obituaries, he was *en route* to Indianapolis or vicinity to fight rough-and-tumble Chuck Wiggins, who outweighed him a good 30 pounds.

The primrose path was where he did his heavy roadwork. On the eve of a fight his manager knew where to find him – bouncing up and down the stairs in the red-light district, a hussy under each arm and a brace bringing up the rear, while the madame put in a frantic call for fresh stuff. If there is one thing that will ruin a fighter it is clubbiness with a lady before a bout. He knows that if he indulges himself – and it is a temptation that nearly drives him crazy because he can't get from his block-of-granite sparring partners or high roughneck manager the kind of affection rugged youth is fondest of – he will vomit the first time he catches a solid punch around the heart and he will have to swallow it to keep his opponent from getting wise. Greb used to sneak girls into his dressing-room, lock the door and give them the works while his opponent waited for him in the ring. Then he would lope out of there, warm and enthusiastic after such pleasurable endeavours, and turn in the most brilliant performance of his career.

As a result of these high-jinks, all sorts of fables grew up about him after his death. It has been written not once but hundreds of times that he boxed with a glass eye most of his life. Nothing could be more ridiculous. A jarring jolt to the face or a sideswipe across the eye with an open glove would have knocked it out of its socket, to say nothing of what would have happened if a direct hit were scored. Besides, an opponent who wouldn't take note of a glass eye and concentrate his fire on it before the end of the first round would be dopier than Don Quixote jousting at windmills with his lance. Greb was twice a champion. He didn't fight dopes, but this is not to say some of his opponents didn't come under this classification after he had batted them around for eight or ten rounds.

What none of them suspected when he was ranging the fistic horizon, and what only two or three people in the world knew, was that he was blind in his right eye and had less than half sight in his left. He fought at least a hundred major bouts when he was so blind in his 'good' eye that, sitting in his corner, he couldn't tell his opponents from their handlers across the ring in their corner. But he didn't quit the ring because of this. He had reached the stage where, in the street, he had difficulty telling a woman from a man ten feet away save for the swish of her skirt or the smell of her perfume.

'Women,' he said, 'mean more to me than anything else on earth. If I can't see 'em, I can't love 'em, so I'm hanging up my gloves.'

It has been written that he fought six times a week and twice on holidays. 'The only thing wrong with that statement,' he once said, 'is that I drop from ten to 15 pounds in a fight.' He thought the sports writers ought to give him enough of a breather to put some flesh on his bones.

The press, not exactly discouraged by the fighters and their managers, paid plenty of attention to boxers who came out of the First World War. It referred to Tunney, who usually entered the ring with a Marine insignia on his dressing-gown, as the Fighting Marine. It billed Bob Martin, the AEF heavyweight champion, as Soldier Bob. It went off the deep end for Georges Carpentier when he came here to train for the Dempsey fight 25 years ago. With no desire to play down this advantage in one of the most stupendous publicity build-ups ever given a prize-fight, Carpentier came into the ring that July afternoon behind a squad of France's famous fighting Blue Devils, the tricolor dangling from his silk boxing trunks, the band playing 'La Marseillaise'.

It was all very colourful. Sports writers loved to dish it out and the public loved to read it. It paid handsome dividends at the turnstiles. It was smart from every angle, and this is no attempt to criticise it, but . . .

How many people knew that Harry Greb, who got enough bad press notices to break the heart of a less rugged individual, enlisted in the Navy soon after America entered the war in 1917, that he mopped up on everybody in the Atlantic Fleet and boxed in inter-allied bouts in London following the armistice? Outside of Pittsburgh, his home town, you could count them on your fingers.

If newspapers outside of Pittsburgh knew about it they kept it secret. There were some mighty odd men on some of the more remote journals back there when Greb was in his prime in the early '20s. A handful of them tried to shake him down with promises of writing beautiful words about him, but when you shook the Greb tree you could expect the falling fruit to knock your brains out. One of these journalistic pimples came up with a sore backside and another lost a mouthful of teeth. Still another waited until Greb died. Then, in his column, he labelled him as 'a tightwad who somehow managed to die broke'. Greb wasn't a tightwad and he didn't die broke. He made a million dollars in the ring, but spent most of it taking care of broken-down athletes, buying fancy clothes, and having gay parties.

He was a stranger to the reporters who picked on him. They had seen him fight, yes. But they didn't know him personally, had never even interviewed him. If they had they might have handled him the way Harry Keck, Havey Boyle and Chester Smith handled him in Pittsburgh. They gave him hell when he needed it, which was often, but they threw him bouquets too. His explanation for unnecessarily rough tactics got him out of many a tight squeak: 'Prize-fighting ain't the noblest of arts, and I ain't its noblest artist.'

One reporter in particular viewed him through jaundiced eyes. Covering Greb's fights as he saw them, some of his stories were classics. A fairly typical lead ran like this: 'They tossed pop bottles, clubs, rocks and pig-iron at Harry Greb as he left the ring last night. Maybe if Harry had kept his thumb out of his opponent's eyes long enough to let him get his bearings it would have been a different story.'

Greb would huff and puff and send word to the reporter that they were through forever, the end of a long and beautiful love. Then he would turn in a nice, clean fight in which he wouldn't have thumbed his opponent more than a dozen times, or nudged him ungently with his knees in the clinches, or stepped on his feet, and the reporter would write that Pittsburgh's Little Lord Fauntleroy had performed creditably indeed. Greb would be delighted and the next day he would hustle around to the reporter's office and tell him he was his sweetheart and demand to know whoever said he wasn't in the first place.

This reporter didn't always pat him with such lighthearted barbs, but he always gave him credit for being on the dead level. When the referee said '. . . and come out fighting', that's the way Greb came out. No one on earth could tamper with him. One day a gangster handed him a bale of $50 bills and told him to drop the decision in his next fight, a couple of days away. It was a fight of no consequence. Greb wouldn't have cared much if he lost it provided he gave his best – and he always gave his best. He threw the money in the thug's face, knocked him down and kicked him all over the street. Only a few feet away, crouched behind a machine-gun in a parked car, sat three killer pals. Greb knew they were there and they knew he knew it. They didn't have the guts to cope with that kind of courage and they got out of there in a hurry, leaving their man gasping for breath and bleeding in the gutter.

Fast as sin and indestructible as rawhide, Greb was seldom knocked down, but when he was he bounced up off the canvas like a jealous stallion, charged with the ferocity of a rattlesnake and clubbed you silly with as hateful a pair of hands as the prize-ring has ever seen.

It has been written so often that his name was Berg that a large percentage of sports fans – and many sports writers, too – think it was. He was born Edward Henry Greb, but changed his first name to Harry when he started boxing. An older brother who died was named Harry. Edward Henry, who idolised him, took his name. Greb's father, Pius Greb, now dead, was of German–American descent, his mother, still living, Irish, which throws down the story that for business reasons he changed his name to Greb simply by spelling Berg backwards.

He never bothered to deny inaccuracies like these so long as they weren't insulting. Consequently, some of the boys went the limit when they hadn't anything else to write about. Shortly before his retirement in 1926, a magazine ran an article about him that was wrong in almost every detail except that his home was in Pittsburgh. A friend bumped into him a few days later and wanted to know if he had read it.

'I heard about it,' Greb said unconcernedly.

'You didn't read it?' asked the friend in amazement.

'No, but I hear it was a lulu – wrong from start to finish.'

'You can make the magazine retract it, and you should.'

'Why should I?' Greb grumbled, irritated at being pressured. 'Some cub probably wrote it and if I denied it it might get him into a jam with his magazine.'

'Cub my eye,' the friend hung on courageously. 'He's a syndicated columnist and he's as well known as you are.'

'Just the same,' Greb said, simmering down, 'he didn't say anything mean about me and maybe it gave the readers a laugh.'

He stepped back and looked down his nose like a bad boy about to admit a truth that was going to hurt.

'I'm no angel, bub,' he said. 'Ha, ha, ha! I done some things myself which wasn't so cosy and I'm not gonna beef about a story I never read and don't intend to read. If he [the author] had a good time writing it, swell; I had lots'a good times myself.'

He wasn't lying, either. He had lots'a good times. He had a perfectly marvellous time one night in Grand Rapids, Mr Harry Greb of Pittsburgh v Mr Chuck Wiggins of Indianapolis. They had had lots'a marvellous times together, but this one was outstanding. It merits the 'Mr' before their names. 'Mr' lends dignity. This was a dignified evening.

For the younger generation, a little background on Mr Wiggins; he was a tough cookie. Known as the Hoosier Playboy, he fought all the good heavyweights, tangling twice with Tunney, and he gave them fits. Fighting was what he was fondest of and it didn't matter whether it was in the ring for money or in the street for relaxation. He ran amok in an Indianapolis hotel lobby one night and it took a squad of policemen and several firemen to tame him. 'The lobby was a shambles,' said an Associated Press story, leaving it to the reader to deduce that Mr Wiggins wasn't. He got mad at his brother-in-law one day, swatting him on the jaw, and in return stopped a bullet with one of his thick ears, peeling off a sizeable hunk of non-edible cauliflower.

Mr Wiggins's weakness was whisky. Mr Greb's women. When Mr Wiggins had finished with the bottle he amused himself and his friends by corralling cops and bumping their noggins together. Of him it was said he could name the town in a given locality in which the cops had the toughest and most tuneful noggins. Of Mr Greb it was said he could name the town in which the girls' skirts were the swishiest and their manner the most obliging.

So on this evening in Grand Rapids – this outstanding evening – Mr Greb, his hat pulled down to hide his cocked right eye into which a thousand thumbs had been stuck, sauntered into Mr Wiggins's hotel room. It was only a few hours before they were to engage in fisticuffs at the local arena, and Mr Greb said like this: 'Hullo Chuck o' pal. You lookin' in the pink. Say kid, there's no use in us killin' each other like we been doin'. Whatcha say we make it a nice clean fight tonight? No rough stuff.'

Mr Wiggins, who looked like a man any sensible bulldozer would choose to skirt, was in a jovial mood and he replied as follows: 'Hullo Harry old sock. You're lookin' good yourself. I can properly state, with reference to tonight's engagement, that you have took the words right outta my mouth. We made a lot of cabbage fightin' each other and we will make more. We won't pull our punches tonight, but we will make it a nice clean fight like you say. Shake.'

It was an agreement between men who respected each other and it was meant to withstand the vicissitudes of time.

Everything was sweet and lovely in the ring, with Mr Greb complimenting Mr Wiggins on his gentlemanly behaviour at the end of each round and with Mr Wiggins doing likewise. Comes up Round Four. For some reason unknown to science Mr Wiggins lunged in a most ungentlemanly and dastardly manner at Mr Greb, who stuck his foot out and tripped him. Mr Wiggins fell headlong through the ropes, his head coming to a thudding rest on the ring apron. His large backside did not follow, however, but stuck upright inside the ropes. Mr Wiggins eased his feet to the floor gently, as in a slow-motion movie, leaving his backside exposed across the middle rope. He didn't remain in this position long enough for nature to grow a pair of hands to protect this seldom-exposed bulge, nor did it occur to the referee to hang a warning light on it, so Mr Greb leaped in and sprayed it with a dozen resounding wallops. When Mr Wiggins got his backside in an unexposed position and his head inside the ropes there was a lot of hilarious fun. At the end of six rounds of butting, heeling, biting, kicking and other forms of delightful deliriums, Mr Wiggins was walking backwards and complaining of bells in his head, and Mr Greb's faith in humanity had suffered an irreparable blow.

'I will never again trust a man who tells me "I can properly state that you have took the words right outta my mouth",' said Mr Greb mournfully. 'But in all fairness to Chuck, I can properly state that he is the best butter I ever butted against.'

Greb was no waster of punches. He aimed them at his opponent, but if they missed and hit the referee – well, what was wrong with the referee? Didn't he have two hands and two feet the same as Greb? Suppose Greb gouged his thumb into an opponent's eyes in the heat of battle, or sank a tooth into his ear, or used his head as a battering ram, or ripped the skin off the face by taking an open glove down over old cuts, or 'sneak' punched on the break-aways, or jumped gingerly on his feet in the clinches? Maybe you wouldn't run across anything like this at Eton. It isn't likely a governess would advise it as rudimentary training for her young charges. But it was the kind of treatment Greb liked to dish out, and when he got it back he didn't yell teacher.

The night he piled up off the floor in Pittsburgh after picking a thumb out of his right eye – a retaliatory thumb to be sure – and knew the sight was gone forever, did he squawk to the referee? On unsteady legs he lowered his head of pain, charged, and handed Kid Norfolk the pasting of his pugilistic life. Back in his dressing-room after the fight he swore to secrecy Happy Albacher (a character with whom I shall deal later), then dismissed the tragedy with 'That black boy's got a tougher eye than I HAD!'

He came on from there, blind in one eye and with no more than half sight in the other, to win the American light-heavyweight and world's middleweight titles before he died following a minor operation on his nose in an Atlantic City hospital and to inspire such soubriquets as The Iron City Express, The Invincible, The Pittsburgh Windmill, The Inexhaustible, The Wildest Tiger.

He was fistiana's Peck's Bad Boy. Boxing officials threatened to throw him out of the ring at the first suspicion of a foul. Newspapers condemned him. Crowds booed him, not always but frequently, no matter if, as was often the case, he was 60 pounds lighter and six inches shorter than his opponent. Sometimes he fretted on the eve of an important fight, not because he was afraid of his opponent but because boxing commissioners were gunning for him and he didn't want to get the bounce. But he wasn't built to fret long and by ringtime he was relaxed as a cud-chewing cow, the picture of peace and contentment.

'And why not!' he used to answer when you asked him why he wasn't nervous. 'I'll be fighting in a few minutes, won't I?'

That was it. He was a fighting man from the tips of his artistic fingers right down to the gnarled toes of his big feet on which so many retaliatory heels had been ground. Fighting was his profession and he loved it.

It was the same old story when boxing officials stormed into his dressing-room, shook their fingers under his nose, called him every vile name in the book and then, winded, shouted: 'And we'll throw you out of the ring and bar you from boxing in every state in the union if you heave a single foul punch tonight.'

And it was the same old story when his dressing-room door flew open and he shuffled up the aisle to the ring in a nice clean dressing-gown, his black hair plastered down, his face freshly scrubbed and his eyes as innocent looking as a fawn's. This old story went 'Boo boo boo boo boo boo!' By the time he had reached the ring the customers had revved it up, leaving out the spaces between the boos, thus: 'BOOBOOBOOBOOBOOBOO!'

It was no laughing matter and Greb didn't laugh. He slid into his corner as quickly as possible and sat there, his face as sombre as a mortician's. He didn't make himself conspicuous by jumping up and bowing around the ring when he was introduced, but bowed with the timidity of a backward boy unsure of the reaction.

Once the gong rang he was a fox behind leather paws. His lithe body was made of rubber and when he was performing in front of a particularly hostile audience he yanked himself up at the waist and took in foul territory punches that otherwise would surely have landed in fair. Speed was what he had an abundance of and when he turned it on plenty was buzzin', cousin. He ran in on body swings so fast that their timing was destroyed and they often landed in the vicinity of his shoelaces.

The customers couldn't believe it no matter how many times they saw the performance. Here was reputedly the ring's dirtiest fighter, yet here he was being fouled at every turn, never once fouling back, never once looking protestingly at the referee – just a sweet dumpling who had been wantonly maligned.

Pretty soon the referee was warning Greb's opponents to 'keep'em up!' And by this time the customers who had been booing him were yelling 'Foul him back, Harry!' Greb usually acknowledged this welcome advice with an owlish smile and from there in, his good character established, you hoped there was among the spectators someone who would notify his opponent's next of kin.

Commander Gene Tunney, retired and only living undefeated world's heavyweight champion, will tell you Greb was the wildest tiger who ever clawed beneath klieg lights. They fought five times. The only defeat in Tunney's career was at Greb's slashing hands in their first bout. It was one of the bloodiest fights in ring history, with Tunney the bleeder.

For this fight he came in at 162¼ against 174½ for Tunney. His frame was beginning to creak under the strain of nine years of savage ring warfare mostly against opponents who outweighed him from 20 to 50 pounds, and the sight in his good eye was getting dimmer. An even worse handicap was the whispered threat that he would be thrown out of the ring if he roughed Tunney as he had Gibbons.

Tunney, on the other hand, was young and strong and coming along. He had seen Greb fight and he thought he had what it took to bring him down – patience, and a right jolt to the heart, which he practised assiduously in the training ring. It was sound logic, but he never got a chance to use it against the wily Greb, who, before the clang of the gong had died in the opening round, rushed him to close quarters and upset his plans.

It was one of the bloodiest and most one-sided championship fights ever seen in the professional ring. Save for the third, fourth and seventh rounds, in which Tunney held his own, Greb couldn't have won more decisively if he had knocked him out a dozen times. With the first flurry of punches, delivered before the bout was 20 seconds old, he broke Tunney's nose in two places. A moment later Tunney's face was drenched in blood and, fed by a long, ugly gash which Greb opened above his left eye, it remained that way throughout the fight. Greb's gloves were soggy from slushing in the blood. The blood and sweat, like grease, were deflecting his punches. He would step back and hold out his gloves and blood-bespattered Kid McPartland, the referee, would wipe them off with a towel.

Tunney fought back gamely, doggedly moving forward. He wouldn't quit. He was a champion and the kind of champion he was doesn't know how to quit. Greb would rain a fusillade of blows against his face, down which blood cascaded, then push him away and ask McPartland, 'Wanna stop it?' McPartland would ask Tunney how about it and Tunney would say, 'Don't you stop it'; sometimes, when his throat was clogged with blood and he couldn't talk, he would shake his head no. Greb would leap in and resume the carnage. He would slam Tunney into the ropes and smash him with knife-sharp blows to body and head, and it was awful to watch. In almost every one of those frightful rounds he would either push Tunney away or move away himself and hold his blood-soaked gloves out. McPartland would wipe them off – he must have used half a dozen towels – and Greb would say, 'Wanna stop it?' McPartland would look at Tunney and Tunney would say, 'Don't you stop it.' McPartland would shake his head futilely, as much as to say, 'If this man doesn't know when he's whipped, it's not for me to interfere.' Then he would move from between the fighters and Greb would leap to the attack. His fists, like leather-encased bludgeons, would thud against Tunney's face, down which streamed blood not only from his left but from another gash above his right eye, and McPartland, whose clothes were blood-caked, would duck to avoid further splashing.

Weak from the killing, relentless pace, Tunney would wipe with his forearms the blood that was blinding his eyes as it flowed into them from those open wounds, stumble into the ropes, and paw weakly at his tormentor with arms that were heavy, aching, leaden things. He smiled, too. It was a tired, half smile – the smile his fellow Marines flashed as their Jap captors kicked them and clubbed them on that bestial Death March of Bataan – but it was disdainful and it said, 'I'm the champion and if you want my title you'll have to fight me until I'm incapable of defending it.'

No one knew better than Greb what Tunney was thinking. He knew he would not surrender until he could no longer stand, and as long as he could do this he could hold his hands up, if only in semblance of protection. If a title had not rested on his decision McPartland would surely have stopped the uneven contest. But a referee with a heart will think hard when a champion is unflinchingly taking a beating and pleading with him not to interfere.

There was no other course for Greb than to try to pummel Tunney into submission or, failing this, to beat him so thoroughly as to leave no doubt in the minds of boxing officials who had won. So when Tunney staggered into the ropes Greb went close and pounded him until he had to retreat or be obliterated. Following one of these manoeuvres Whitey Bimstein, who later was to second Greb against Tunney and then Tunney against Greb, slipped into the press section. He had seconded a boy in an early preliminary and now he was a spectator.

'Cute,' he said of Greb's work in close, 'awful cute.' (Cute is ring parlance for a very wise owl, one who knows everything and never fails to press an advantage.)

At the end of 15 brutal, terrifying rounds Greb gave Tunney over to his handlers, a bleeding, helpless hulk, and loped off with his title. Staggering uncertainly, Tunney mumbled through swollen lips, 'Well, Harry, you were the better man – tonight.'

'Won the championship,' Greb said crisply as one of his men kissed him on his unmarked countenance and dragged him away.

Half blind, sick, his body bruised from ceaseless battering, his face a pulpy mask, Tunney stumbled towards his dressing-room, blood dripping off his face on to his chest. He collapsed before he got there and his handlers carried him the rest of the way. The moment supporting hands left him, he fell back with a thud, the back of his head striking the rubbing table.

'Nature surrendered,' he said.

Greb, fresh as a frisky colt, hustled uptown, rented a nightclub orchestra and danced until the musicians fell asleep.

Though nature surrendered, Tunney's heart didn't. He had taken the worst, the most sustained, beating I ever saw in any ring, yet as he lay on the rubbing table, in complete control of his mental faculties but too weak to sit up, he was recalling the fight from first to final gong. He wasn't discouraged.

'I discovered through the early part of the fight that I could whip Greb,' he said. 'As each round went by, battered and pummelled from post to post as I was, this discovery gradually became a positive certainty.'

It was Tunney's first and only defeat – Tunney who four years later was to startle the world by dethroning the mighty and supposedly invincible Dempsey and to prove, a year later, that it was no accident by picking himself up off the floor in their return match that night in Chicago's controversial and forever-to-be-discussed Battle of the Long Count.

Give Him to the Angels
Smith and Durrell
New York, 1946

A Man Must Fight

Gene Tunney

The most remarkable thing about the remarkable Gene Tunney was why he wanted to box in the first place. The son of comfortably off parents, he was intellectually astute, widely read, a confidant of Shaw and Thornton Wilder and other literary figures, a navy commander during the war, an extremely successful businessman and married to a wealthy heiress; the very epitome of the beau ideal.

At an early age his parents had tried to dissuade him from pursuing a career in the ring but ambition brooks no argument. Tunney did not bother to box the compass, he was too busy eliminating rivals on his way to the top. His ultimate goal – the world heavyweight championship.

After that hiding from Greb (his only professional defeat) Tunney spent a week in bed recovering and planning revenge. He took it on four subsequent occasions. Eventually he challenged the formidable Dempsey for the world title and outboxed him over ten rounds at Philadelphia in 1926.

The return contest a year later in Chicago, ever after to be known as 'The Battle of the Long Count', was eagerly awaited. Tunney himself takes up the story.

Through some mistake in the signals I kept Jack waiting in the ring a couple of minutes. This was unintentional. Jack greeted me as I entered the ring: 'How are you, Gene?' 'Quite well, Jack, and you?' I replied. Soon after my arrival the announcer bellowed what had been printed a million times – 'This is a fight for the world's heavyweight championship' – and announced the principals.

I was standing in my corner and made the usual gesture in acknowledgement of the cheers and jeers. Suddenly a grey-haired man, whom I had never seen before to my knowledge, climbed through the ropes and stood in a neutral corner. The announcer turned to him and shouted, 'The referee, Dave Barry!'

My heart dropped into my stomach. Dave Barry! Jimmy Bronson's old antagonist and the man that Jimmy warned me against permitting to referee the match! Well, now I was in for it good and plenty. 'You must make the most of it!' I told myself.

Then followed the introduction of the two judges, prominent Chicago businessmen, George Lytton and Sheldon Clark. I had never seen either of them before. We were called to the centre of the ring. Flynn and Jerry the Greek stood with Dempsey, Gibson and Bronson with me. The referee said: 'Both you boys have received a book of rules of this Boxing Commission. They are the rules under which you are going to fight. They have been discussed by your representatives, I understand, for several days at the Commission.'

Gibson and Bronson assented to that.

'The rabbit and kidney blows are barred, of course,' continued Barry. 'In the event of a knockdown, the man scoring the knockdown will go to the farthest neutral corner. Is that clear, Jack?' – turning to Dempsey – and, 'Is that clear, Champ?' – turning to me. We both nodded 'Yes'.

'Now, in the event of a knockdown, unless the boy scoring it goes to the farthest neutral corner I will not begin the count until he does. Is that clear, Jack?'

'Yes,' nodded Dempsey. 'Is that clear, Champ?'

'Yes,' I said.

'When I tell you to break, I want you to break clean and step back without hitting . . .' He paused impressively. Then: 'Shake hands now and come out fighting.'

We shook hands and went back to our corners. The bell rang. We came out fighting.

In my anxiety to end the fight by a knockout, I threw and missed more rights than I ordinarily would have in 20 fights. I scored often with my left, only occasionally with my right. So did Dempsey. Dempsey, however, was fighting a considerably different fight from the one in Philadelphia. He was very cautious. Because of this, I was unable to get him into positions that would make him a target. He left very few openings.

At the end of the fourth round, I finally nailed him with one of those wild rights on the temple. He staggered back into a corner. He was considerably dazed, but conscious enough to cover up. The bell rang. He went to his corner in an unsteady stride.

Sitting in my corner, I thought that the end was near and that I should probably get him in the next or following round. Much to my surprise, he answered the bell for the fifth round as clear and strong as he was at the beginning.

'He has marvellous recuperative powers!' I thought. 'Well, it is only a matter of time until he will be weakened from the loss of blood.'

I had opened two cuts on his face, both of which were bleeding. The fifth round passed without much heavy damage being done, though there was considerable action. I felt I was leading by a big margin on points.

We were both fencing carefully. I was trying to manoeuvre him into an opening so that I could get a shot at his jaw; he was attempting to cross my left lead with a long, straight right. The sixth was similar to the fifth. My right-handers were landing high and Jack's cross-counters were either missing or grazing my jaw. At close quarters I tied him up. This, however, was more to prevent his using the rabbit punch than a disinclination on my part to infight.

Despite repeated warnings from the referee, he continued to use the rabbit blow whenever I failed to tie him up. This rabbit blow is the most dangerous blow in boxing. It was barred originally through the action of Jack Dempsey in his fight with Bill Brennan in Madison Square Garden. After Brennan had started to the canvas from a body blow, Dempsey hit him a fearful blow on the back of the neck on his way down. This left Brennan prostrate on the canvas. When I asked Carpentier what effect the rabbit blows had on him in his match with Jack, he pressed his temple and said, 'Zis is where zey hurt.'

The rabbit blow is particularly dangerous and damaging because it is directed at the point where the base of the skull and cervical vertebra meet – the lower brain stem, called the medulla oblongata. This nerve centre is actually the centre of life. It controls respiration, heart action and locomotion. Many doctors are agreed that it is the twisting of this brain-stem by a blow or jolt that causes the so-called knockout. No man can stand 80 or 90 rabbit blows from the fists of a heavy hitter like Dempsey, as I did in each fight, without feeling the effects. It brings a deadening headache which seems to rest in the base of the skull. There is a numbness which reacts on the whole nervous system. The blow was barred by all Boxing Commissions because it is not a scientific blow that you make an opening for, but one that is used when men are locked in a clinch, animal fashion. It is about as scientific as a blow of a hugging bear. There is no defence against it but to tie up the hands of an opponent.

My bodyguard, Sergeant Bill Smith, of the Chicago Police Department, who was in my corner, became wildly excited because the referee was apparently doing nothing to stop Dempsey's rabbit punches. Between the fifth and sixth rounds he climbed to the outer platform of the neutral corner in which the referee was making his notes and yelled: 'You blankety-blank-blank, if you don't stop those rabbit punches you'll be carried out of here dead!' The faithful bodyguard was feeling each blow more than I.

In the seventh round, after some 50 seconds of jabbing, feinting and mixing, I led a straight left which Dempsey crossed with a long right. This hit me high. I realised it. So did Dempsey. I danced back a step or two. Dempsey followed. With a long left swinging hook, he hit me on the right side of the chin. It was a savage punch and shook me up. To this day I cannot understand how I missed seeing it as it came.

I got furious at myself for being hit by that kind of swing. It had actually been telegraphed. How stupid of me! Such was my reaction. Suddenly a right followed which I partially rode. My back was to the ropes. I leaned against them quite relaxed. Rebounding with a spring I raised my guard.

Dempsey slipped in with another left hook that got inside my guard and hit me as I sprang from the ropes. This blow had the added force of catching me as I hurled myself forward. It landed again on the right side of the chin. It was a terrific blow. I began sagging against the ropes. It was the fourth he had landed in quick succession.

As I slowly crumpled to the canvas, being partially supported and held up by the ropes, he followed with a hard right, a left, and another right. By the time the last right landed, I was just short of sitting on the canvas. Seven vicious punches in all. I have no recollection of the last three.

This was the first time in my life I had ever been knocked down. After getting to the floor, I slowly went back towards a reclining position. Before my shoulder blades touched the canvas, I instinctively reached out with my left hand and, taking hold of the lower ropes, pulled myself into a sitting position.

My first conscious reaction was one of comfort. Gosh, the padded floor felt good! I noticed that the distance between my eyes and the canvas seemed short – I was sitting on it. I must be down. I must be down!

'You must have been knocked down,' I told myself rather foolishly. 'You must have been knocked down. Look here, Tunney, you must get up. Sure, sure, get up! But . . . What shall I do when I do get up?'

I looked over at my corner. Bronson and Gibson were wild-eyed, beckoning me to stay down. I nodded, recognising them and their message. I looked up. There was the referee. I heard him say 'Two'. I had lots of time – lots of time.

What to do when I did get up became the problem. Although I had never been knocked down before, I had thought of the possibility of it from the early days of my career. I had decided that one of two courses might be followed to try to ward off defeat after a knockdown. Every thoughtful boxer goes on the assumption that sooner or later he will have the experience of being knocked down. To anticipate is to be prepared.

Since a man who has been knocked down usually loses the power of locomotion, it follows that he must clinch if and when he rises. I had never seen a man completely knocked out or seriously knocked down get up and propel himself out of danger. When a complete knockout is administered, the recipient usually has to have his legs lifted up so that he may get through the ropes and out of the ring. Because of the belief that this partial paralysis of the legs always followed a knockdown, I decided it would be wiser to clinch with an opponent and hold on until my head cleared. Moreover, a clinch affords one a chance to take a light blow on the shoulder or chest as an excuse to go down for another count. These extra nine seconds would enable one to clear one's head entirely and get back the strength of the legs.

But now I had to dismiss this first alternative because of the danger of Dempsey's rabbit blow, which I know he would use if I attempted to clinch when I got up, and which would probably cause a complete collapse.

There was left the other alternative. It was to gamble with an opponent. Usually after a fighter knocks another down, particularly when it is unexpected, he gets excited in spite of himself. In this excitement and his desire to 'kill', he usually leaves himself open. At this moment a well-placed punch, properly timed, is apt to turn defeat into victory.

I realised that Dempsey, by constant conscious effort in his training bouts, shadow-boxing and road work, had learned to keep his chin on his chest. This constant precautionary measure developed an instinctive habit of keeping his chin tucked down when in action. In the 21 rounds I have boxed Dempsey, I never once landed a hard punch on his chin. It was always on the forehead, the cheek, the upper jaw, behind the ear, or on the nose. But never once on the chin. This was only because of Dempsey's subconscious habit of keeping his chin buried. I missed many well-aimed attempts!

Because of this habit, I knew that Dempsey, as he came at me for the 'kill', would be a bad gamble. My blow would probably land on the top of his head or on his forehead, while his would undoubtedly hit me on the chin or jaw. Another blow on either, after getting up, was not going to help me. That I realised.

Therefore, in those few seconds I rested on the canvas waiting for the referee to say 'Nine!' I had to discard the plans that I had thought of for years and expected to put to use in such an emergency as I now faced.

I decided that I must avoid allowing Dempsey to close in on me when I got up. I remembered that in the early part of the fight, as I feinted him and moved away, he would flounder after me. This was the cue to my safest course; to get up and make him chase me. This was my decision.

To the average person the possibility of all this thinking, weighing, rejecting and deciding seems incredible in so short a space of time. Considering that thought in the normal person is instantaneous, I can readily understand the development of a faculty for emergency thinking.

Resilience, precision and decisiveness were needed. My years of training had provided them. Determined to get the last part of a second that was mine, I rose as the referee raised his hand to say – TEN!

There has been considerable question about the length of time I was on the floor. Many newspapermen at the ringside said that the referee lost two seconds in taking Dempsey from behind me and putting him into a neutral corner. Leo Flynn, Dempsey's chief second, said that the stop-watch in his corner registered 14 seconds from the time I went down until I got up. It was agreed by all the experts to accept Flynn's timing. Even photographs were taken of this magic watch, the next day, registering 14 seconds. Wonderful provision and thoughtfulness there, dear Percival! I have never found out what the official timekeeper's watch registered. It did not matter.

Realising, as do all professional boxers, that the first nine seconds of a knockdown belong to the man who is on the floor, I never had any thought of getting up before the referee said 'Nine!'. Only badly dazed boxers, who have momentarily lost consciousness, and 'show-offs' fail to take the nine seconds that are theirs. No boxer that I have ever known has carried a stop-watch on his wrist going into the ring. Boxers always go by the referee's timing. Whether 29 seconds or nine seconds had elapsed when the referee said 'Nine!' would have made no difference to me. My signal to get off the floor was the count – Nine! The action of the referee in not taking up the count immediately when I went on the floor, regardless of where Dempsey was, is another question.

Football, tennis, baseball, swimming, golf, and all the popular sports have rules by which the contestants abide. There is usually an arbiter in the form of an umpire or referee to see that the rules are enforced. Dave Barry, in his refusal to count until Dempsey had moved from behind me and had gone to a neutral corner, was merely enforcing the rule insisted upon by Leo Flynn, Dempsey's manager, and agreed upon by the promoter, the Commissioners and the boxers. Any other action of Barry's would have been in direct contradiction of the Illinois Boxing Commission rules, under which we boxed that night.

It will be argued, 'What right has the Illinois Boxing Commission or any other commission to change the established tradition with regard to knockdowns?' For the benefit of those individuals who live by tradition I will say – by the same right that Washington changed the form of government of the 13 colonies, or by the same prerogative that the Marquess of Queensberry exercised when he changed the London prize-ring rules to a new code named after himself. In the Marquess of Queensberry rules it was compulsory for a man scoring a knockdown to step back ten feet and not advance until the fallen foe gained his feet.

Each state makes its own rules, which become a part of the law legalising boxing. There is very little of the original Queensberry code in the various states' rules governing boxing. But each state has as part of the law the clause regarding knockdown so that it becomes not only an 'unsporting' thing to stand behind a fallen opponent, but unlawful.

Had Dempsey and I been boxing under the old London prize-ring rules, the round would have ended at the knockdown and I should have had 389 seconds in which to come to scratch. The matches under the old London prize-ring rules were always to a finish with bare knuckles. The only virtue about this kind of fighting was that it put each man to the final test.

They were most boring spectacles, however, for after the hands got sore and disabled, the contestants became wrestlers. These ten-round fights for the world's heavyweight championship are entirely too short in which to establish the really better man. They are decidedly disadvantageous to the skilful man who goes on the principle of the constant drop of water wearing away the stone. It could only be by sheer accident that a man of my style could knock out a man of Dempsey's strength, resistance and courage inside ten rounds. Fifteen rounds is the minimum number of rounds in which a man can establish his superiority as a champion fighter unless a knockout intervenes. However, I am in favour of 20-round matches for heavyweight championships.

'Your legs are fine,' was the first thought I had after rising. Dempsey was darting towards me from the corner. He was crouching forward. His head was about four feet from the floor. A savage scowl covered his face as he looked up from below his heavy eyebrows. With his right hand up as a guard, the left hand dragged along the floor until he got within hitting distance.

'This time,' I said to myself, 'you will catch that left and not be sucker enough to walk into it again!'

I waited until it got three-quarters of the way on its course and then picked it off. In doing so, I started to circle to his right. This was to stay out of the way of his left hook.

After circling the ring once and avoiding eight or nine swings, I realised that I could circle him faster than he could follow. I bided my time, remaining physically relaxed. Presently, I decided it was time to try to nail him. I slowed up until he got within hitting distance, suddenly I lunged forward with a straight right that hit him on the temple. This was unexpected. His knees buckled a bit. We exchanged five or six blows in close before the referee separated us. I then circled to his left side. He made several futile attempts to catch me with long swings. Slowing up again, I lunged forward with another right-hand punch and hit him on the cheekbone. Again his knees buckled. We clinched. The referee separated us. I renewed circling to his left. He sensed that if he kept up this futile chase, he would be knocked out. Either of the two blows that I hit him with had sufficient force for a knockout if placed on a more vulnerable spot.

He then decided on a grandstand gesture. The ridiculousness of the situation can be most appreciated by a professional boxer. Here was I, just up from a count, and, while avoiding his attempts to put me down again for keeps, being beckoned by my opponent to come in so that he could land the finishing punch or punches!

I thought this gesture an acknowledgement of discouragement; so, cautiously moving about, I got what I thought was an opening for a right at his body. I lunged forward with the same power of the other two blows and hit him under the heart. He grunted.

I want to say here that Dempsey's actions after this blow proved to me that he possessed the stick-to-it-iveness that makes him great among champions. He made no attempt to go down, but, bending forward, his arms close to his body, weaved until the bell rang.

In the spring of 1929, while coming north on the train after promoting the Sharkey–Stribling fight at Miami Beach, Dempsey went into the compartment of Roy Howard and Ray Long, the publishers. After talking a little while about the Chicago fight and, in particular, the seventh round, Dempsey exclaimed: 'The right-hand punch under the heart that Tunney hit me when he got off the floor in the seventh round was the hardest blow I have ever received. It was not a question in my mind of being knocked out – I thought I was going to die. I could not get my breath. A second rubbed away the congestion around my heart when I came back to my corner, but for that I would not have been able to come out for the eighth round.' Gus Wilson, his worshipping trainer, has told me the same story.

Following the knockdown at the opening of the eighth round, Dempsey again demonstrated the kind of courage he has. Every newspaper account of those last three rounds describes Jack as a human punching bag. Yet, aside from the knockdown in the early part of the eighth, he was never off his feet.

When the decision was given, I walked across to Jack's corner. He advanced to meet me and said, 'Congratulations, Gene! It was a good fight! I did the best I could.'

Back in the penthouse of the Sherman Hotel after the fight, a group of friends gathered. We staged a party. Learning that Mayor Thompson was living at the same hotel, I went down to ask him up to our celebration. 'Sure I'll come up – would love to, Gene!' was his reply. During the course of the evening, after many toasts had been drunk, Mayor Thompson said: 'I will admit I bet $8,000 on Dempsey, but that is because I had not met you.' Big Bill was always a good politician.

The following day Eddie Sullivan, alderman for my old Greenwich Village district, and Jimmy Eagleton ran into Al Capone at the railway station. Al had come down to see some friends off for New York. Eagleton had been to his hotel, the night before the fight, where Al was showing to the out-of-town visitors the warm and generous hospitality of Chicago.

Capone said to Eagleton and Sullivan, who were about to board the train: 'I lost $45,000 on the fight, but I don't give a damn because Tunney is from New York. Before the fight I heard Tunney was up in his training camp with a lot of lavender boys in golf clothes and that they did not know what it was all about. I couldn't understand fellas like Gibson and Tunney coming from New York being so dumb. So I says this to the guys that told me to go and bet as much as I wanted on Dempsey and that everything was okay. One of these guys tells me: "They're all saps. They gotta couple college guys up there with them runnin' the camp. Tunney's too busy wid his books. He's a mug, I tell yer!" So against me best judgement, I bet against Tunney. At five o'clock I had word that the Commission had switched the referee. I did not have time to get off, but what the hell! These mugs in Chicago think New Yorkers are all suckers. Why, I came out here from Brooklyn seven years ago and they ain't made a sucker of me yet.'

There was talk of a return match. There was still a question in the minds of many as to who was the better man.

I felt as badly about the incident of the seventh round as Dempsey. The subsequent publicity made it obligatory for us to meet a third time. Realising this, I decided to give Dempsey a third match, only stipulating that it should be for at least 15 rounds.

At a conference at the Union League Club in New York between Tex Rickard, Richard Hoyt, chairman of the board of the Madison Square Garden Corporation, Bernard F. Gimbel, George Whiteside, my lawyer, Rickard's lawyer, and myself, Rickard was authorised to meet any demand that Dempsey might make that was within reason for a return engagement of 15 rounds. It would surely have been the largest purse ever paid a challenger.

But Dempsey turned a deaf ear to Rickard's constant pleadings and, finally, in a telegram which Rickard subsequently showed us, said, 'Count me out, Tex.'

With Dempsey out and no likely looking opponent around, I began to lose interest. Tex did not ask to tear up the contract which he had signed a few days before the Chicago fight in which he agreed to provide an opponent for me during the year 1928 in the event I was still champion, and for which he was to pay me a guarantee of $525,000.

To meet his contract Tex selected Tom Heeney, who had the best record of all the 'tournamentalists' as my opponent for that year. Sharkey would have been ideal from the point of view of gate receipts, but just when he had the match in his hand, Tom Heeney bested him, so Rickard thought. After the Heeney fight, Sharkey lost again; this time to Risko in a 15-round bout. This unfortunately eliminated him as contender. Heeney subsequently got a decision over Risko and, though Heeney turned out to be the poorest drawing card Rickard could have selected, he was entitled to the match on achievement.

Before the Heeney match I became engaged to be married. I decided this would be my last ring contest. During the training period for this fight, I was completely free from annoyance and worry. The fight with Heeney, I believe, was the most skilful performance of my career. It was not the most satisfactory, personally. Everything clicked in unison. Heeney was stopped in the eleventh round after putting up a most courageous resistance.

After this fight there was considerable speculation on the part of newspapermen and fans as to why I had backed away, refusing to hit Heeney in the eighth round when he was in obvious pain and helpless from a blow over the left eye. It was laid to timidity by some, to sportsmanship by others and, by the more fiction-minded, as conclusive proof of the lack of a 'killer instinct' – 'that indispensable quality of the successful fighter'.

I have always been amused by that phrase, 'killer instinct'. It has been written of exhaustively as a virtue. It was coined for prize-fighting; it is now being employed in describing football and other athletic contests. In pugilism it is defined as that fierce urge to beat one's opponent helpless, hang him on the ropes, push him out of the ring, knock him unconscious, kill him, win.

In my humble opinion, a great deal of what is described as the killer instinct is merely a burning desire to win, to win brutally or skilfully, fairly or foully. It is the emotional reaction to violent physical competition. The higher in human development one goes, the more controlled one finds this reaction. Acting on instinct has always meant to me a suspension of reason. How does one adhere to rules in such circumstances? All the killer-instinct boys of my acquaintance obey the rules – when the referee is looking.

For myself, I was always guided by reason in the ring. For everything I did, I had a reason. When I moved back from Heeney, an experience of a friend, a splendid little fellow, had come to my mind.

While in Hollywood making 'the greatest serial ever produced' – *The Fighting Marine* – I attended a fight show one night. Gene Delmont, my friend who seconded me in some AEE matches in France, was in the star bout. Gene went very well for the first three rounds, winning rather easily. At the beginning of the fourth, Gene stepped into a terrific right-hand punch that seemed to land on his forehead. There was an instant reversal of form. Gene backed away. He clinched. He hung on. The referee had a hard time breaking them. The crowd started razzing. Gene was stalling. The fifth round was a repetition of the fourth. Delmont's opponent started getting to him in the sixth, pounding him rather severely. The audience continued booing. The eighth, ninth and tenth rounds were tests of endurance for little Delmont. Leaving the ring, Gene got an unmerciful booing and razzing. The brave ones in the audience called him profane names.

I believed something was wrong, so I went back to the dressing-room. Gene was weeping; the names he had been called as he left the ring had hurt. I asked him what happened in the fourth round. And this was his answer.

'I got a punch over the left eye that didn't hurt much. I thought it closed my eye. I couldn't see with it. When I got back to my corner, I told one of my seconds that the eyelash was in my eye. I asked him to open the eye and turn the lash out.'

'"Your eye is open," he said.

'"Stop kidding me," I said, "I can't see a thing. Open it."

'"I tell you it is open," he insisted.

'Like a death sentence I realised I was blind in that eye. The doctor now tells me I am going . . .'

And so I could not hit Heeney again.

A Man Must Fight
British Publishers Guild, Jonathan Cape
1933

The Joe Louis I Remember

Jimmy Cannon

Jimmy Cannon was one of the most knowledgeable sports writers of the 1940s and 1950s. This episodic treatment he gives to life with Louis is rather like a straight-faced version of Rowan and Martin's Laugh-in. *The understatement works brilliantly and emphasises the greatness of his subject.*

The truths of our youth often become falsehoods in our middle years. It is the fee we pay for being alive. We tolerate leniently the rotting of the flesh and the defeat of beauty, but it is harder to accept the decay of ideals. So I am grateful I am still able to admire Joe Louis for what he was. We were young together and he has survived in my estimation. It is because he was a symbol and a force for good, and because he is a decent man.

We have a tendency in this country to praise athletes beyond their worth. It is natural because we are essentially a lighthearted people and this is an age of turbulence. It is a tribute to us that we were able to appreciate Louis. He is a simple man with little education, but the truths he uttered gave him a special radiance. Perhaps his observations were ungrammatical. But often they seemed profoundly witty because they were told with a candour that was unblemished by cleverness. I've never known him to seek the sanctuary of a lie. And I was there from the beginning.

He was an historic heavyweight champion. The others were John L. Sullivan and Jack Dempsey. They were before my time. But I know Joe Louis improved the fight racket with his presence. He ducked no one and he bragged less than any champion I've known. He is a good-humoured man who had pride in what he was. The night that Rocky Marciano knocked him out, people who didn't know him wept in Madison Square Garden. Their grief was not restricted by colour.

On his fortieth birthday Louis refereed a wrestling match in Decatur, Illinois. Stooging for these comedians of sport demeans a man who was the greatest fighter I've ever covered as a sports writer. I telephoned him long distance to wish him a happy birthday. I expected him to be cranky. Wrestling is a slum, and in this squalid bazaar Louis was selling his tarnished splendour for a night's pay.

'Have you,' I asked, 'any regrets?'

'No,' Louis said. 'I had a wonderful time. I still can make as much as I want to make.'

I expected him to claim the second fight with Max Schmeling as the finest night of his life or, maybe, the night he beat Jimmy Braddock out of the heavyweight championship. He chose neither. It was, he insisted, the Max Baer fight. 'I felt better that night,' he explained. 'I felt like I could fight for two, three days.'

'What was your worst fight?'

'Arturo Godoy,' he answered. 'I guess I try too hard with him. I was stale. I couldn't do nothing.'

So there he is, now nearing 41, on the road, performing in the clumsy tableaus of the wrestlers. It is sad, of course, but there is little joy in the fight racket. Maybe Louis is fortunate. At least he doesn't have to bleed for the money he picks up working with the clowns. Maybe I'm being too drastic about it but I wish he could find another way to exhibit himself. Of course, Dempsey did it and so did a lot of other great fighters. The hours are short and the pay is good. But Louis doesn't belong in a ring to incite laughter. Neither does any other fighter who suffered publicly to make the toughest dollar an athlete earns. We find it hard to forgive the likes of Louis for submitting to these indignities. We want to remember them as they were, and who was greater than Louis? Let me tell you how I think he really has changed. Of course the years took the skills with them. They made his body a burden. But he never became bitter and nasty, the way some champions do. The history of his fights is in the guides. The matchless record is public knowledge. So this will be a personal recollection of Louis. It is not complete and there will be much that is missing. But none of it is in the files or the books. It is out of my mind and my heart.

The first time I saw Louis fight he humiliated Primo Carnera. The knockout didn't impress me as much as the first left hook that tore Carnera's slack mouth. It was a small punch but it ripped Carnera's high-curved upper lip and his mouth seemed to be crawling up the sides of his face in an agonised grin. The eyes in the big head rolled in terrible wonder, marvelling at the force of the blow. Ask me the way Louis punched and I'll tell you about Carnera's mouth breaking into that idiot's smile.

After the Baer fight, Louis's hands were bruised. Baer was sick with despair. Afterwards, Jack Dempsey, who worked his corner, said that Baer had been bragging in the dressing-room about what he would do to Louis. But a man shouted it was time for the main event to go on and Baer began to pant.

'I can't go on,' said Baer, according to Dempsey.

Dempsey regarded him with loathing and amazement.

'I can't breathe,' Baer insisted.

'I conned him into the ring,' Dempsey remembers. 'After the first round, Max came back to the corner and said he couldn't breathe. I told him I'd kill him with the water bottle if he didn't go back out there and get knocked out.'

It wasn't Baer, removing his mouthpiece and waving goodbye to the crowd as he sat on his legs, that I remember. It wasn't Louis's face when Baer hit him after the bell. Louis's hands were down and he took the punch and a grimace of contempt puckered his face. It degraded Baer, that brief glance. It told what Baer was and what Louis was and never was the difference so clear. The referee didn't have to count.

Instead of an opponent, Paolino Uzcudun seemed more of a confederate. No one gave him a chance. People wondered how long he would last.

Paolino wasn't clever and he couldn't punch much. But he fought with the vanity of the pug who is a fighter in his heart. He stopped over and hunched forward, his face concealed behind the stockade his crossed arms made. The corner had told Louis to be careful. They were afraid he would break his hands on Uzcudun's head. So Louis jabbed, carefully, precisely, lightly. He was patient and cautious. It happened in the fourth round. Paolino looked up and his head came out of the cage of his arms. One punch did it. It was a right hand and Paolino was down. Gold teeth sprinkled on the dirty canvas, the way tiny charms might fall off a woman's broken bracelet.

Paolino began to push himself up. His back was to Louis. But he was in another country, lost and hurt through. The boxing journalists forgot they were reporters. They stood up and shouted to referee Arthur Donovan.

'Stop!' they yelled. 'Stop it!'

And Donovan stopped it.

The sports editor of the old *American*, the late Eddie Frayne, called me into his office. I had a choice of assignments. Did I want to go West with the Yankees or stay in New York to cover the Schmeling–Louis fight? There was a kid with the Yankees who was making his first road trip. I decided I would rather travel with Joe DiMaggio.

'Schmeling's all washed up,' I told Frayne. 'It won't be much of a fight.'

We were in Detroit. I went to Tony Lazzeri's room. We sat around the radio. Clem McCarthy broadcast the fight. I remember him shouting above the tumult of the crowd.

'He's down!' came McCarthy's hoarse, excited voice.

'I told you,' I said.

But it was Louis who was down, and he would be knocked out that night. In the city of Detroit people lit red flares and a parade of automobiles rolled through the downtown streets to celebrate the knockout of a home-town kid. I never understood that.

Let the others tell you how stately Jimmy Braddock was in defeat. Go to the library if you would know how Louis won the heavyweight championship of the world. But what belongs to me was what Louis said after it was over. It is not important now but it impressed a sports writer who was still young enough to be moved by a champion.

I had to shove my way into Louis's dressing-room. The special cops on the door barred my way. There was a pushing crowd behind me. They threw me into the room, past the cops who fell and were walked upon. There was a radio announcer clinging to Joe, holding a microphone in his face. I collided with Louis and he grabbed me to hold me up.

'This is Jimmy Cannon,' he said, 'the assistant heavyweight champion of the world!'

I remember that.

I was in the army when Louis was matched with Lou Nova. I came to New York on a pass and went up to the Polo Grounds early. I was sitting in my seat when John Roxborough, who was one of his managers, came down to the working-press section.

'Joe wants to see you,' he said.

I went back to the dressing-room. It was a half hour before the fight. But Joe was asleep, burbling little snores. The crowd sounds awakened him and he sat up. We talked about the army and about people we knew.

'Time to go, Chappie,' one of his handlers said, taking up Joe's robe.

'I got to go to work,' Louis said.

As long as I've been on the sports beat, I've never seen a cooler guy.

There are those who are small-hearted and forever afraid, and they shall always fail in every crisis of their lives. But more unfortunate than these are the ones with sufficient courage who betray themselves intentionally by relying solely on caution. When a fighter discards recklessness as though it were a vice he had conquered, it is possible he will survive, but with such a gesture frequently he also abandons his dignity. It was not cowardice that I saw in Jersey Joe Walcott the first time he fought Louis and knocked him down. It is the penalty the mediocre man must pay when he tries to counterfeit greatness. I made Walcott the winner over Louis, eight rounds to seven. But Louis, although knocked down twice, was still the champion because Walcott refused to reject his concocted meekness and replace it with even an imitation of boldness.

The great champion felt disgraced after that night. He ducked into seclusion and no one could see him. It became a big story because he hadn't told his version of the fight. I made a telephone call to a friend of Louis's. I told him I wanted to see Joe, alone. The champion called me back himself.

'You want me?' asked the thick, soft voice that had awakened me.

'Yeah,' I said.

'Come up the apartment then,' Louis said.

'Where are you?' I asked.

He gave me the address of an apartment house in upper Manhattan. He told me not to mention his name to the elevator boy but come directly to the flat which was rented in a friend's name. He had been there a week and hadn't been out. He opened the door himself. He wore pyjamas and a black-and-white striped cotton bathrobe. The left eye was still pinched by a discoloured mound of flesh. His face was bloated. The knuckles of his right hand were swollen.

'What happened to you?' I asked after we had chatted about inconsequential happenings.

'I made the fight tough for myself,' Louis said. 'He didn't make it tough for me. He did so many wrong things. I saw every opening. But I couldn't go get him. It was a lousy fight. I saw him when he made the mistakes. It's like a guy running. You can't make a sprint near the end. Your legs feel you can go but you feel bad in the pit of your stomach.'

'Sounds like you're getting old,' I said.

'Diet and drying out,' said Louis, who had weighed 211 pounds for the fight. 'I wanted to weigh 12,' he continued, omitting the 200 as most fighters do. 'I should have weighed 14, I weighed 15, and sometime the day before the fight I killed myself taking off the four pounds. But that ain't no excuse. It was a real lousy fight.'

'When did you dry out?' I asked.

'I don't know,' he said. 'I guess I figured it was a good weight.'

He pointed to a thicket of roses standing in a white vase on the table in the room. 'If I water those flowers every day,' he said, 'and then I don't put no water on them, if I don't keep them alive – the flowers got to die. That's me. The day before the fight I had four lamb chops. No juice. Nothing else. No water all day. I eat no more – not even water – until two o'clock the day I fight. You got to have strength to go to a guy. I was weak.'

'When did you know you weren't right?'

'In the dressing-room,' Joe said. 'I was warming up in there for 15 minutes. I knew I didn't have the strength in the dressing-room.'

'The punch that knocked you down in the first was a sucker punch,' I told him.

'You can see it coming when you're weak,' he said, 'but you're late getting up there. I saw every right hand, but it hit me anyway. One thing I'm happy to know . . .'

'What's that?' I asked.

'I made it tough for myself,' he said. 'He didn't.'

Had he been persecuted into panic by the knowledge that he was losing the title? I told him I thought he had lost the fight and didn't deserve the decision.

'On my little daughter —' he said earnestly, 'I never thought at any time I lost the fight. I chased his tail all the rest of the night. You knock a man down, you're supposed to go at a man. He knocked me down and then . . . run . . . run . . .run.'

'Suppose they had given him the decision?'

'If they had given it to him,' he said, 'I wouldn't have cared about it. What I mean is it would have been all right with me. What the decision says – you got to go by it. I wouldn't have mentioned it.'

'But you were so sore,' I reminded him, 'you tried to leave the ring before the decision came down.'

'I was mad because I was so silly,' he said. 'Getting hit by them sucker punches. Seeing them coming – and getting hit. This is no excuse – what I told you – it was a lousy fight. Everybody say something. Everyone give a reason why you do this. No one knows what's in your mind, but you do. I can tell you how I feel but you don't know how I feel. I know I had no excuse for a lousy fight.'

Not once during the three hours I spent with him did Louis call Walcott by name.

I found out afterwards that the people who live off Louis had tried to discourage him from giving me an exclusive interview.

'You'll make a lot of enemies if you give this to Cannon,' one of them said.

'Cannon's my friend,' he said, 'if I win or I lose.'

The second time he knocked Walcott out and announced he would fight no more. The night after the fight I had dinner with him in the dining-room of the Hotel Theresa in Harlem. There were a lot of people standing on the sidewalk when we came out. With us was his wife, Marva, and Leonard Reed, a vaudeville actor, who was his closest friend. The people didn't nag him for autographs but followed him quietly as he walked through the Saturday night crowd to the Alhambra Theater, which is across the street from the Theresa. The usher took us to the loge, off to the side, and from this angle the figures on the screen were thin and very tall. The fight movies started as we sat down. The audience was amused by Walcott's skipping and shoulder-shrugging and they reacted as though they were watching a comedy. They shrieked with laughter as Walcott made his preposterous and solemnly funny gestures. Louis didn't talk to me until the ninth round when he reached Walcott with a solid jab. He nudged me with his elbow. 'Got him now,' he said.

The audience stood up and shouted when Louis knocked him out, as though the finish was unexpected and had surprised them. We went out through a side door, unnoticed by the majority of the crowd, and strolled back to the hotel.

'It was dreadful,' Mrs Louis said.

'I thought it was terrific,' Reed said.

'It might have been the other way,' Mrs Louis said.

'It's all over now,' Reed said.

'I hope so,' Mrs Louis said. 'But you know how it is . . . like an opera singer with a new role – but I hope not.'

'Did you enjoy the picture?' I asked Louis.

'It had a real nice ending,' Joe said.

We went up to the two-room hotel suite after the movies and Louis took off the dark glasses. His left cheek was puffed. The flesh around his eyes was scraped and bruised. He believed he was finished with fighting forever. I asked him about his financial condition.

'I won't ask anybody for nothing,' he said.

'Suppose,' Reed asked, 'you could get a soft fight for, say, half a million clams?'

'If they put half a million in my hand – I got half a million,' he replied. 'But this way – retired – I can make a hundred thousand a year the rest of my life. The championship is an annuity like.'

There was a night in Philadelphia when he drifted through a four-round exhibition with Arturo Godoy. The dressing-room was humid but Louis lay under a woollen blanket on a rubbing table, kidding Ike Williams, who was then the lightweight champion. They were talking about golf.

'If Ike keeps his head down, he's a real good 85 shooter,' Louis said.

'That's not me,' Williams protested. 'My score's 72.'

'How about a match for a thousand?' said Blinky Palermo, who managed Williams.

'I don't want to take his money,' Louis said. 'It would be pitiful. They put people in jail for taking money that way. Seventy-two – he better buy shoes for his caddie. The caddie would wear out his shoes kicking the ball for a 72.'

'Do you like these exhibitions?' I asked.

'Sure,' Louis said. 'There's a lot of difference between fights and exhibitions. Exhibitions. Big gloves. Don't have to fight hard. Expenses ain't much.'

That night 7,285 people paid to see him.

They put Louis in with Joe Chesul, a main-event fighter from the obscure clubs of New Jersey, on the exhibition tour. There was a referee to do the counting if there was a knockdown. The seconds acted as though these were genuine contests. But it was show business, not the fight racket.

The cast was the same when I went down into the basement of the Newark Armory. There were cops on the door and inside were the vague hangers-on you know you met before but can't remember where. There was always a guy carried strictly for laughs. This was George Nicholson, who used to be a sparring partner for Louis. There was Manny Seamon, who still trained Joe. There was Marshall Miles, who did the business for him. I had visited Louis in so many bleak rooms like this in so many towns. But the excitement was gone and so was the strain. There was no guessing. Nothing was at stake. It was just another pay night.

Into the place came a guy with a fighter's face. 'You remember me, Joe?' the guy asked.

'How are you?' Louis stalled.

'Steve Hamas,' the guy said.

This was Steve Hamas, who once licked Max Schmeling who, until Marciano did it, was the only man ever to knock Louis out. Their conversation was limited to fighters they both knew. After a while, Louis got up and went out to earn his touch.

'Whatever became of Ezzard Charles?' a guy yelled.

This was before Louis fought Charles, and I wonder now what caused the guy to say that. The people there, about 5,000 of them, grumbled when Louis's weight was announced as 228½.

I realised what the years had done to Louis when a kid like Chesul made him miss and lunge. The grace was gone and so was the quickness of hand. I was positive that night that Louis would never try to fight again.

I was a war correspondent in Korea when Louis was beaten by Ezzard Charles. There had been no mail for us since we made the landing at Inchon. The last radio I had heard had mumbled with static. On the sports page of the last copy of *Stars and Stripes* I had was a photograph of Louis, placid and immense, staring drowsily at Charles. There was no talk about the fight in Korea. But I thought about it one night when I couldn't sleep in a cottage on the road to Seoul. One of the guys was snoring with a whimpering moan. There was the smell of feet and the sound of men turning stiffly in their blankets. I went around to shield my cigarette in the blackout of the command post.

Much of my life had been spent writing about Louis or hanging around his training camps. My youth was gone with his and middle age was upon the both of us. I felt especially old among the very young Marines. That photograph of Louis had aged me. My thigh bones ached from sleeping on the ground. I was weary with a deep tiredness that never diminished and only seemed to increase. Shaving with cold water had chapped my face. I had worn the same clothes for six days. I was the only sports writer there and I found no companions who cared to argue fights.

I knew Louis couldn't win. But I still had faith in him. At dawn I sat down at a typewriter and filed a sports piece. I wrote that Louis would knock out Charles in six rounds. I was homesick and tired of combat and feeling my age. I wanted to be there when they fought. It seemed to be wrong to be against Louis when I was so far away. So I picked him. It didn't surprise me when I was told that Charles had trimmed him. But it depressed me.

Of course, Louis won his fight with Cesar Brion in Chicago. I told him I thought he should quit. But the liars said he still had a couple of more good fights in him. He was 36, but older than Methuselah in the fight racket. One observation he made clarified it all.

'My right hand don't leave me no more,' Louis said. 'I got to think to throw it now. When you're young, you see an opening and throw punches you can't even remember throwing.'

It was said quietly. Louis wasn't being dramatic about it. But here was a guy giving me his own obituary as a fighter.

I went to Pompton Lakes where Louis worked to get ready for Lee Savold. He was obstinate in a courteous way when I asked him about his condition. I told him that he should have taken Brion out because he had a lot of shots at him.

'I ain't lost my punch,' he said stubbornly.

'You nailed Brion,' I said.

'Not so good,' he said sadly, 'not so good.'

'How's training this time?'

'Very nice,' he said. 'Very nice. But it's tough to do what you want to do. When you start in boxing, you want to throw a punch but you can't do it. You have to force yourself.'

We walked out of the gymnasium and into the glade where the ring was pitched. There was a pigtailed young woman waiting for him with a clump of photographers. She wore boxing gloves, white trunks and a white T-shirt. On the T-shirt were the figures of two women boxers. Above them, in blocked blue letters, was the legend, 'Female Joe Louis'.

'I got 17 knockouts in 22 fights,' Female Joe Louis said. 'I fight boys and every-thing. I'm a champion, too.'

I asked Female Joe Louis where she boxed.

'Mexico City,' Female Joe replied. 'I'm fighting a girl there for the champ-ionship very soon.'

'What's her name?' I asked.

'It's in the contract,' Female Joe Louis said. 'It's an odd name. I don't remember it. I like to fight men. The harder I pop them, the better I like it.'

'You scare me,' Joe Louis said to Female Joe Louis.

They knew what he meant even after they had beaten him. It embarrassed Rocky Marciano a little when he knocked out Louis.

'They didn't like me,' he said, 'because of what I done to Joe.'

Small remembrances return to me as I write this piece. Now it is the dressing-room after the first Walcott fight. Louis sat on a rubbing table. He got the decision but he looked like the loser.

'How is your cold?' was the first thing he said to me.

I had been laid up for a couple of days. It impressed me that a guy, bleary and angry, could be that considerate of a friend in such a spot.

I was in Chicago for a football game. Louis telephoned me and said he had a surprise for me. Would I, he asked, come to a nightclub on the South Side? He wouldn't tell me what would happen. I went and there were people standing in line outside. There was an immense photograph of Louis in the lobby. There was a sticker pasted across the chest. The legend on it read 'In Person'. He did a comedy act with a straight man. It was very bad and Louis broke up and laughed away the punchlines. The people liked it. Afterwards, Louis came to my table and I asked him why he did it.

'Some friends got the joint,' he said. 'I give them a hand. But don't print that. Just say I'm having some fun.'

There were stories in the newspapers that Louis was broke. I met him at Mike Jacobs' offices which were then in the Brill Building on Broadway. I asked him if it were true he had been trimmed.

'No,' he said. 'I'll let you see my books.'

He paused. 'I made some investments with friends,' he said. 'They turned out bad. Look at the books but don't put that in.'

There was a hot day at Yankee Stadium when the Red Sox were playing the Yankees. I came upon Louis, who was sitting behind third base.

'You know Ted Williams?' he asked.

I said I did.

'A good hitter,' Louis said.

'Would you like to meet him?'

'Yeah,' he said.

I took Louis back to the Boston dressing-room. Williams was in his underwear, standing before his locker. They looked at one another and Louis spoke first. He didn't wait to be introduced.

'My,' he said, 'you skinny.'

Frankie Harmon, whose father Paddy built the Chicago Stadium, promoted an exhibition match between Louis and Billy Conn when both were finished with fighting. Louis dropped by Harmon's office before the fight and asked him: 'What percentage Billy getting?'

Harmon told him.

'Take five per cent off my end,' Joe said. 'Put it on Billy's.'

He never told Conn that.

Gee Walker, who played the outfield for the Tigers, was the ballplayer Joe admired most. He talked about him continually and explained what a thrill it was to see Walker play. I said the records showed Walker wasn't the best. I told Louis to prove he was.

'You know a man's the best,' Louis said, 'he's the best. You don't have to prove it.'

There was a season when Louis toured with a softball team and played first base.

'What did you hit?' I asked him.

'Round .200,' he said.

We talked a while about other matters. Louis returned to the topic of softball. 'You don't have to put my average in the paper?' he asked.

'I do,' I said.

He thought about it a while. 'You're a bad hitter,' he said. 'I guess you're a bad hitter.'

There was a time when the late Paul Small, a theatrical agent, arranged a profitable movie deal for Louis. The managers sat at a table and discussed terms. They finally reached an agreement.

'This all right with you?' Small said to Louis.

'Can my softball team be in the picture?' Louis asked.

And that was the only question he asked.

The rest is in the book, but what he was isn't there. There was conceit in him but he controlled it. There was a lot of pride in him, too, but it never took charge of him. He was shy and he hid in silence when there were strangers around, but he was easy-going and good company if you were a friend. I admired him but I tried to see him clearly. At the end, when he needed help, I was sympathetic but I knew he was a goner and I said so. He never complained about it and it never spoiled our relationship. He was a great champion and I'm glad he was a champion in my time. He was mean at his work but he was able to leave it in the ring. The cruelty was there, all right. The poverty of his boyhood formed him as it does all fighters. But he was never resentful and he always did the best he could. His best was wonderful.

The night Marciano knocked him out, a guy said it was pretty sad to see him go that way.

'I've knocked out lots of guys,' Louis said.

He was a fighter. Many a guy makes a good living fighting for money and many become champions. They can show you licences to prove they're fighters, and there isn't any way I can dispute them. But Louis was a boy's dream of a fighter. There was joy and innocence in his skills and this gave him what the others lacked. There have been others but I'm sure of Louis.

Joe Louis was a fighter. It is the finest compliment I can give him.

So I'll stop right here.

Sports Magazine
1955

A Rare Interview with Max Schmeling

Dr Laurence F. McNamee

Max Schmeling is the only boxer to win the world heavyweight championship on a foul. Two years later, in 1932, he lost it to the same man, Jack Sharkey, on a disputed points decision. These facts, however, only surface as an afterthought when his name is mentioned. Outside the fight game Schmeling is known solely for his encounters with Joe Louis.

Having brought about what was probably the biggest upset in boxing history by knocking out the 'Brown Bomber' in 12 rounds, Schmeling was destroyed in just 124 seconds in the return in June 1938. Racial hatred poisoned the atmosphere because of publicity from the Nazi Party proclaiming that the German was fighting for the white race. Noting his jet-black hair and bushy eyebrows, compared to the café au lait complexion of Louis, the press gave Schmeling a moniker – 'the Black Uhlan' (a cavalryman armed with a lance). Sitting alongside 70,000 screaming fans in the Yankee Stadium, British sports writer Peter Wilson was moved to remark: 'He looks nearly as dark as that famous Aryan Hitler.'

Despite the shellacking from Louis during which he received a kidney punch that fractured vertebrae in his back and caused him to scream in agony, Schmeling bore no grudge and indeed struck up a lasting friendship with his conqueror.

In 1992, Laurence McNamee went to Hamburg to interview the then 86-year-old Schmeling shortly after the former champion had been inducted into the Boxing Hall of Fame. As the wealthy owner of the Coca-Cola Corporation of Germany, Schmeling was far removed from the stark surroundings of his early career, but that did not prevent him giving precious insights into those momentous times.

The first thing you notice about Maximillian Siegfried Schmeling is his vibrancy. Sure, the shoulders are a trifle bit stooped and the once jet-black hair has grown thin but the panther-like movements that propelled him to a world title are still there.

As I came into his office I found him behind his desk, leafing through a large tome. Significantly, it was a history of the 1920s, a decade that became known as 'The Golden Age of Sports'. There could be found all the familiar faces: Jack Dempsey, Gene Tunney, Babe Ruth, Red Grange, Bill Tilden and Bobby Jones.

Schmeling looked up. 'It's like looking at a silent movie,' he mused. 'The cheering died long ago. And now the only voice I hear is my own.'

It wasn't just that Schmeling had walked with the crowds and kept his virtue or talked with the kings and never lost his common touch. It was more. For here was the last remaining link with that long-ago decade, a man who had survived a Depression, World War II and a despot named Hitler.

As he sent out for Coca-Cola and his special brand of lemonade, I asked him how he had survived; how he managed when it seemed that he had been dealt so many bad cards from the bottom of the deck – called 'fate', for lack of a better word.

Schmeling thought a minute and then answered. 'I always trust the Dealer and try to make the system work for me. I look for a weakness in the opposition, an opening.'

Trying to get more specific, I asked him about his second fight with Jack Sharkey, back in 1932, when he lost a 15-round decision for the heavyweight title that everyone at the ringside thought he had won, including the mayor of New York, who later apologised to Schmeling for the unjust decision. Why, I asked, had he been first to congratulate Sharkey after getting the proverbial short end of the lollipop?

'I was right there in the ring, closest to him,' Schmeling answered with simplicity. 'Besides, all of my opponents became my friends. Especially Joe Louis. He'd come over here and sit with me for hours.'

I interrupted Schmeling's train of thought by asking something I had once heard: had he paid for Louis's funeral?

'I didn't think anybody knew,' Schmeling answered, softly. 'Actually,' he hurried to add, 'I just sent over a small sum. Maybe it did pay for the funeral.' And then, as if to end the embarrassing line of questioning, he said, firmly, 'Let's get on to the next question.'

Well, since the subject of Joe Louis had been broached, I wanted to know more about his two fights with Louis, two that indelibly linked their names forever in the annals of boxing. Why had Schmeling, 31 years of age and supposedly on the downside of his career, taken the first fight with the supposedly invincible Louis? Especially when the leader of the German people, Adolf Hitler, was afraid Schmeling would lose to a black man and embarrass the so-called 'Master Race'?

'I knew I was going to win,' Schmeling responded. 'I had studied clips of Louis's fights and detected a weakness. When he would throw a left, he would drop that left before throwing a second one. I saw he was open for my right. So, I made a special trip just to watch Louis fight – and knock out Paolino [Uzcudun] and look for that weakness. It was there. I was jubilant. I knew I'd win after that.'

But, I interjected, he had lost the first three rounds and his eye was almost closed.

Elaborating, he went on, almost as if he were giving a course in Boxing 101: 'But you notice that when I hit him in the fourth he went down. I knew then for sure I would win the fight. He was still dangerous until the twelfth when I knocked him out. But I had found the weakness.'

His bout with Louis was called an upset by all the major New York papers, but, I asked him, hadn't they also reported that he had become Hitler's darling and that he and his wife had had dinner with Der Fuehrer?

'It's normal for a head of state to have a reception for a successful athlete,' he explained quietly, his hands extended as if to give his remarks emphasis. 'The papers were correct. I wonder, though, if they mentioned how many times I turned Hitler down? Did they ever mention that I had had dinner with President Roosevelt? That he used to come to my training camp? That I used to correspond and exchange stamps with Roosevelt and Jim Farley, his campaign manager? No,' he sighed. 'Hitler really embarrassed both me and my wife.'

His references to his wife brought up something that had never been mentioned before. Why, I asked him, hadn't his wife accompanied him to the States in 1938 when he fought Louis in the rematch?

'Because,' he explained, 'Nazi propaganda minister [Joseph] Goebbels kept her in Germany as a hostage so I would not defect. Dempsey had always been after me to defect. My mother was also still in Germany. I was trapped. It was a very unpleasant period. Hitler knew what I thought of him. And yet, when I came back to the States, the American press identified me with Hitler. When I entered the ring before the second Louis fight, not only was I jeered but I was pelted with fruit. The debris hurt, but it was also the disappointment which hurt most.'

Why had his wife been kept a hostage? Wasn't he, I asked, more than somewhat nervously, a member of the Nazi Party?

'You're talking to a guy who had Joe Jacobs, an orthodox Jew, for a manager. I used to go to the synagogue with him. You're talking to a guy who was slammed into the paratroopers and had two promotions in three years to become, what? A sergeant.'

And so, as a sergeant in the paratroopers, Schmeling had parachuted into Crete in 1940 during the invasion and been captured. After the battle, Goebbels had ordered him to give an interview to the American press from a hospital bed about the alleged 'British atrocities'. What was his injury, I wondered aloud, battle wounds?

'Nothing so sensational,' said the soft spoken Schmeling. 'Actually, it was a bad case of diarrhoea. But when I told the Americans that the so-called "British atrocities" never took place, he had me court-martialled.'

Why had he returned to the ring after the war?

'I was penniless,' he explained, matter of factly. 'I went back on my forty-second birthday. But I was no George Foreman. I really admire him for that comeback.'

Skipping ahead, I asked how Coca-Cola had come into the picture and how he became head of Coca-Cola Germany.

'It was 1954 when I learned that my old friend, Jim Farley (once head of the New York State Athletic Commission, then Roosevelt's campaign manager and Postmaster-General and now head of Coca-Cola International), was in Essen. So I went over and he made the arrangements. The rest is history.

'It has been a great pleasure, but also profitable . . . very profitable.' And then, as if to put a fine point on just how profitable, he continued: 'I'm sure you've heard about the Schmeling Foundation. Originally, I put one million marks (a mark is worth 60 cents) into the Foundation and now, from the interest – which is up to 100,000 marks, we can address worthy causes. Like we just restored an old church in Hamburg. And we've helped a lot of poor people too. So that is my hobby . . . making money with one hand and giving it away with the other.'

Something else occurred to me, something I had long heard rumoured, so I asked him about helping Jews escape from Germany during *Kristallnacht*, the night of terror in November of 1938.

'It wasn't anything dramatic, like an underground,' he said, slightly uncomfortable at the question. 'All my wife and I did was to let them hide at our home until they could get out. A lot of other Germans were doing the same thing and I just had more to lose – especially because I was suspect.'

And then, almost as if he wanted to turn the discussion back to something that made him more comfortable, he added, 'But ask me more about boxing.'

All right, enough probing, I thought, back to the basics, to boxing. And with that I asked him who he thought was the greatest heavyweight of all time.

'I get that question a lot,' he answered, 'and I'm always evasive.' And sure enough he was as he went on, 'The heavyweight champion of a certain time is the best fighter for that time. I repeat, for that time. And to compare him with a champion of another time is all theory, generally emotion and something to do in a bar after closing time. They all had a speciality. Take Ali . . . No one was better than Ali in the centre of the ring. No one could stalk an opponent like Foreman. No one could hit like Max Baer. Joe Louis, I guess, was the best finisher. And Jack Dempsey the most vicious and aggressive. But,' he concluded, still moving, panther-like, around the corners of the answer. 'I never tried to compare champions.'

Since he hadn't mentioned Mike Tyson, I thought I'd try. And since the latest on Tyson was his trial, I asked Schmeling what he made of it.

'I'll be biased because I've met Tyson and really like him a lot. His problem was that he made too much money while he was still so young and didn't know a lot of people want that money. As for the trial, it's so simple. She came up to his room at 2 a.m. What did she expect, a cup of coffee?'

After an hour and a half, we had touched on almost everyone, from Dempsey to Louis to Ali to Tyson. Now it was time to wind it down. As a final leave-taking question, I asked Schmeling what three things he had learned in his four-score and seven-odd years.

'The first would be tolerance. So would the second and third,' he answered.

And then the great man got up and shook my hand, concluding that rarest of rarities, an interview with the former heavyweight champion of the world. Max Schmeling – a man who has always trusted the Dealer and always looked for an opening. And who has been treated well by both life and the Dealer in to the bargain.

Boxing Illustrated
1992

Main Bout (Somebody Up There Likes Me)

Rocky Graziano and Rowland Barber

Rocco Barbella was the archetypal 'underprivileged East Side kid punching his way out of the gutter'. Constantly in trouble with the law, he took the name Rocky Graziano and legitimised his street savagery in the ring. A ferocious hitter, Graziano had slaughtered world welterweight champion Marty Sevro in a non-title fight to earn a shot at Tony Zale's middleweight crown in the autumn of 1946.

Here is Graziano's own account in conjunction with Rowland Barber, of the first two of his three-fight series with Zale. Shortly before the contest, Graziano felt that he had at last crossed over into the licit world; not only did he own a Cadillac, but his house had twice been broken into and possessions taken: '(All right) that made me sore. So now I was one of the others. I was one of them that get stole off, instead of them that stole.'

On the night of 27 September, 40,000 people packed into Yankee Stadium to watch me in my first title fight. Nowhere had that many people ever come to watch two middleweights before. 'We got a record crowd, a record crowd!' Irving kept saying down in the dressing-room.

'We're going outa here with the title,' says Jack Healy.

'Crowd – title – nuts,' says I. 'How much money am I making tonight?'

'Don't worry, Rocky,' says Irving, 'we'll cut up half a million.'

We cut up almost $350,000 it turned out. A good thing it was that kind of money, because I didn't like what happened that night in the stadium. For the first time in my life, I get knocked out.

In the middle of the first round, Zale got me mad. He come out with some cautious jabs, feeling around, then he lands a stiff left hook on my chin. It hurt and it surprised me and the next thing I knew I was sitting on the canvas. I looked up at this guy. He looked big and he looked tough and I knew he was fast and he looks like he thinks I am ready to be killed off. We will now see who does the killing around here. I get to my feet. My head is a little dizzy. He presses in at me, throwing left and rights. I hold up my arms and stop most of the punches. Then my head clears. I slam into the son of a bitch. I shove my left hand at his throat. I crash a right on his jaw, haul back, crash a right to the side of his head, haul back again, let him have another on the jaw. He begins to wobble on his feet. One more walloping right and he will have his face bleeding in the gutter. I haul back. Just then the bell rings.

I can't wait to get back out there. I got the hungry-thirsty feeling for the kill rising up in my throat and I got to smash this guy who has become my enemy. The bell rings and my blood boils and there's fire in my guts that's got to bust out through my fists. He hits me back, in the ribs, on the head. I don't feel a thing. I swing faster and I swing harder and he's hurt and I feel like roaring like a bull and ramming my fist right down his throat. The crowd and the noise and the lights are gone. There is only him and me on a square of canvas in the middle of the night, and the only sound I hear is him sucking in his breath when I slug him. Now there is blood; I have split his lip and the bright red shows there and I aim for it, smashing at his mouth.

Wham! A perfect long right connects on his jaw and he's down! Now I can hear the crowd again, and they are bellowing so I can't hear Ruby Goldstein counting. I wait in the neutral corner. My feet are light, like there are springs in my shoes. I open and close my right fist. I got the feeling in my throat and the itch in my fist to cut loose with that last shot, the ramrod right-hand punch. I've got packed in there what I want to shoot at everybody who ever made me afraid, everybody who ever made me hate them, everybody who ever knocked me off my feet. The noise gets louder. Zale gets up to his feet and Goldstein has stopped counting. I hear somebody screaming. 'Rocky! Rocky!' It's Whitey and I realise the bell has rung and I have lost my chance to put him away that round.

They pull me over to my corner, Whitey and Frankie and Irving. They don't talk much. They are happy but they got their fingers crossed. 'You're ahead, kid, just keep it up, and don't change nothing. Go for his head. Keep going for his head and you'll finish him if you watch out for his left.' Something like that is what Whitey said. I don't know exactly. I just kept opening and closing my right fist while they rinsed my mouth, and wiped off the sweat, and massaged my shoulders. I was going to go out there and take over exactly where I left off one minute ago. The bell rung and I charged out to the middle of the ring and the noise rose up all around me in Yankee Stadium like I used to hear the surf come in by Ulmer Park when I was a kid out looking for driftwood for our stove. Like it was part of the programme, an airplane flew over low with its motors blasting, and the third round began.

But I had lost it. The feeling for the kill was lost between the rounds. My throat was dry now, the sweat gone off me. I heard everything plain, even Jack Healy yelling to come on, Rocky Bob, come, Rocky Bob, go for his head, boy. I went after him. I never threw so many punches in my life. Left, right, left, right, wham, whop, blam, whop, and he would wheeze and suck in and gasp and hold out his hands and try to catch my shots on his arms, his shoulders. I knocked him all over the ring. I didn't just shoot my right. I swung plenty of lefts. But I had lost it. Gone from his face was the look I saw in the second round, the look that said he knew what was going to happen, what he couldn't help from happening.

I can't take him. I hit him and hit him and he staggers, but every time I haul back for the killer, he has got me standing off balance. The bell rings when I am landing them on his jaw and his head, and he is still standing. It's like every split second I start my long swing somebody invisible pulls him back just half a step, and the punch whistles off his skin. I start to punch faster and faster.

The bell rings the end of the third.

The fourth round is worse. He comes after me, banging me in the ribs and in the stomach. A shot in my side almost takes my mind away, and I back off. He follows me and catches me with a couple of lefts in the face, before I can get my balance. Every time I try to rock back on to my feet he catches me with a left to the head, a left and a right to the ribs. He's too fast, too frigging fast. I am jumping back and sideways and waiting for the bell, listening for it, when it rings.

In the corner I tell Whitey, 'Okay, I got him opening up now. I'll let him open up a little more. This round. This round.' Whitey gives me a whack on the knee and says, 'Go get him, kid!'

In the fifth he's even fresher. His eyes are clearer and his lip looks closed where I split it open. Good. Let him think he's on top of me. Let him hammer me a few. He goes for my body again, trying to catch me between breaths, trying to pound the wind out of my lungs. I back away. I wait a second. Now. I start for him with a left and a right and a left and a right and for a minute the blood begins to boil again, and all the sound fades away except the singing in the back of my head. A left, a right, spin his head this way, that way, snap it back. He's wobbling on his feet again. Now! Now! a right to the chin. Haul it back. A right to his head. Grab his throat, grab his throat. Another shot to his face. He starts to stagger backwards.

The bell rings.

In my corner I don't say anything. This guy is tougher and he is quicker than anybody I ever fought in my life. This is a fighter, this Tony Zale. Anybody else I ever fought would be dead now.

The crowd is yelling and they're clapping. I know what they want. They want blood. They want the kill. They paid to see the wild, filthy-mouthed, dirty-punch East Side Guinea punk knock out the champion from Indiana who was built of steel like the mills he come from. That's what the papers told them they were going to see.

All right. All right. Just give me some wind, give me my breath back and get the sweat rubbed off, and I will give them what they paid for.

The time was going faster. Warning buzzer. Whitey snatches the stool and disappears. The bell rings. I wheel out to the middle. If I don't kill this guy soon, I am going to be too tired to move. I threw everything at him but the ring posts and my house and my car and all the chairs in Yankee Stadium, and still he rushed at me with lefts. I start swinging. I get him caught in the crossfire, left, right, left, right.

Then it was like the ground exploded up and hit me in the stomach. The lights spin in a fast circle, then dim down to a little spot like through the wrong end of a telescope. I try to yell out and I can't make a sound. I am deaf again, in the middle of Yankee Stadium. I am deaf and I can't talk and I can't lift my right hand or my left hand and I am falling. There was a big plane flying over the stadium and not making any noise but just its little red and green lights blinking off and on.

All at once everything was clear. I wasn't hurt, I just had the wind knocked out of me in the middle of Yankee Stadium with 40,000 people watching me and Tony Zale hanging over me and Ruby Goldstein the referee and this airplane up there flying by.

I got up. Tony Zale wound up with a left. I saw it coming. I couldn't stop it. It hits me. It was like the time the truck knocked me against the johnny pump. The jolt shot from my head down to my feet. The feeling went out of my feet and I went whang on the canvas like I didn't have any feet at all. The referee is swinging his arm down over me and counting.

I keep working at my feet and finally I get halfway up, leaning back against the ropes. Then my feeling comes back, the blood comes boiling back in my veins, and my lungs are full of air again and my ears are ringing with the sound of the crowd.

Somebody is pumping my arms back and forth. Then is the first time it comes to me. I have been counted out. I have been knocked out. I have been beat by Tony Zale in Yankee Stadium. But now I got all my fight back. Let me at this son of a bitch! He didn't beat me, he just knocked out my wind and caught me a punch after that. Let me back at him. This ain't no fight! Look at the guy – he's hurt, he's bleeding, his mouth is hanging open. I can tear him apart.

I knew what it was like for the first time in my life to be KO'd.

What I got out of that night in the Stadium was $100,000 and a guarantee to fight Zale again for his crown, and the stubborn idea that I had to get revenge on any guy ever knocked me out. I wasn't in no hurry. Let me enjoy my dough first, then I will take care of him.

The night I took the ten count was a tough night for Norma. When I come home she was hysterical and I couldn't stop her sobbing. She was afraid I was really hurt, and when she saw I wasn't she wouldn't let go of me and she wouldn't stop crying and it woke little Audrey up and she begun to cry too.

Before the fight, like she done before all my fights, my grandmother went and prayed for me and lit a candle. When she heard over the radio I got beat, she went back to the church at midnight and prayed again for me.

Up in Sing Sing, Terry Young busted two windows that night and got thrown in the Hole for trying to start a riot when they told him that Zale knocked me out.

Me it hurt the least of all. I put way back in my mind where I would never forget the idea of revenge for this knockout. Then I took my dough and I took Norma and Audrey and my mother-in-law and father-in-law and we all went to Florida.

It was my first long trip away from the city since they took me out to Leavenworth, Kansas. I was scared when I got off the train in Miami. I walked off and I saw all these white buildings, and all the traffic moving so quiet, and the funny trees all over the place in the middle of the town, and all the people I never saw before in my life, and I wanted to get right back on the train and take it right back to New York and go straight to the East Side.

I couldn't tell anybody this. I stuck it out. It was a weird place, Miami. The only joints they got there to hang out in are your own house, or maybe some big white drug store or saloon with the front door open. You can't find any regular kind of candy store or cigar store or poolroom. There aren't even any docks by the water to swim off of. You have to walk out on the sand before you jump in, like Coney Island.

At first I hate Florida and don't want to move out of the house, but by the time I got to go home it's not so bad at all.

When the Commissioner leaves he gives me a dirty look. I see what it meant. It meant one false move, brother, and the world is going to know that Graziano is a bum and a no-good criminal, a punk. Graziano is the scum out of the slums and he never changed. All right, Mr Commissioner, I was thinking, I got your look. So keep your eyes open and you are going to see a fight.

He saw a fight all right, and so did 20,000 customers, a fight like nobody ever saw before. They saw two guys come out in the ring and rip each other apart and never stop until it was over.

This was no boxing match. It was a war and if there wasn't a referee, one of the two of us would have wound up dead. Today I still can't look at the pictures of that Chicago Stadium fight without it hurts me and I get nightmares that I am back in the ring on the hot July night and I am looking out through a red film of blood.

In the first round we both come roaring out looking for an early knockout. Zale is slashing at me and rocking me and stinging me, and I am throwing long rights and I clinch three in a row on his jaw and knock him back on his heels. He comes back at me, hammering at my ribs, then catches me with a stiff shot to my left eye. It was like he crashed a gun butt over my eye. I couldn't see out of it no more, and the blood starts pouring out.

They closed up the cut over my eye but in the second round Zale goes right for it with short jabs, left right, and the pain starts beating in my eye and the blood is running again. He is hammering away at my ribs and my stomach, and in the heat my breath is coming shorter and shorter. I can't get set to land one square on him. I swing and miss, swing and miss.

The third was the worst round I ever lived through in the ring. Before I could put a glove on Zale, he belts me a right on my jaw and the arena is spinning and when it stops I am sitting on the frigging canvas looking up with one good eye, blinking through the blood, I smile at him. It is a smile that means I am going to kill or be killed, and if anybody thinks I am going to stay down they are crazy. I jump to my feet before there is even a count. But before I can square off he is all over me again, whamming me in the middle, trying to cut off my wind like he done in Yankee Stadium. He caught me an awful whack like a policeman's bat socked me across the belly and it doubled me over. Then he quick goes for my head. I can't see nothing for the rest of the round, only this red blur that comes at me, fades away, comes at me. I can't see the jolts coming. My head is knocked to the left, to the right, like it is going to come right off my neck. I hold up my hands but he smashes them back into my face, and my gloves slither in the blood and the sweat. I lunge out at the blur, but when I swing there is only air. My arms and legs feel like they are made out of lead and I almost topple over on to the canvas.

When the bell rung I ached from my head to my feet. I could have laid down in the middle of the ring and gone to sleep and not cared if I ever woke up. I dragged back to the corner. Whitey swabbed out my eye and squeezed the sponge over my head. The first thing I saw when I looked up was the referee examining me and shaking his head. Irving was saying, 'Looks pretty bad, don't it?'

I could feel what they were all thinking. Everything was coming to an end. They were going to stop the fight!

I couldn't talk. I shook my head and hammered my fists together. Whitey must have seen how desperate I looked. 'Give Rocky one more round,' he said. 'Just one more round?'

The referee made a face. I must have looked like something that got up and walked off a slab in the morgue. He shrugged his shoulders. 'If this wasn't a championship fight,' he said, 'I would never a let him last out the third round. One more and if he don't come out of it, I got to stop it. They give you the chair for murder in this state.'

The bell rung for the fourth round and that is when I stopped remembering. The only thought in my head was they are going to stop it. If I let up from swinging for one second, if I go off my feet just once, they are going to stop it and I am through, I am nothing, a nobody, and everything I got is lost. I had forgotten all about cutting up half a million bucks. I had forgotten all about Norma by the radio in the hotel, and my family by the radio in New York, and my grandmother praying in the church.

I was an animal in a cage of ropes, a bleeding, cornered, half-blind, aching, sweating, snarling animal who had to kill or be killed. I don't remember no bells ringing or no crowd or no referee. The figure of Zale was a blur sometimes, then the blood got wiped off my good eye and he was sharp and splotched with red and moving slower and slower under the hot lights in the steambath air of the arena. I followed him and followed him swinging out, punching, belting.

He tried to swing back and he missed, and went sprawling on his hands and knees. I growled a curse and jumped at him, but something stopped me. It was the referee. It was the end of the round.

Then I got a second wind, like a breeze of cool air come from heaven and I sucked it deep in my lungs and I felt new strength tingle down my arms and legs and I yelled that I was going to kill that stinking rat bastard and I tore into him and never stopped. I hit him until both my fists go numb. I hit him until he can't hit back no more, he can't hold his hands up. He sways over and I grab his throat and straighten him back up and hit him. He sways again, and I belt him up straight.

Somewhere a bell must have rung and I must have gone to my corner to get the blood wiped off but I don't remember.

I am back out there in the sixth round, and he is helpless and I am ripping him up and tearing him apart. I'm breaking every bone in his body. I'm stoving his head in and punching his guts out. I don't even know any more who I am killing, whether it's a cop or a guard or somebody who ratted on me or Tony Zale or who.

Suddenly there is a sharp whack across my face. My good eye comes into focus. I am standing in the middle of the ring in the Chicago Stadium and 20,000 people are going crazy. I have been trying to belt out Jack Healy, who is out there with me, and it is Whitey Bimstein who slapped me and who is saying, 'Rocky! Rocky! Come out of it! Rocky, you're the world champion!'

I had laid Zale on top of the ropes and he couldn't get back on his feet and the referee had took one look at his glazed eyes and stopped the fight.

I am world champion and my eyes are blind with blood and tears as I ask Jack to help me over to Tony's corner so I can shake his hand. I am the world champion and then the radio guy comes up there in the ring with the microphone and says, 'Rocky, how does it feel? What do you have to say to our listeners, Rocky? Ladies and gentlemen, the new middleweight champion, Rocky Graziano.'

I think of all the long, tough, hungry years, stretching like the dirty stairs in the dim light up to the top floor of the tenement house in First Avenue. Up there in the hot front room of the railroad flat, they are listening to what is happening in Chicago. That is why I said into the microphone, 'Hey, Ma – your bad boy done it!'

Consul Books, World Distributors (London)
1965

Raging Bull

Jake La Motta with Joseph Carter and Peter Savage

Rocky Graziano and Jake La Motta (Giacobe La Motta) were two of a kind. Born a month apart on the wrong side of the tracks in New York in 1922, they came from Italian backgrounds and were boon drinking companions. Shared experience extended to spells in jail and to having the mob at their elbows. They also wrote assisted autobiographies from which films were made – Somebody Up There Likes Me and Raging Bull, starring Paul Newman and Robert De Niro respectively. And above all, of course, they were both extremely tough, aggressive world middleweight champions with similar attacking styles. The wonder is they were never matched. What a fight it would have been.

'The Bronx Bull', as La Motta was known, had to wait eight years for a title chance. At last, at Detroit on 16 June 1949, he climbed into the ring to meet the champion, French-Algerian Marcel Cerdan. Cerdan had won the title by disposing of Tony Zale who in turn had regained the middleweight crown from Graziano in the third of their battles.

L adies and gentlemen . . . for the middleweight championship of the world . . . at a hundred and fifty-nine-and-a-half pounds . . . the great French champion . . . from Casablanca, Morocco . . . Marcel Cerdan!'

Cerdan is a very popular champion around the world and gets a great roar of applause. Then the announcer goes on: 'And in this corner, from the Bronx, New York, the challenger, at one hundred and fifty-eight pounds, the Bronx Bull . . . Jake La Motta!'

I'm sorry to say that even though I got as noisy a reception as Cerdan, half of it was boos. You know the old saying about giving a dog a bad name. It had gotten so that no matter what I did, it was wrong. Six months before the championship I had fought Tommy Yarosz, and I stopped hitting him when he was helpless on the ropes. The crowd booed me and Jimmy Cannon, who was a columnist on the *New York Post* then, wrote that I was 'probably the most detested man of his generation'. Well, that covers a lot of ground. I could mention – well, never mind.

There I was in the ring with Cerdan and the fight started and it was one hell of a fight because we both had styles that were a lot alike – go, go, go, punch, punch, punch. Both of us were willing to take punches in order to hand 'em out, and both of us had a punch. The very first round was a lulu. I was charging out of my corner and fighting the only way I knew how, hard and fast. He came back at me good and hard, and somewhere around the middle of the first round he wanted to go into a clinch but I didn't, and I was half-punching, half-shoving him to get him off me when he went down. What caused it – whether it was a punch or the shoving or a slip, or a combination of all three – I still don't know. Anyway, he went down and the referee motioned me to a neutral corner, but Cerdan was back on his feet before the ref could start counting. Cerdan looked all right to me, but after the fight was over he claimed he hurt a muscle in his right shoulder when he fell.

Maybe he did, but it didn't feel that way to me from some of the lefts I took during the fight and there are still movies of that fight around, if you'd care to look at them and make up your own mind. Also, the records show that Cerdan won the second round on the cards of everybody who was scoring.

In the second round, as a matter of fact, I also got a knuckle pushed out of joint, and the trouble with a boxing glove is that it isn't easy to get out of in a hurry, or to manipulate. You can get your seconds to manipulate it, but if the knuckle doesn't go back in, you don't have the time to take the glove off and fix it up. Anyhow, this was on my left hand, and I had enough confidence that I could jab with it but not hook, and from the second round on I was getting to Cerdan. That again is on all the record cards. The third, fourth and fifth, I won on all the scorecards, and in the sixth and seventh, Cerdan began covering up a little and I could hear my corner men, Al Silvani and Al DeNapoli, yelling to me, 'That's it, Jackson! That's how to go, Jackson!'

By the eighth and ninth rounds, I knew I was winning. I heard afterwards that Joe Longman wanted Cerdan to quit before the eighth and ninth round and Cerdan told him: 'If you stop the fight I will kill myself.'

He was both brave and proud, which is what a champ should be, and if he was going to lose, he was going to go down fighting.

But after the ninth round, the referee, Johnny Weber, saw how much trouble Cerdan was in, and he went over to his corner and took me by the wrist and led me back to the centre of the ring and raised my hand up and all hell broke loose.

The noise was so loud you couldn't hear yourself think. It sounded like it would lift the roof off the joint, and the aisles were filled with people, and my brother Joey jumped into the ring, and then the seconds, and they threw their arms around me, yelling and screaming and pounding, and the cops piled up there all around the ropes to keep these jokers from climbing in, and the bell kept gonging away for silence till it quieted down enough so the announcer could get down the overhead microphone again.

'Ladies and gentlemen . . . Marcel Cerdan is unable to answer the bell for the tenth round . . . The winner and new middleweight champion of the world . . . Jake La Motta!'

United Artists Corporation
1980

Hymn of Love: Piaf and Cerdan

Dominique Grimault and Patrick Mahé
(translated by Barbara Mitchell)

The story of the love affair between Marcel Cerdan and chanteuse Edith Piaf was realised in what could be called a factionalised account by Dominique Grimault and Patrick Mahé. As the drama unfolds, the mercurial Piaf and the frustrated Cerdan seemed helpless to influence events.

Marcel was in the depths of despair. He had lost the title he had fought so hard to win and to a decidedly dubious opponent in a decidedly dubious atmosphere. This alone was enough to depress him. But there was something else. His injury, for example, remained mysterious. A few minutes after the end of the fight, Dr Vincent Nardiello, the official doctor attached to the New York Boxing Commission, diagnosed a tear or supraspinatus strain of the elevator muscle probably with a haemorrhage. The next day in New York the same doctor took an X-ray of Cerdan's shoulder in Saint Clare's hospital. He announced shortly afterwards that the X-ray showed absolutely nothing. Another official doctor, Dr Joseph Cahallan, examined Cerdan. He came to the same conclusion: there was no external sign of injury.

And now, to make matters worse, the sports journalists were raising questions both about Cerdan's training and Lew Burston's over-confidence before the fight. And why did Marcel agree to go into the ring immediately after a game of *jacquet* when he was suddenly informed that the fight had been brought forward? Significantly, La Motta had spent the previous half-hour shadow-boxing to warm himself up. Were these simply mistakes or were they signs of negligence?

When Loulou Barrier met Marcel at Saint-Lazare station he hardly recognised him. Marcel immediately asked him how Edith had taken it.

'She's waiting for you,' Barrier replied. 'She's completely demoralised.'

Edith was in a state, angry at herself for not having gone over to the States. 'Marcel,' she said, 'I should have been there with you.'

'Do you think so?'

'Of course! But I'm never going to leave you again. And we're going to get out of here. I'm fed up with this house. It feels sad.'

'Do you think so?' He would have gone along with anything she said.

A few days later they bid goodbye to Auteuil and moved out, lock, stock and barrel. Edith had found a magnificent house on the edge of the Bois de Boul-ogne, at 5 rue Gambetta. There were rooms everywhere, columns, a spiral staircase, terraces, a bathroom in pink marble, attics, basements and a large room destined for Marcel's training.

When she was shown round, Edith immediately concluded that the man who built the house must have been mad. His name appeared on the facade: Emilio Terri. He had made a bet in the thirties that he would build the largest possible building on the tiniest plot in the neighbourhood.

Edith soon imposed her own inspired chaos. It was as though a theatre set were being assembled instinctively, any old how, yet with a sense of conviction. It was like living out of a suitcase. But in the midst of this flurry of furniture, American goods, fur coats and plants, Edith maintained a sanctuary for herself, a few square feet of peace. It was her room – their room. It was dominated by a white piano and the latest model of TV set. There were pictures by primitive artists on the walls, not a modern picture to be seen.

'One day,' she said to Marcel, 'we'll buy ourselves a Rembrandt and a Corot.'

'Oh yes, why?' asked Marcel.

'Because they're really good painters.'

Marcel went off to Rome. He was bound by the terms of his contract to make a second film, *Al diavolo la celebrità!* (To Hell with Fame!). There was no way he could get out of it. Edith's view was to hell with obligations. But boxing films were all the rage at the time. The Americans had a stock of them. They had just released *The Champion* with Kirk Douglas, and were already announcing another boxing film with Robert Ryan. The prospect of earning a few million francs dispelled whatever doubts Marcel might have had about signing. There was no point in looking a gift-horse in the mouth, even if the plot did end badly for Marcel: he was due to die at the end, following a car accident.

Edith and Marcel met up three weeks later in mid-August in Cannes. She was in the middle of a summer tour. It seemed as though they hadn't seen each other for close on a century. They discovered each other all over again. Her movements were delicate. He became bashful. Afterwards, she laughed till she cried listening to him telling stories about the shooting of the film.

'No, it can't be true, Marcel. You didn't really, did you?'

'I did, I swear, but it wasn't on purpose.'

'But what did the director say?'

'He said it was very good and that on no account was the scene to be altered in any way.'

Marcel had been explaining to Edith how, in the middle of shooting, he had pulled off an amazing KO which wasn't in the script. The victim was an Italian by the name of Fernando Janilli, a real boxer. 'Let's have a real fight,' Marcel had said to the Italian. In the heat of the moment he delivered a left hook and put Janilli right out of the game.

'Was he cross with you afterwards?' asked Edith who couldn't contain her laughter.

'No, he was a good guy, but what got him was that the sequence is to stay in the film.'

Edith thought Marcel looked superb, positively radiant. His suntan suited him. 'How handsome you are, Marcel,' she kept telling him, fluttering her eyelashes at him . . .

Jo Longman soon caught up with them. He had received a cable from Lew Burston telling him to get ready: La Motta and his 'gentlemen' had decided to offer Cerdan his return bout without delay. The fight was planned for 28 September in the Polo Grounds in New York.

'Wonderful!' cried Edith. 'This time, I'll be there with you.' She had just signed a new five-month contract with the Versailles where she was to open on 15 September.

Marcel turned to Jo: 'When do you want to go?'

'As soon as possible,' replied Jo somewhat impatiently. 'It's time we shut them up.'

'What do you mean?' asked Edith.

'Lew's got me a bit worried,' said Longman in embarrassment. 'There are all sorts of strange rumours going round over there. People are claiming Marcel let himself be bought or that he gambled on La Motta. Bullshit like that. But they're serious charges.'

There was a silence. Marcel was disgusted. 'How can people say things like that! They're going to pay for it!'

To take his mind off it, Edith took him out to Juan-les-Pins in the evening. She was singing. There was a festival with fireworks. Marcel agreed to give the starting signal for a race of home-trainers. They made him ride a bicycle. He didn't have it in him to refuse. The audience of holidaymakers made him feel warm inside. They treated him as if he had already regained his crown. He swore to himself he would.

The story continues with Cerdan going to New York, only for La Motta to pull out with an apparent shoulder injury. With no definite date for a rescheduled meeting, Cerdan returned to his wife Marinette and family in Casablanca, leaving Piaf, together with her friend and companion Genevieve Lévitan, despondently continuing with her booking at the Versailles in New York.

Then came the news Marcel was waiting for. La Motta's agreement was imminent. Marcel had to get ready to return to Paris. The day before his departure, after a last family meal at the Sidi Marouf farm, to please Marinette, Marcel suggested they go out to the Don Quichotte, a big nightclub in Casablanca. There was no holding him back. He led Marinette out on to the dance floor. She liked dancing with him. He had taught her the tango, the samba and the bolero.

The next day, 23 October, Marcel flew to Paris. He didn't want Marinette to accompany him to the airport. While she was packing his case, he told her: 'This'll be my last fight. Don't listen to the radio. I'll win.'

In Paris, Marcel stayed at Jo Longman's house in the rue de Provence. He was a bundle of nerves. A first cable announced that La Motta was on the point of signing. Burston asked Jo and Marcel to stand by. There would be another message soon . . . A few hours went by. Burston was playing a tight game in New York. The organisers had had difficulty finding room in Madison Square Garden's heavily booked programme. La Motta had seemed to agree to 2 December. Now, all of a sudden, he was pulling out to get publicity. And, to top it all, he was demanding an extra $1,000 for the television rights.

La Motta went too far. They ended up threatening to relegate him to the list of 'ill or unavailable boxers'. There was even talk of leaving the title vacant should Jake continue to be awkward. Jake finally agreed to sign. Burston immediately alerted his friends in Paris. His telegram said that La Motta had given him every assurance and that the world championship would take place on the date planned.

Marcel jumped for joy in the flat. 'Wonderful!' he shouted. He wanted to leave for America immediately.

Longman calmed him down. 'Marcel, don't forget your exhibition bout at Troyes.'

'I haven't forgotten,' replied Marcel, 'but nor have I forgotten that I've got to be on the spot at least 25 days before the fight.'

Why did she have to phone him then?

She wasn't okay. She was in a terrible mood. She was having rows with everyone in New York. She could do nothing but find fault with her friends. She and Genevieve had a scene over nothing. They went to see a ballet arranged and danced by Roland Petit. At supper Genevieve had felt she ought to pay him a compliment. She said she had particularly liked a *pas de deux*. Roland Petit had nodded his assent. Edith had sniggered. 'Poor Genevieve,' she had giggled, 'it was the only movement Roland had nothing to do with.'

They had walked back to the apartment. Edith had launched into Genevieve again as if she had taken a sudden dislike to her. 'What a clanger you dropped, my dear.'

Genevieve let her finish before striking back somewhat haughtily: 'Frankly, Edith, you overdo things.'

Edith was cutting. 'And who on earth do you take yourself for, Madame Lévitan?'

Genevieve was in the process of packing her bags when Edith appeared in her room. 'Forgive me, I didn't mean it. I can't stop myself.' Then she burst into tears. 'Why must I destroy everything?' Genevieve held her in her arms.

She heard his fluty laugh on the phone. He was euphoric. They were on opposite sides of the Atlantic. They were half happy, half sad. He told her everything.

She pressed him: 'So, you'll be here soon?'

'Yes, I'm going to arrange it. We'll take the boat as soon as possible.'

'The boat? You must be joking. Take the plane, Marcel, I need you.'

So he promised her to be there even sooner. The next day, an article signed by Marcel Cerdan and written by René Dunan made the *France-Soir* headlines:

Once, through stupidity, a silly accident, La Motta got me. Once is enough . . . It won't happen a second time. I must beat La Motta, and beat him I shall. I will be at my peak on 2 December. Believe me, I shall return to France with the world middleweight crown firmly on my head. Unfortunately, the Evans Hotel, where I usually train, is now closed. It is too late in the season. But Jo Longman is negotiating with several training camps. We shall set ourselves up in the middle of the countryside, most probably about 60 miles away at Greenwood Lake. Willy Ketchum, who trained me for the match that didn't take place in September, will be back with us.

Marcel, Wednesday, 26 September 1949, Troyes

Marcel resigned himself to the exhibition bout. It was organised by Charly Mittel, one of the founders of the Club des Cinq and a close friend of Jo Longman's since the African campaign with the 2nd Armoured Division. Mittel ran an off-the-peg clothing shop in the rue du Commerce, in the fifteenth arrondissement in Paris. His made-to-measure motto was; *Honi soit qui mal se vet* (he who dresses badly shall be held in contempt). He promised that 'anyone referred by Marcel Cerdan shall be entitled to a reduction'.

He had organised the fight in the municipal circus to celebrate the opening of a new branch in Troyes. To please Charly and for old times sake, Marcel graciously agreed to attend all the receptions given in their honour. A reporter on *France-Dimanche*, Jacques Chapus, kept a careful note of his busy timetable.

Marcel arrived in Troyes around ten in the morning. Wherever he went – to the newspaper, the *Petit Troyen*, to see the mayor at the town hall, and in the headquarters of the local club, *L'Energie troyenne* – he had a smile on his face. It was one of his open, slightly teasing smiles. He was happy, calm and very much in control. He was inundated with questions. He told everyone: 'I'm leaving tomorrow for New York. It's the most important trip of my career. I want to become world champion again. Firstly, for myself, for my own personal pride, but also for all of you who've put your faith in me.'

There was applause. He had lunch in the restaurant *La Bourgogne*, then went on to Charly Mittel's shop, *A la ville de Paris*. There was a scrum. He signed autograph after autograph. He gave photos of himself to everyone, children, women, sportsmen and would-be sportsmen, always adding a kind word.

Longman shouted at him: 'Stop, take a break.'

Marcel waved him away. 'It's okay, Jo, I'm not tired.'

The municipal circus was crowded that evening. The programme had already started when Marcel arrived. He drank in the atmosphere. He gave his bag to Longman. 'Take it to the cloakroom. I want to see the boxing.' He mixed with the other spectators and got caught up in all the amateur fights which opened the show. Then came his turn to get ready. He joined Jo in the changing-rooms. It was a circus dressing-room, covered with photos of film stars.

Jo and Paul Genser watched him dress. Marcel got on to the scales. He weighed 162 pounds.

'If you only knew, Jo,' said Marcel, 'how well I feel.'

'Too well, I fear,' replied Longman. 'You are too fit, too light, for someone who still has six weeks to go to the world championship.'

'It's not a serious problem,' said Marcel. 'We'll lounge around in New York for four or five days. You'll see, I'll put on weight again.'

'Won't you stay in Paris for a few more days?' Longman was trying to get Marcel to change his mind. 'You know,' he went on, 'we really could leave next Tuesday. We'd be able to go to the *Palais des Sports* on Monday evening. That would give us time to get ready for the journey.'

'No, no, Jo,' said Cerdan excitedly, 'we can't wait. Friday's a good day to arrive in New York. We'll make all the weekend newspapers.'

Longman was tired of arguing and gave up. He made a joke of it: 'My word, Marcel, so you're a businessman now, are you?'

Marcel smeared his face with vaseline, put on his purple American Everlast shorts, threw his robe over his shoulders and went back to mingle with the crowd in the hall for a few more minutes while he waited his turn. He watched the ring, isolated like a brilliant raft in a sea of shadows. Then he was called. At 10.15 the master of ceremonies Tafanelli announced him to the public.

Tafanelli cleared his throat and said in a voice everyone could hear: 'Every time I have the honour of introducing Cerdan, I try to find a new way of doing it. But whatever I come up with is a waste of time.' Tafanelli waited for silence, and with a theatrical gesture, held his arm out to the champion's corner, raised his voice and, emphasising each syllable, he announced: 'Here is Mar-cel Cer-dan!'

Marcel sprang over the ropes. He was received with noisy applause. Valère Benedetto, a young welterweight from Arles, had been chosen to fight him. He was very intimidated and drew near to Cerdan to whisper in his ear: 'How do we play it?'

Marcel reassured him: 'Don't worry. Hit me and I'll try and hit you.'

But Benedetto had learned his lesson by heart. He had been told that in the last seconds of each of the three rounds, Longman would blow on a whistle. At this point the boxers would face each other and do a few staged sequences. People loved these rhythmic exercises.

The three rounds went very quickly. Marcel gave the impression of great strength and lightness. He ended with a left hook – the left which had let him down when he fought La Motta and which he had since worked on. The audience was delighted and cheered wildly. Marcel thanked them and Tafanelli took up the microphone again. He had one last announcement to make: 'It gives me great pleasure to be able to say that Marcel is handing his fee over to local charities.'

Marcel was in no hurry to leave. He savoured his triumph like a beginner. Paul, Jo and Marcel didn't leave the dinner table until two in the morning, when they decided to go back to Paris.

Andy Dickson, then a junior reporter on the *Parisien Libéré*, remembers that day:

I was the only Parisian sports reporter that evening at the Troyes circus. Marcel, who had boxed wearing a leather helmet, made a strong impression on me. He had literally knocked the wind out of his opponent, who had a reputation for being very fast. I was preparing to go back to the hotel, thinking I would take the first train in the morning, when I met Jo Longman. He immediately suggested that I go back with them.

People in the boxing world were very friendly towards me, not because I was a young journalist but because I was the son of Jeff Dickson. My father had been a great figure in the Vélodrome d'Hiver before the war. He was dead – he had been a pilot and was killed in 1943.

There was room for one more in the car. We had to squeeze up. Paul Genser sat to the right of the driver. I was directly behind him. Marcel was in the middle and Jo Longman on the other side. It was very late when we set off. Marcel fell asleep straightaway, or almost straightaway. When we came to a bend his head would fall on to Jo's shoulder or mine. I didn't dare move. I was too star-struck. Paul, Jo and I talked incessantly. Marcel was going to beat La Motta. It was obvious to all three of us. He had all the trumps in his hand. We competed with each other to list attributes that would win him the match. It was a foregone conclusion. We were driving quite fast.

Marcel woke briefly between Nogent-sur-Seine and Provins, listened to us for a few seconds as we discussed his forthcoming world championship and put in his word; 'Listen, leave me in peace, I'm going to beat this La Motta, but let me get some sleep.' I can still hear him saying it. We arrived in Paris at daybreak. They left me at the metro stop on the Quai de Bercy. I was living with my mother in Sartrouville.

By lunchtime, the comfortable flat shared by Jo Longman and Jacqueline on the fifth floor in the rue de Provence looked like the Marx Brothers' cabin in *A Night at the Opera*. Jo and Marcel were throwing things into their cases. It was a scene of busy but lighthearted chaos. The atmosphere was relaxed. Marcel kept playing his favourite record: 'Riders in the Sky'.

They grabbed a quick snack. Jacques Meyran, a variety artist and one of Edith Piaf's confidants, had offered to take them to Orly. Marcel had on a grey tweed overcoat over the blue suit he wore for luck whenever he flew. Carrying his heavy suitcase on his shoulder he rushed down the stairs, followed by Jo. He sat in the front of the royal blue Pontiac Jacques Meyran was driving. Jo and Paul Genser sat in the back.

Meyran was about to start when Longman, who had been checking to see they had everything, cried out: 'Damn! We've left the passports behind. I'll go back and get them. Wait for me, Meyran, I won't be a minute . . .'

Finally they left. It was late. Longman was jumping up and down. The plane would be taking off in two hours' time. And then Marcel had an idea. 'Let's go and say goodbye to the girls.'

Jo didn't agree; 'We haven't got time.'

Marcel stuck to his guns. 'We can't leave without saying goodbye.'

The Pontiac drew up front of the *Ambassade de l'Opéra* in the rue Saint-Anne. The little restaurant was still empty. Marcel went behind the bar and embraced Mado Fondo, Irene de Trébert, his buddy Jacquot the barman, and Denis, known as Néné, Mado's brother, who was devoted to him.

An edgy Longman appeared on the threshold. 'Hurry up, we'll miss the plane . . .'

It was eight o'clock according to the big clock in Orly airport. All of a sudden, the word spread through the hall to the ticket counters: 'Cerdan's here!' The photographers were waiting for him and jostled with each other. Ten microphones were held out at the same time. Marcel faced up to the flash like an old hand, spoke into one microphone and leaned comfortably over another, repeating the same thing: 'I shall be bringing back the crown I lost. I'm going to fight like a lion. I shall be starting my training in three days' time. I can't wait to get back to New York and the Madison Square Garden ring. If I could have left earlier I would have. I had to lean on Air France to get a priority seat on the Paris–New York flight.'

The whole of France was listening. For millions, Cerdan's departure overshadowed the fact that after three weeks of unhappy experiments, the French President, Vincent Auriol, had finally found a new government leader in Georges Bidault.

Marcel added: 'I shall use every ounce of strength I have to regain the title which I was stupid enough to lose. At the age of 33, with 116 fights behind me . . .'

'Wrong, Marcel. A hundred and nineteen,' someone whispered.

'A hundred and nineteen then,' he smiled. 'It makes no difference. I feel nowhere near worn out or too old.' Marcel was very articulate that evening. 'When the time comes, I'll know how to stop without being pushed.'

Longman was more down to earth. 'We're slipping away like thieves,' he apologised. He raised his eyes. 'But we simply can't keep him here a minute longer. If he had taken my advice we would have spent the whole week in Paris. We would have flown on Tuesday. It would have been much simpler. But no, we had to go now. I have the feeling we've forgotten half the things we need.'

Marcel signed his autograph on cards, handkerchiefs, metro tickets. A taxi driver brought him a boxing glove to sign. He thanked him, crying like a child. A voice was heard: 'Are you wearing your blue suit, Marcel?'

He nodded and gripped the lapel of his jacket. All his fans knew how superstitious he was. Strangely enough, no one paid any attention to the predictions made by the palmist Arista. He had asked to see the champion. The meeting had taken place at Paul's in the rue d'Orsel. Arista had looked at Cerdan's hand and warned him in an earnest voice: 'You fly too often. Watch out . . .'

'I can't help it,' Marcel had replied. 'I have to travel.'

Later on, Arista had stretched his 'professional conscience' to ask for a copy of Marcel Cerdan's birth certificate from the town hall in Sidi Be Abbes. He had then drawn up his horoscope. There it was for all to read: 'Try not to travel by air, especially on Fridays.'

Now Marcel was being pressed into having his photograph taken with Ginette Neveu. He grimaced. It was not that he had the slightest grudge against the great violinist who had just given a triumphant recital at Pleyel of the 32 Chacone variations by Bach; but Cerdan was wary of posed photos which could always be used against you. It had happened before . . .

Nevertheless, he let himself be persuaded. 'For posterity', he gazed respectfully at the Stradivarius which Ginette Neveu had taken out of its case, and he now gripped in his thick fingers. She played a few chords for the photographers. The reporters were happy. Marcel then took his friends off for a last drink. Maurice, the barman at Orly, knew what he liked. He had already chilled, without freezing it, a bottle of extra dry champagne which Marcel drank slowly, as befits a connoisseur. Jo Longman, visibly preoccupied, forgot to drink.

Marcel kidded him. He remarked to Maurice that Jo was like a wet blanket that evening. Luckily, his friend Paul was at his side, full of beans, laughing and humming a tune, the life and soul of the party.

And now the time had come to say goodbye. Marcel grabbed the hands held out to him, shouted a joyous 'See you soon' to Maurice and went off to the newspaper kiosk. He gave the saleswoman 50 francs and hurried off.

'Your change, Monsieur Cerdan,' she cried.

He turned round and replied with a smile: 'Give it to me next time.'

It was a cold, clear night. The passengers pulled up the collars of their coats as they climbed the gangway in single file. The steward said there were 37 of them.

Three passengers had had to give up their seats at the last minute: Mr and Mrs Newton, a recently married American couple and Mme Erdmann, a Parisienne. Marcel, Jo and Paul were given their seats. The three of them were ushered down the gangway by Monsieur Guirant, the manager of Orly airport, who had been a friend of Cerdan's for ten years.

Marcel and Jo sat side by side, in the middle of the plane, Marcel next to the porthole. Paul was behind Jo. Opposite them, on the other side of the aisle was Bertrand Boutet de Monvel, who painted American high society, fine horsemen and polo players. He designed the posters for Ingrid Bergman's films. Americans paid a high price for his portraits. His painting of Jeanne d'Arc had won him international renown.

Seated in front of Marcel was Mme Jenny Brandière, aged 40, and her daughter, Françoise, who was 21. Four months earlier, Mme Brandière had rushed to her daughter's bedside, after she had been seriously injured in a car crash. Françoise was considered beyond hope. She had recovered, and mother and daughter were off again to Cuba where they lived.

In the first row was Mrs Hennessy, a face well known to Air France. She had arrived late at Orly. They had tried to turn her away. She had thrown a tantrum and insisted. She got her way in the end.

Sitting at the very back were five Basques flushed with excitement. Three of them were from the village of Aldudes. They were shepherds. They were called Siquilbide, Chourrout, Aduritz, Etchepare and Arambel. They had never been further than Bayonne. They were going to the American West to make their fortunes, as the pioneers had done before them.

There was also Guy Jasmin, a journalist on *Canada Montréal*, and his wife; Mr Kay Kamen, director of the Walt Disney Studios; and Jean Paul, Ginette Neveu's brother, who sat next to his sister. From the departure area you could see Marcel's familiar wave at the porthole.

At 9.06 p.m. the Constellation FBA-ZN, equipped with four 2,500 horse-power Wright cyclone engines, took off amidst a deafening roar. There were 48 people on board, including extra cabin staff, who had been brought in especially. The plane was full in terms of total weight, passengers and freight. There was nothing unusual about the take-off. Planes took off all the time for New York. It was no more significant than the departure of a train for Marseilles. Forty planes crossed the Atlantic every day. Since 1 July 1946, Air France had carried 52,000 passengers on 1,972 crossings, each taking 17 hours. There had never been an accident. The Constellation was due to make two stops *en route*: the Azores and Gander (Newfoundland), before reaching New York, at 9.30 a.m.

The captain of the FBA-ZN was Jean de la Noue. A former sailor, he had been a pilot since 1935 and had trained numerous commercial pilots. He had been flying the North Atlantic route for the past two years. He had crossed the ocean 88 times and had accumulated nearly 7,000 hours of flying time. He was 37 and had three children.

At 11 p.m. Paris time, the Constellation gave its first position: west of Rochefort. The second position was communicated at midnight: AOK. Third position, 1 a.m.: AOK 200 miles west of Portugal. Fourth position, 2 a.m.: AOK. The plane indicated that it would be arriving in the Azores at 3.50 a.m..

3.50 a.m. : The plane asked for landing instructions from the control tower on Santa Maria, the most southerly of the islands in the archipelago. It was midnight in the Azores. It was clear; visibility 12 miles. The island of Sao Miguel and the Rodonta peak (3,500 feet) were on the right.

The control tower replied that everything was ready for landing and that the plane should come in from the south. It was to reduce speed to 260 miles per hour.

The FBA-ZN replied: 'Okay. We're at 3,000 feet. We land in five minutes.'

EPILOGUE

Si un jour la vie t'arrache à moi . . .
(If life should tear you from me one day)

Edith, 28 October, New York, 1.30 p.m.

Edith screamed and collapsed. Loulou Barrier's silence had told her everything. The others – Chauvigny, Bonel, Burston, Genevieve Lévitan – were all impotent and helpless, caught up in their own sorrow. They were all mourning Marcel in their different ways. It was Barrier again who tried to pick Edith up. Everyone in the apartment was overwhelmed. Instinctively, they all kept an eye on the windows, watching Edith closely. Poor little woman. Her crying had given way to moans. She threw herself against the base of a lampstand near the sofa. Genevieve put an arm round her shoulders and guided her gently towards her room. She offered her a glass of water but Edith shook her head. She crumpled up on the end of the bed like a rag doll or an abandoned puppy.

Lew Burston had been fully aware of the tragedy for a while. The phone had rung in the middle of the night in his Manhattan apartment. It was a reporter. Lew had been fast asleep and had been surprised that anyone should disturb him so late. He had been about to hang up on this intruder when he heard him ask in a breathless voice: 'Lew, have you heard the news?'

Burston couldn't sleep for the rest of the night. When he got up at 7.00 a.m., his brown hair had turned grey, as it remains to this day. Burston felt he had a mission: to protect Edith in her suffering and to ensure respect for Marcel's death . . .

There were about ten press photographers and reporters in the stairway still battling for a comment or photo. They all used different lines to try and get a foot in the door. One of them cried out that there was still hope. Burston pushed him aside: 'Please leave us alone.' He called a doctor. The doctor had to push his way through the crowd outside before he could get to the apartment. He made Edith take a tranquilliser.

Barrier spoke to Clifford Fischer on the phone: 'No, Clifford, forget it, it's impossible.' Fischer wanted to know what sort of state Edith was in.

'She's lost everything, Clifford, everything.' Barrier asked Fischer to warn Provys, the manager of the Versailles, that Edith wouldn't be singing that evening.

Since he had given her a second chance after the Playhouse two years ago, Provys had always gone out of his way to show Edith the kind of consideration she appreciated. It was typical that he should now come over with Fischer, bearing a flask of soup. It was his way of warming up his little French woman's body and soul. Piaf had got into the habit of drinking his bouillon every evening before going on stage at the Versailles.

Provys opened her bedroom door carefully. He leaned over Edith and spoke a few tender words. He talked to her about Marcel who he knew well. 'He was my friend as well, you know.'

She lifted up her head and thanked him with her swollen eyes.

'It's terrible, terrible for everyone,' Provys went on. 'Don't worry about this evening, I'll sort something out.'

She came down to earth. 'There's nothing to sort out. I shall sing . . . for him.'

She had always had an incredible instinct for survival. She agreed to see a reporter-photographer from the *Daily News*, Tom Baffer. But no one else. She knew she had to meet her responsibilities towards the public. She also knew that the whole of New York knew. She had to face the city as well.

She posed for two photos. The reporter then plucked up his courage and asked her a question. 'And now, Madame, what are our plans?'

Edith burst into tears. 'Oh, Marcel!'

Lew Burston signalled to the photographer to withdraw.

Edith collapsed into the arms of Genevieve, who proceeded to dress her for the show.

She usually left the apartment around 9.00 p.m. and arrived at the Versailles half an hour before she went on. It was 7.30 p.m. that evening when she went down into Lexington Avenue. Together with Mrs Lew Burston, Genevieve and Loulou Barrier, she let herself be taken to the first church they saw. It was a block away in St Vincent Ferrier Street, on the corner of 66th Street.

She wanted to persuade herself that Marcel was still alive. She lit a candle.

There were more photographers when they came out. Loulou kept them away and hid Edith behind his wool coat.

There was a feverish atmosphere outside the main entrance to the Versailles. Everyone was caught up in the drama. People wanted to catch a glimpse of Edith as she went in through the main entrance. And the tables next to the stage were going for $100 each.

In Madison Square Garden where a big basketball evening was in progress, the announcer's voice could be heard above the excitement. 'Marcel Cerdan was killed in the Paris–New York plane crash.' The excitement faded. There was a short silence, a few murmurs and then the crowd sang the American anthem. A few people could be heard singing 'La Marseillaise'.

At 10.10 p.m. Marc Bonel clung to his accordion in the Versailles, his eyes full of tears. He had just started to play 'La vie en rose'.

Edith embraced both him and Robert Chauvigny, her pianist. She had calmed down. She had tried to put some life into her chalk-like face.

The audience gave her a frenetic welcome with an enormous round of applause. She stopped them.

'This evening I shall be singing for Marcel Cerdan.'

She was supposed to sing eight songs. She sang only four.

She started to sing 'Hymne a l' àmour':

> Le ciel bleu sur nous peut s'effondrer
> Et la terre peut bien s'écrouler
> (The blue sky can collapse on us
> And the earth can give way)

All you could hear now was the music. Eventually, a few more words came out:

> Si un jour, la vie t'arrache à moi
> Si tu meurs, que tu sois loin de moi . . .
> (If one day life tears you from me
> If you should die, and be far from me . . .)

She fainted. The curtain came down, shrouding her.

LETTER TO FELIX LEVITAN, WRITTEN FOUR DAYS AFTER THE EVENT

New York 3.11.49
Dear Felix,
I'm in such a state, all I can do is cry. It's terrible, Felix, terrible. Your wife must be with you by now, keep her close, never leave each other again; it's too awful when you realise what you've lost. I'll never get over it. All I want to do is die. Why can't God have pity on me? I want to be where he is! I know how much you loved him and you know how I adored him. To think how happy we should have been and how miserable I am now. Write – your letters do me so much good. I need to hear from you. Thank you for lending me your Genevieve. Now she has gone, my burden of sorrow is even greater. We were so cheerful when we left Paris. O Felix, it's too cruel!

I don't know what else to write, my heart is empty.

I embrace you in the depths of my sorrow.

Edith

Edith Piaf lived another 14 years, but her life was never complete again.

from *Hymn of Love*

A Quick Flashback and Sandy and Me

Willie Pep with Robert Sacchi

Without doubt, world featherweight champion 'Willie the Wisp' Pep was one of the greatest boxers of all time. A supreme artist, fleet of foot and with lightning reflexes, he could bewilder and demoralise opponents with an infinite variety of moves. Aesthetically he was the boxing purists' delight and likened by one writer to 'a tap dancer with gloves on'. Another compared him to autumn wine and rhapsodised about watching 'his televised shadow flitting across the screen you knew that time cannot wither nor custom stale the little desperado's incomparable gifts . . . Willie as Manolete and Michelangelo in the handy pocket-sized package.' All of which shows that Willie Pep was special.

In Friday's Heroes *Pep reminisced to co-author Robert Sacchi about his early career.*

I was around for a long time, and retired in 1959 after 21 years in the ring, though that didn't stick. I came back later for a time. I was a champ, featherweight champion of the world, for nine years. I fought them all and I had a good career. You know, I made over a million bucks fighting. Of course, we didn't have very good money managers in those days, but times have changed. Today a guy like Ali gets two and a half million for one fight. One fight! And that kid Buchanan got $150,000 to fight Rocky Duran just a while ago. But I've got no complaints. I got $92,000 when I defended against Saddler, and that was hard work. Saddler was one hell of a fighter.

Like I said, boxing was good to me, very good. Where else would someone like me have gotten that kind of dough? I took care of myself and I lasted a long time. I had 62 amateur fights and I lost three of them. Then I turned pro and won 62 in a row, winning the title in the fifty-sixth. I was the first guy to win a title undefeated. Later on I had a streak of 73 in a row. Those are the two longest undefeated streaks in the history of the game. I went on to have 241 pro fights, losing only 11 of them. That's a career I'm proud of, but it's funny how fast they forget. But I've no complaints – no money, but no complaints. You can't live in the past; you've got to look to the future, and as long as the people around me are happy, I'm okay.

One morning I packed my things, had a quick late breakfast and I was on my way. The plan was to pick up some of the guys in town and meet Chico and the others at Newark airport. Now Wethersfield, Connecticut, is just a stone's throw from Hartford, where I grew up. I rolled my blue caddy slowly through town, especially with the roads being a little slick, yet nobody paid any special attention to my WPEP licence plate. People are nice, but, like I said, they forget – even little reminders.

I took my little detour past the big white house I bought my mom and dad when I was champion. And that house always brought back memories. It was a long way up from my beginnings. My parents were from the other side, as we Italians say. My old man was from Syracuse in Sicily and couldn't read or write in English. He was a construction worker and things were pretty tough during the Depression.

I started fighting amateur back in 1937–1938. I was 15½ years old, and I got eight or nine dollars for a fight. After the fight I'd run home to my mother and give her the money. Later my father would come into the room and give me a buck. Well, naturally, that didn't go too good with me.

One night up at Crystal Lake I boxed twice and at the end of the night I had $50. I also had my eye on a sports jacket and pair of pants that cost $10, but I knew that if I took the $50 home, my father would give me only a couple of bucks. So I took $10 and hid it. I went home that night with $40, and Ma said, 'Willie, where did you get this money?' I told her I made it boxing. At that time my father was working at the WPA for $15 a week. When my dad came home Ma said, 'Willie brought home $40. Maybe he did somethin' wrong?' You know, after all, they didn't really know, and I'd been gone all day. So my father took me into the other room, closed the door and said, 'Where did you get this money? You can tell me. You know your mother.' I said, 'Dad, I boxed tonight. I boxed tonight and I got $40.' All this time the $10 was almost burning in my shoe. He said he thought 40 bucks was good money for boxing and then he reached over and gave me $2. Then he said, 'If you fought tonight and you got $40 see if you can fight twice a week from now on.' My old man, he was a sports fan.

That's how I got my start. The guy who was fooling around, training me at the time, said to my Pop, 'Willie, he's a pretty good fighter. Be sure he gets to bed every night before 11 and be sure he does his roadwork every morning.' So my dad became like a part-time trainer. For example, I might be out on the corner talking with someone and he'd come out and say, 'Willie, go home. You gotta fight next Tuesday.' And I'd say it was only nine-thirty. But he could only say, 'No, Willie, go home.' So I'd go. Next morning he'd wake me up at six o'clock and say, 'Willie, you gotta do your roadwork, you gotta fight next Tuesday.' So I'd get up. Then, naturally since I was up I figured I might as well do the roadwork. Of course Pop, he'd go back to bed, naturally, because it was only six o'clock. He was a big sports fan, my Pop.

Pretty soon I was heading up out of town towards the Merrit Parkway. I don't use the new throughway. Like I said, I don't drive fast and I'd rather take the old roads I used to take. Soon I passed the Dunkin' Donut shop they put up a couple of years ago. I laugh to myself everytime I pass it. Since I was a kid I've had a passion for doughnuts. When I was about 15 years old, boxing amateur, I had a manager that, well, he was really tough on the buck. He didn't spend money too freely. For example, on the day of my fight he would bring me in a restaurant and say, 'Willie, what do you want for breakfast?' Well, I was just 15 and I was used to crackers and milk at home, so all I could think to say was, 'Could I have a doughnut and coffee?' As he patted me on the back, he'd say, 'Willie, that's what some of the best fighters in the world train on.' To the counterman he'd say, 'Give this kid two doughnuts and a cup of coffee.'

Now it's still the day of the fight and when we came back for the meal which was supposed to be a steak – at that time a pretty nice steak dinner would cost about $1.75 – he asked me what I wanted and I said, 'Well, gee Buster, I'd like some scrambled eggs.' 'Give this kid three scrambled eggs,' he told the waitress, without a smile. He didn't care. Though there were a few people like Buster in the fight business there were also a lot of nice ones. I guess Buster was just Buster.

We used to fight out of Norwich, Connecticut, sometimes at this place called DU-WELL AC. I always got a kick out of that. The DU-WELL AC. I was amateur flyweight champion of Connecticut at the time and we used to fight the Salem-Crescent AC from Harlem, New York. Black kids who could really fight. Anyway, I saw this real tall kid come in and when I said to my manager, 'Who's that?' he said, 'That's the guy you're gonna fight.' I said, 'Be serious, look at that guy.' You see, at that time, I was a flyweight. I weighed about 105 pounds, and this guy was about 128, a featherweight. So Buster said, 'Don't worry, don't worry. He can't be any good fighting you.' Well, I fight this guy and he's all over me. He's too good. Too big. He's punching me and punching me and I'm just trying to hang in there. When it ended and the guy won I heard his name was Ray Roberts. Later on I find out that, too, is a phony name because he was really Sugar Ray Robinson and he was also the Golden Gloves featherweight champion. Since Ray, who fought his amateur career under his real name, Walker Smith, was amateur, he couldn't pick up any money in New York, and so he came to Connecticut where amateurs were allowed to fight for money. This was in 1938. I had changed my name at that time myself from Gugliemo (William) Papleo to Willie Pep. Pop, he didn't like the idea but I felt I needed a fighting name. Anyway, I got eight dollars for that fight and my manager took seven. One thing about Buster, he was consistent.

Yes, that was my manager but you would think I would learn, even if I was just a kid. Later on he had me fighting another 128-pounder named Angelo Rodano. Now Angelo was a great amateur fighter who could take a lot of your professional featherweights today. I had won 20 straight at the time and I didn't want to lose. Buster said, 'Willie, don't worry. It's more like an exhibition. You just go out and hit him.' So I went out there in the first round and I hit him and I knocked him down. When he got up you could see he was mad. He swarmed all over me. I think he knocked me down four times in the first round, three times in the second, and twice in the third. I was getting stronger, but not fast enough, unfortunately. Rodano took it in four. He got crippled during World War II and that ended his career. But he would have been a great pro and a great crowd pleaser when television arrived and brought so many fighters out of the clubs and before the public.

As I drove closer to New York, I thought about the early days of my pro career. I began by parting with my 'doughnut manager' Buster and getting the manager and trainer I had throughout my career. My trainer was Bill Gore, the man who trained the light-heavyweight champion of the world, Emilio Bettina, and he was a great trainer for me. Most recently, Bill trained Cleveland Williams, Roy Harris, and Manny Gonzales when he fought Emile Griffith for the welterweight title. Bill is now 84 years old and is in Florida. What I owe this man can't be expressed in words, except it's a great deal. My manager was Lou Viscusi out of Florida and he managed me up to my retirement in 1959. What a change in the money. When I was boxing for Lou it was 50–50, though that's not how we began. (When I came back, George Shepard, he was my agent, would take only ten per cent, a big drop from 50.) The contract read that I would get two-thirds and Lou would get one-third. Expenses would come off the top. But there was some small lettering that if I ever got to be champion it would go to 50–50. Being champion seemed somewhat far away then. But I was fortunate and two and a half years later I was champion. So it was 50–50 for the next nine years. But as a champion he also took care of expenses, so it wasn't all that bad. It was high, 50–50, but what are you going to do? It wasn't coffee and doughnuts. He was a good manager and he treated me fairly.

It was awful tough at the beginning. I was 17½, a four-round fighter, and not getting much work around New York. So two fellas and myself jumped into a car and drove to California from Connecticut. We went Route 66. When we got to California we were all broke and very, very hungry. I had my boxing stuff with me, so I went up to the Main Street gym in Los Angeles, which isn't there anymore, and told this fella that I was a fighter. I wanted to fight. He said, 'Okay, kid, I'll be your manager. You got any money?' Since I was broke he said, 'Okay, you can get a dollar a round if you spar with that guy over there.' A dollar a round seemed fine at the time.

The guy's name was Manuel Ortiz, a good fighter, being he was the bantamweight champion at the time. I boxed him three rounds a day for a week, and that three dollars a day was our feed bill. Because of this they got a four-round fight for me in the Hollywood Legion Stadium, where I got to meet George Raft, my idol at the time, who was sitting at ringside. I won my fight, too, but the funny story was I got officially $50 for the fight. But my manager said, 'Listen, it's $5 for the licence, $5 for the gym use, $5 for this and that . . .' In the end he handed me $15 and said, 'This is your end, kid.' Now I had already paid the bus fare – we had sold the car – and I knew we were short. So I borrowed $5 from him against my next fight, and the next day we got on the bus and came home. That was his end.

I came back home, I trained, and a couple of years later I fought for the title and won. Then I fought Manuel Ortiz. In some pre-fight publicity his manager had said, 'I remember him very well. We paid him a dollar a round in California and he isn't worth much more than that. We won't have any trouble with him.' Well, I won seven out of ten rounds and $20,000. Manny passed away about three years ago. He was a good man.

The city loomed up in front of me before I knew it and I headed south on the West Side Highway to make a pick-up at Jack Dempsey's. I would be picking up Steve Belloise, who is always ready to help out at benefits. Jack Dempsey's is right in the strip, the Broadway and 8th Avenue area around the old Madison Square Garden. Stillman's gym used to be there, with all the promoters and fight managers hanging around. We called it 'Jacob's Beach', after fight promoter Mike Jacobs. This place was especially alive through the late '40s and early '50s when the really good fighters, the cream of the crop, got a chance to fight on television. And there seemed to be dozens of good, tough fighters in those days. Of course the small clubs suffered, too. Maybe that's why you have fewer good fighters today. That and the fact that it's easier for a kid to make a living now. Anyway, television took to boxing and boxing took to TV. Now that was the real good marriage.

I would like to feel that, in a way, I had something to do with it at the beginning. I was fortunate enough to be a pro for just two and a half years when I got a shot at the featherweight crown and I won it. I won it from Chalky Wright, who was a great champion. That was in Madison Square Garden on 20 November 1942. I boxed him again on 29 September 1944 in the Garden and defended my title successfully. It was the first time ever a fight was televised from Madison Square Garden and it started the long series of Friday Night Fights that ended around 1964. Chalky and I each got $400 for the television rights that night. (Chalky, who I had beaten for the third time in 1945, accidentally drowned in a bathtub in 1957.)

TV fights started when Mike Jacobs, the Garden promoter, made a contract with the Gillette Safety Razor people for them to sponsor the Friday Night Fights from the Garden. The deal covered my second fight with Chalky Wright. Of course, nobody had a television set in 1944, and then World War II came around. It wasn't until 1948–49 that the television fights really started to boom. I guess the fights along with Uncle Miltie – Milton Berle – really sold television sets during this period. But once everybody had a television set, the television stations began losing their interest in boxing and started programming other things. But boxing sold many of the first TV sets and so I think the television and fight business owes a good deal to those guys who did the fighting.

In the '40s and '50s we all got a standard rate of $4,000 for the television rights, except for the big fights, like me and Saddler. In that case we got about $15,000. Of course, by today's standards it's not that impressive. Today, with the closed circuit television fights, a man can make quite a bit of money. Take the Ali–Frazier title fight a couple of years ago. They both made well over $5 million. But in the '40s and '50s TV fights were 'free' – 'home TV'.

Then we had a guy named Tiger Jones who used to fight almost every Friday night it seemed like. He was a crowd pleaser, what we call a trial horse. I don't mean he wasn't a good fighter; if you were a little out of shape he'd trounce you. And there were a lot of other guys who were always on TV. Chico Vejar was one. He was a good classy fighter. And then Kid Gavilan, a great champ. The 'Kid' was perfect for television because with him every round was exciting. He was what we call a clock watcher. He wouldn't do much until he had about 45 seconds in the round. Then he would explode. It would catch not just the fans' eyes but also the judges' eyes, too.

Of course, some guys got rushed because of television, meaning after four or five fights they were already getting a TV fight. I think Chuck Davey was rushed. Chuck, popular with the home viewers, got rushed into a fight with Kid Gavilan. The 'Kid' was the first really good fighter Davey had fought and Gavilan destroyed him.

But that's the way it goes sometimes. Television helped a lot of guys but then it ruined the source of new fighters – the small clubs where the kids are developed. I think maybe TV will do the same to baseball someday.

As I drove along, I thought about the guys and the magic of television. In those days, when I wasn't fighting myself, I was sitting somewhere watching those Friday night fights. A lot of those guys would be at the benefit and others wouldn't. But they were all worth remembering, like heroes maybe, or Friday night television.

> . . . *If Willie had chosen a life of crime he could have been the most accomplished pickpocket since the Artful Dodger. He may be the only man that ever lived who could lift a sucker's poke while wearing eight-ounce gloves. In action he's a marvel, and in the record books he's a downright hoax.*
>
> *It is accepted as a fact of life in the ring that the little fellows don't last long. Many of them start young and are burned out by the time they're 25. Willie had been fighting, as amateur and professional, six years or more when he won the featherweight title from Chalky Wright, and that was away back in 1942.*
>
> *Sammy Angott was the lightweight champion then, Red Cochrane had the welterweight title frozen, Tony Zale was succeeding to the spot left vacant by Billy Soose among the middleweights, Gus Lesnevich and Joe Louis bossed the big fellows. Where were they this year, 13 years later, when Willie was fighting once a month and winning 'em all?*

Red Smith, *Chicago Sun-Times*
1955

Sandy and Me

The sense of foreboding in these cameos of Pep's life is heightened by our knowledge of what was to come. In 1947 he was seriously injured when on a non-scheduled flight. The plane overshot Newark airport and came down in woods in Middleville, New Jersey. Five passengers were killed and Pep was ferried to hospital suffering from a broken leg and vertebrae. His back injuries were undetected for some time and if they had remained so for only a little longer, he would have been crippled for life. To the amazement of his doctors, Pep rapidly recovered and was in good enough fettle to return to the ring six months later. Another watershed was in the offing.

In 1948, I fought Sandy Saddler for the first time. Now it's funny the way things happen. There's a story about me and Sandy that not too many people know. See, my manager, Lou Viscusi, had been friendly with the Johnston brothers for years. There was Jimmy, one of the best managers around, and Ned, who handled Jimmy's fighters, and Charley, who learned from Jimmy and became a great manager himself. And finally there was Bill, who started out managing boxers but later switched to wrestling. Anyway, Bill came to Lou one day and said he had a kid who he'd like to get started and couldn't we put him in a four rounder. So Lou says okay and the kid comes up. He's a tall, skinny Negro kid and he wins his fight and we forget about him. A couple of weeks later Bill calls again and asks if he can't get the kid in a six. So Lou puts him in against Jock Leslie and in the third round Leslie knocks him out.

Now that's all we knew about the kid. His name was Sandy Saddler and nobody ever heard of him. We forgot about him. The next thing we know Bill Johnston has turned Sandy over to his brother Charley and Charley started to move him. He had him fight some in New York, but mostly out of state, in New Jersey and Pennsylvania, Detroit and Boston, New Orleans and Caracas, Jamaica and Havana, Aruba and Honolulu. Almost any place where he could get him in.

Sandy was coming along but nobody in New York paid much attention. Then suddenly he's the number one contender. So Charley Johnston came around to Lou again and asked to get Sandy in a main event in New York to show what he could do. The arrangement was with Bobby Thompson and he wins but he doesn't look all that good. The boxing writers therefore said that Willie Pep doesn't have to lose any sleep worrying about Sandy Saddler.

However, Sandy was the number one contender so we made the match. But I wasn't even a little worried. I had just stopped Jock Leslie, who had whipped Sandy. I had won 73 fights in a row and I didn't think any kid named Sandy Saddler was going to beat me. So we fought. It was in Madison Square Garden on 29 October 1948. I started out feinting as usual to get a feeling for him and he ignored it completely and waded in and caught me cold. I was completely surprised. He knocked me down twice before the fourth round and then he stopped me.

We had a rematch. It was set for 11 February 1949, and you better believe I was ready for him. Most of the writers were picking Sandy, but I was ready for him. I was dead set on beating him no matter what. That night we had the fight of our lives. A lot of people who know what they're talking about rate it as one of the greatest fights, and I just happen to be very proud of that fight. As Casey Stengel would say, 'You could look it up.'

Nat Loubet's report in The Ring *gives a graphic account of the fight.*

Boxing's most dramatic fight of 1949 took place in New York's Madison Square Garden on 11 February. It was a thriller between Willie Pep, former world featherweight champ, and the man who relieved him of the crown, Sandy Saddler. The hatchet-faced Italian from Hartford, Conn, amazed a throng of

19,097 by regaining the championship in 15 torrid rounds. So keen was the interest in the fight that a new high for a world featherweight championship contest was recorded, with a $87,563 gross. In a previous affair, on 29 October 1948, the Nutmeg Flash was knocked down in the fourth round and lost the championship.

A careful screening of thousands of professional bouts held during the past year failed to bring out any contest that could match this epic battle for thrills. In consequence, the Saddler–Pep return engagement has been designated by *The Ring* as 'The Fight of the Year'.

It was a contest that had everything the fight fan could desire – clever manoeuvring, hard hitting, and even gory manifestations, without which a fight is meaningless to so many of the fans.

Those who crowded into the House that Tex Built expected a sensational fight and were not disappointed. They saw a former champion, burdened with advancing years after a long and busy career, stand up and fight like a youngster.

Pep's four-round KO by Saddler had led many to believe that the Pep of old was gone. They also saw Saddler, the new champion who, as an underdog a few months before, had scored a stunning victory over this same Pep.

The odds on the contest at ring time were 6–5, take your pick, but the wise heads picked Saddler and blamed the even-steven odds on the sentimentality of Pep fans, going all out to back their idol.

From the opening gong through the 15 action-packed rounds, there was not a moment that wasn't filled with suspense and drama. Both fighters left the ring, blood-smeared faces a mass of punch-puffed lumps that left no doubt as to the punishment they had absorbed and dished out.

Pep was once again the featherweight king, but he knew he had been in a real scrap. The fight put up by Saddler was such as to make a return between these two one of the stand-out attractions for 1950.

The lad from Hartford had 11 stitches sewed into his face and around his eyes and Saddler required seven.

The first round set the pattern for the fight. Pep, using every trick in his repertoire, moved rapidly. He spun Saddler from side to side and the Negro attempted to land with his most potent weapon, a left hook to the head and body, the latter thrown in close while holding with his right.

It was this technique that Saddler had used so successfully to win the crown. But as the bout progressed, it became evident that this strategy could not be executed.

Willie outgeneralled Saddler. Pep moved in and out, hooked with his left, jammed three and four times before the slower Saddler could move out of range. Willie ducked under Sandy's guard to maul and push him off balance and then, when set up, moved with his speed of old, launching a two-fisted bombardment that bewildered the champ.

Saddler was the aggressor throughout the entire fight. He stalked Pep, attempting to move in close where he could land his vaunted body blows. Now and then he'd corner the elusive Old Master and in the exchanges that followed

Pep took a great deal of punishment. But Saddler was unable to land hard enough or often enough to swing the course of the battle.

At the end it was a victorious Pep who left the ring, but of the two, Willie had suffered more physically.

At the two-thirds mark, although Saddler had been moving into Pep, Sandy was far behind the challenger on points.

The fans were as breathless as the contestants at this stage of the bout. The struggle had been a two-fisted slaughter with neither fighter asking nor giving quarter. It was only the vast assortment of tricks that Willie pulled out of his bag that kept him from being tagged.

The tenth saw Saddler break through Pep's defence and nail him with a terrific right to the chin. Pep's legs sagged, his eyes became glassy. He was a tired fighter.

Saddler was in at his foe like a tiger and he chopped away with both hands in an endeavour to end it all.

But Pep still had his main asset – the knowledge that he had amassed over years of successful boxing – ring savvy. That came to his aid now as he covered, back-pedalled, and fought his way out of danger.

In the next three rounds, Pep came back strong while Saddler tired. And so the battle see-sawed.

In the last two rounds Saddler ripped Pep with savage rights and lefts to the body and head and it appeared that the challenger would go down. But his fighting heart and keen brain got Willie through those last two sessions.

The final round was a sight that had the entire gathering on its feet for three solid minutes. Saddler, realising that his one chance for victory now lay in knocking out his challenger, threw caution to the winds. He piled into Pep with everything he had.

Lefts and rights smothered Willie and he was on the verge of sinking to the canvas a number of times. In the last minute, only the courage born of desperation and dogged determination kept Pep on his feet.

When the bell rang ending hostilities, it was an exhausted Willie who went back to his corner. He had made it but only by a hair's-breadth. Had Saddler won more of the earlier rounds or had he not blown those near the finish he would have kept the title.

The decision was unanimous, with Judge Frank Forbes calling it 9–5–1, Judge Jack O'Sullivan giving it to Pep at 9–6, and referee Eddie Joseph calling it 10–5 for Willie.

Another year has been recorded in the history of pugilism. The struggles, hardships, joys and sorrows, victories and defeats all are down in the annals. On that page reserved for all-time thrills is listed the second Pep–Saddler fight, which of all has to be given the call as the Fight of the Year 1949.

The Ring
February 1950

I had my title back. And besides the packed Madison Square Garden, thousands and thousands throughout the country had seen it on television, way back in 1949. It was a great fight for lots of people.

We fought again in 1950 and that was a good fight, too, only rougher. It was going along close with me leading on points when all of a sudden my shoulder snapped and it hurt bad. I couldn't lift my arm and there was no way I could continue unless I wanted to fight Sandy with one hand. It was around the eighth or ninth round. I couldn't continue and Sandy was the champ again.

We fought for the last time on 26 September 1951, in one of the roughest, toughest fights of all time, and in some ways one of the most controversial. Not that there was any doubt about who won. After all, I was cut and couldn't continue. This time my left eye was completely shut and I was fighting with one eye. I was ahead on points by the end of the eighth round but I couldn't continue, so the fight had to be his.

But there was controversy. First of all it was a real brawl, like the old-time bare-knuckle days, with wrestling, heeling, eye gouging, tripping, thumbing – you name it. A lot of writers thought that we should have both been thrown out. They thought Ray Miller, the referee, let it get out of hand, that he should have followed his own instructions. He told us he had the power to penalise us and he wanted a clean fight. Well, I've got to admit he didn't do much. However, I'm not blaming the referee; it was me and Sandy who did it.

And that's the second point of controversy. Who was most to blame? Who started it? Now, quite a few writers said it was my fault, but that's ridiculous. I'm not saying I was blameless, but look at it this way. Sandy was the tough guy; I was the boxer. It didn't make any sense for me to rough it up with him. However, I did it eventually because he started it and I got mad. In the first 30 seconds Miller had to warn Sandy to lay off holding me around the neck and hitting me with his free hand. I didn't do anything that early in the fight. In fact, I was boxing good and won most of the early rounds. I know if I kept it up I would've beat him and become the only guy to hold the featherweight crown three times.

But that wasn't to be. I got mad and tried to outrough him, which wasn't my style. And the referee didn't do much, so we kept it up. In fact, one writer asked how come they bothered with a referee at all.

Anyway, my biggest problem was that he caught me in the second round and cut my right eyelid. I was hurt. I couldn't see and later in that round he knocked me down with a left to the body. There was no doubt about the fact that he really hit. After that round I boxed him good for a few rounds, making him miss and then countering. But I couldn't see well and sooner or later he would corner me and the rough stuff would begin. It wouldn't end until we were both wrestling around on the canvas or the referee was actually outside the ring trying to pry us apart.

In the seventh round we were wrestling around and somehow my leg got tangled up around Sandy's and the referee rushed over to untie us. The referee wound up getting tangled himself and we being off balance accidentally caused him to fall down. It resulted in a very funny scene. The spectators roared with laughter and poor Ray Miller was red with embarrassment.

When he picked himself off the canvas, Sandy still had me tied up like a pretzel. Miller got mad and said, 'Break, break you S.O.B.s or I'll suspend both of you.'

In the next round, Sandy came out and deliberately back-handed me across the face as I was on the ropes. The referee didn't say a thing. So I proceeded to jab and get behind Sandy and deliberately tripped him. Miller warned me. My fans, seeing that only I was being reprimanded, charged the ring screaming at the referee for being one-sided. Charley Johnston climbed on to the ring apron and screamed at the referee for allowing me to trip Sandy. Poor Ray Miller got it from both ends.

Anyway, it went on like that and my eye got worse and worse till I couldn't see at all. You can't fight with one eye, not against Sandy Saddler, and not in a fight like that. At the start of the ninth round I couldn't continue. It was over.

We had wrestled in the fifth, sixth and seventh besides in the eighth. We were strangling each other and there was gouging and heeling throughout. In spite of, or despite, all this, Ray Miller had me ahead five rounds to three on his card. I was also ahead on the judges' scorecards. But I lost; that was my 165th fight and only my fourth loss. It was my third TKO loss, all three by Sandy. He had knocked out 89 guys in 130 fights to that time. He could certainly hit.

A funny bit about this bout was Robert Christenberry, the new boxing commissioner. At the weigh-in he passed the remark that he liked wrestling. He saw it that night. After the fight he didn't say much except that 'these boys don't like each other'.

Of course the boxing commission was not happy with this brawl we staged and Christenberry, making his first major decision as commissioner, suspended Sandy and me from boxing in the state of New York for an indefinite period. I can't blame him. We had broken all the rules that night.

It took quite a few months for the commission to cool off and when they did we both were reinstated. In the meantime, I had won 15 straight outside of New York and my popularity was as strong as ever. The International Boxing Commission booked me into the first open date – a Friday Night television spot against a rough, up-and-coming Pat Marcune. I beat Marcune bad, real bad, and once again I was in good standing with the New York Commission. Nothing succeeds like success.

Now, a lot of people think there was antagonism between Sandy and me. Maybe there was during our fights – but we're friendly now. I've boxed him several times since in charity exhibitions and we get along fine. When we were fighting for the championship I wanted to lick him in the worst way and he wanted to lick me. Well, we went all out. But I have no hard feelings and we get along. No complaints here.

It's a funny thing about styles. I beat a lot of guys who beat Sandy. Yet he beat me three out of four times. Umberto Sierra beat Sandy and I beat Sierra twice. Paddy DeMarco beat Sandy twice and I beat DeMarco. Strange. If you don't have the right style you're going to get licked, and if you don't fight your own fight you're going to get licked. I tried to get rough with Saddler and you usually can't beat a man at his own game. Not that man.

A year after our last bout, Sandy got drafted into the army. This was early in 1952. The National Boxing Association thought it would be a good idea to have an 'interim champion' to help keep the interest alive in the featherweight division until Sandy got back. The 'interim champion' not only would fill in for Saddler during his absence but would automatically be recognised as the number one challenger against the returning Saddler.

Percy Bassett became the 'interim champion' and the European boxing officials went along with this by matching Bassett with France's Ray Famechon. I had beat Ray several years earlier in a title bout. Anyway, Bassett stopped Famechon and was now the undisputed 'interim champion'.

But Bassett never did get that crack at Sandy. Instead, he was asked to meet Lulu Perez in an elimination match and the winner would positively be given a go at Saddler. Bassett stopped Perez, but neither man got a title shot.

After he was discharged in 1954, Sandy continued his tune-up bouts and still wasn't ready to defend his title. But, he said, he would consider the winner of a Bassett–'Red Top' Davis match.

So Bassett got into the elimination against Davis and he lost in 12 rounds at Madison Square Garden. Poor Percy, after all that fighting and no title bout with Saddler.

In 1955 Sandy met Davis in his first title defence since the last one he had with me in 1951 and KO'd Davis. He went on to KO Lulu Perez and then lose a non-title decision to Joe Lopes that year.

The same year he lost a non-title bout to Flash Elorde. As a result, a title bout was set with Elorde in 1956 because of Flash's good showing. Sandy KO'd him.

Sandy had his last fight later on in 1956. He took a shellacking from an unranked Jewish kid called Larry Boardman in yet another non-title bout.

At age 30, Sandy had compiled an amazing record. He had a total of 162 bouts, losing 15, and a knockout ratio of almost 70 per cent – 103 knockout victims, including me.

What cut Sandy's career short? Well, Sandy was involved in a crash in July 1956. He was riding in a taxicab and struck his head against the door when the cab crashed up onto the sidewalk.

He was hospitalised for about three or four weeks, and then tried to get back in shape by working out – but it didn't help.

He was constantly bothered by warnings from the boxing commission about defending his title. They finally told him to submit a medical report on his condition.

In the report, the doctor treating Saddler since the accident recommended that Sandy quit boxing if he wanted to retain his sight. And that if he continued there would be a chance of total blindness. At his age, with no 'money matches' in sight and with Sandy's earning power on the downgrade, Sandy took the advice of the doctor.

It was a tough turn of events for Sandy, considering boxing was all he knew and he had worked so hard to get there.

But you know, Sandy had 160 fights and may have been experiencing some eye trouble somewhere along the way like other boxers have. Eye injuries and that threat of blindness is one of the major occupational hazards of boxers. (Sandy made a wise decision.) A lot of guys kid themselves and keep walking into the night.

But like I said, Sandy was just rough and tough and not a 'dirty fighter' as people think. His almost five-foot-ten-inch frame, tremendous reach and the punching power of a welterweight, sometimes had the five-foot-five-inch opponent tangling himself to get inside Sandy.

I have nothing but respect for Sandy. He was voted into boxing's Hall of Fame in 1971.

Friday's Heroes Inc, New York, New York,
distributed by Fell Publishers Plc,
1973

They Must Tike Me for a Proper Mugg

A.J. Liebling

No one was more adept at finding the human story behind boxing's cast of characters than Abbott Joseph Liebling. Dispensing with his Christian names early on – just in case anyone was under the misapprehension that he led a monastic order – A.J. Liebling, as he was universally known, wrote passionately about the 'sweet science'.

A series of masterly essays in The New Yorker *during the 1950s and early 1960s, of which this is one, illustrate the point. Routinely he was in the workplace: 'In the gymnasium there, I often watched him (Patterson) fighting against heavier team-mates with a driving earnestness that transcended pugnacity. It was more like the rage of a literary stylist trying to get something down on paper, or of a painter who thinks he has seen a new colour'; the metaphors so seemingly remote and yet so unerringly apt.*

On a visit to London in 1957, Liebling strayed east. Terry Spinks, later to become British featherweight champion, was the attraction. It does not matter that Liebling's attempt at cockney dialogue is a touch mannered and self-aware, for in his circuitous excursion to one of the byways of boxing he paints pictures that cannot be erased.

While reading my habitual London newspaper, *The Times*, not long ago, I strayed from the kind of story I prefer, such as 'Getting Facts About the Elizabethan Playhouse' and 'Chinese Writers Denounced for Deviations', to the portion of the paper that Englishmen refer to as 'sporting news', which deals largely with cricket. I found little, at first glance, to set my pulses surging with emotion, an effect American sports writers strive for even on a dull day, but in the investment, or racing, section, just under 'Birmingham Selections', I came upon what I thought a promising headline:

BOXER MAY RIDE AT MANCHESTER
TWO MOUNTS OFFERED TO TERRY SPINKS

It is unusual for a professional athlete to engage in two such specialised activities concurrently, and I read the story that followed this announcement with some interest:

> Terry Spinks, the 1956 Olympic flyweight champion, and now a professional boxer, has been invited to ride two horses at Manchester on Friday – Luing, a five-year-old, in the Cromwell Selling Handicap, and

Dominion, a six-year-old, in the Loom Handicap. Both horses are owned by Mrs E. Schmidt-Bodner and trained by E. Gifford at Skipton. Spinks, aged 19, a former stable lad and apprentice jockey, has accepted both mounts subject to permission from Mr M. Marsh, the Newmarket trainer, who has him under apprenticeship. It will be Spinks's first public appearance as a jockey, though he has ridden training gallops on many occasions. He spends much of his time between fights at the Newmarket stables and hopes to be a full-time jockey when he retires from boxing. He will fly to Manchester on Friday morning after training for a fight at Shoreditch four days later. Mr H. Grosssmith, promoter of next Tuesday's fight at Shoreditch Town Hall, London, between Spinks and Ivan McCready (Belfast), said yesterday that he had objected verbally to the Boxing Board of Control against Spinks riding on Friday. 'I can't take any chances against Spinks getting injured,' he said. 'This is to be his first fight over eight rounds.'

My first reflection after reading this was that it was odd of an owner to offer two mounts in one day at a major race meeting to a boy who had never ridden a race. My second was that the story was not calculated to deter *Times* readers from attending Mr Grossmith's show, if *Times* readers ever venture as far afield at night as Shoreditch, which is a fried-fish-and-jellied-eel-consuming autonomous borough about a mile inland from London Bridge and north-east of the Whitechapel district. Customarily, what a press agent seeks from *The Times* is consecration, rather than direct profit.

When I turned to Lord Beaverbrook's *Express*, one of the less serious London papers that serve as morning garnish to my *Times* reading, I saw that its boxing writer had gone for the story in an enthusiastic, Beaverbrookish way. *The Express* sports page carried a picture of Spinks, looking young and truthful, over the same data I had read in *The Times*, plus a bit of extrapolation: 'What a row Spinks started when he let out this stable information.' According to *The Express*, Spinks's manager of record, a recently retired boxer named Sammy McCarthy, wanted Spinks to ride, but the story did not make clear whether this indicated unlimited confidence in his boy's horsemanship or a heroic indifference to his fate. 'I will offer Mr Grossmith a three-figure sum as a guarantee for Terry's appearance at Shoreditch on Tuesday,' the paper quoted McCarthy as saying. 'It would well compensate him if anything did go wrong.' But, *The Express* added, 'Promoter Grossmith, heavily armed with a rule book marked at clause 14, which refers to the right of promoters to restrain a boxer from endangering himself – and incidentally the box office – marched up to the offices of the Boxing Board of Control yesterday ready to do battle for his idea of a square deal . . . And yesterday Spinks, the lad who wants to become a champion jockey as well as a champion fighter, was hoping that his racing licence would be granted before Friday.' The author of the *Express* piece was Sydney Hulls, who is the son of a famous old-time boxing promoter and takes a kindly view of impresarial inventiveness.

The boxing expert of the Labour Party's *Herald*, which I generally read as a political counterweight to *The Express*, is Tom Phillips, whom I first met at the Helsinki Olympics in 1952. He took an Opposition line in his Spinks story, which was headed 'HORSE LAUGH'. Phillips, who has eight children, a couple of them considerably older than the galloping flyweight, also took a paternal line, advising young Spinks in a fatherly way not to lend himself to 'silly publicity stunts' and ballyhoo. The story, he wrote, was 'a dilly' – all 'bunkum' – and in corroboration of this bit of intuition he reported that the husband of the owner of the two horses concerned had been a boxing promoter himself.

The Times had said that Spinks the horseman was currently apprenticed to trainer Marsh. But Phillips, who was a straight reporter before he became a sports writer, had phoned Marsh, and the trainer had told him that he no longer had any hold on the boy – adding, however, that in his opinion Spinks had no more chance of riding at Manchester on Friday than he had himself. Spinks, Marsh said, couldn't ride unless he got himself indentured to another trainer, and that isn't the sort of thing one can arrange overnight in England. As for Grossmith, the promoter of the Shoreditch fight, Phillips wrote, 'Somehow I don't think he need worry.'

Phillips's story, I thought, was the best plug of all for the fight, because I pictured McCarthy, Grossmith, and the others as resourceful and charming characters, who would not be out of place in the Neutral Corner Bar & Grill on Eighth Avenue – a cultural haven to which my thoughts fondly turn when I tire of getting the facts about the Elizabethan Playhouse.

I phoned Mr Phillips to congratulate him on his exposé and found him still spluttering with honest north country indignation over the situation he had unearthed. 'Bloody Barnum could have doon no better!' he said. He pronounced all double 'o's as in 'good'. Phillips likes to remind his readers that he is a Geordie, or coal miner, from County Durham, north of Yorkshire. The Geordie devotes himself to British boxing with the selfless passion that Dr Schweitzer lavishes on his African lepers. Many of Phillips's nights are spent riding on wretched sleeping trains bound for places like Swansea and West Hartlepool to make connections with buses that will carry him to still more peripheral pest spots, where promoters tout him on the local advent of a future British world champion, usually a coal miner. Phillips often arrives just in time to see the fellow being carried out of the ring, though occasionally, if he misses a connection or his bus is late, the phenomenon has already been revived and is back on the night shift in the mine by the time he gets there. This sort of thing never disheartens the idealist.

When Phillips's paper sends him to big bouts in the United States, he repeatedly corners his American colleagues to confide, 'There's a lad in Llanelli' – or Newton Abbot or Eccleston – 'who can bash like Jack Dempsey, but the question is can he take a punch?' The answer is invariably in the negative, but the next time Phillips shows up, he has another false Imam in South Leeds or Birkenhead. No great heavyweight has learned his trade in Britain within the memory of any living man under a hundred. Bob Fitzsimmons, who won the championship in 1897 and lost it in 1899, was born in Cornwall, but he did all his fighting in the Antipodes and in America. As late as the election of Warren Gamaliel Harding, though, there were a few top-notch men in the lighter classes. The last of these illustrissimi, Jimmy Wilde, was, like Spinks, a flyweight.

Over the phone, Phillips said that Spinks was a good boxer, of the stand-away, quick-moving classic type adapted to amateur bouts, which are limited to three rounds, but that it had not yet been established whether he had professional toughness. He was tall for his weight, Phillips said, and, like all boxers built that way, he looked fragile, but there was no telling about him until he had been further tested.

What I had read and heard about Spinks made me want to see him box. I was happy, therefore, to learn from Friday's *Times* that he had been spared the perils of the turf; he had decided not to ride that day. (Of Mrs E. Schmidt-Bodner's two runners at Manchester, I noted the next morning, Luing was scratched from the Cromwell Selling Handicap, while Dominion, carrying a weight of eight stone three, or 115 pounds, ran dead last in a field of ten in the Loom Handicap. This may have been due to the fact that he was ridden by A.J. Russell, one of the most accomplished jockeys in England but obviously an inadequate substitute for the boxer.) Grossmith must have been as relieved as I was at the fighter's decision, and on the following Tuesday afternoon, when I rang through to Shoreditch Town Hall, the telephonist there sounded as pleased as though she had a piece of Spinks. She said that the first bout would go on at 7.45 and that I had better come along early, because the house was nearly sold out.

London is made up of a galaxy of autonomous boroughs that operate within the framework of the London County Council and that – as any visitor who has strayed much beyond Mayfair and the Strand knows – have strong individualities. To pass, for example, from excitable Jewish Stepney – which includes Whitechapel – on the north bank of the Thames, to dour autochthonous Bermondsey, directly opposite it on the south bank, is nearly as striking a transition as crossing the Channel. (The populations of these two boroughs refer to each other as 'the people across the water'.) Shoreditch is a borderland where the rowdy old urban boroughs along the river shade into the faceless respectability of the boroughs that used to be suburbs. In Defoe's day, the breadth of London was reckoned to be 'from the Haberdashers Alms Houses in Newington Butts', on the south, 'to the Stone's End in Shoreditch'. The stone's end was not half a block from Shoreditch Town Hall.

Forewarned by the cheerful woman on the switchboard, who had also kindly given me directions for reaching the scene of battle, I took the tube in time to get down to Old Street, in East Central London – the nearest stop – by seven. A bleak and silent thoroughfare, Old Street was made all the more discouraging by a filmy London rain that threw a protective glaze over the quarter's grime. From the tube station to the Town Hall is a fair walk, and as I plodded along, it seemed strange to me that anybody would think of putting on a prize-fight in this metropolitan equivalent of a Yorkshire moor. But after ten minutes or so I saw an unmistakable municipal building – at once pretentious, inharmonious, and depressing – with vertical human figures covering the steps of a long stairway leading to it. The crowd spilled down across the pavement and over the kerb, like people waiting in front of a church to rubber at a bridal party, its components as indifferent to the rain as the English always are. Inquiry revealed that instead of going into the hall, they were waiting for the arrival of Spinks – a small free part of the evening's entertainment, to be savoured separately, like the pleasure of standing in a queue for an hour before entering a moving-picture theatre.

I made my way slowly up the steps, careful not to jostle any of the men, which would be 'taking a liberty', and they slowly pulled out of my way, one by one, waiting until the last moment but not clocking me absolutely, because that also would be 'taking a liberty'. Among the common people of this freedom-loving country there is no social offence so heinous as the one they call 'taking a liberty', or 'making free'. Trying to sneak into the middle of a bus queue, seeking to attract a barmaid's attention before she has finished serving another customer, and asking a man for more cigarettes in the course of a year than you proffer him in return are specimen crimes. Pushing in a crowd is an aggravated form. So is offering unsolicited advice, although in a crisis an altruist may dare it. At Sandown races one day, a small man who had been shadowing me so persistently that I thought he might be a pickpocket at length came within my speaking range and said, 'Pardon me, sir, I hope you'll excuse me, but your shirt is hanging out, and I thought you'd rather I told you.' Nobody else had taken the liberty, and if I hadn't chanced into the path of this bold eccentric, I don't suppose anybody ever would have. He scuttled away crabwise in the crowd, looking horribly ashamed of his inability to control his tongue.

Once, in a shared-taxi returning to London from another track, I heard a man say to his companion, 'You keep your eye on 'im. 'E's a liberty-tiker, and once you let a liberty-tiker tike liberties with you, 'e'll tread on you.'

'Not much bloody fear,' the other fellow said.

This cult of respect for the other bloke is diluted in the lower middle class, and at higher social levels it is as weak as Scotch whisky bottled for home consumption. Britons trying not to seem common can be uncommonly rude.

Pushing open the glass doors of the Town Hall, I headed for the box office – in ordinary life, I suspected, the information booth at which taxpayers are directed to the borough officials they want to see – and there a bulky gentleman, obviously in good humour, told me that the only seat left in the house was one at two guineas ($5.88), in the first row ringside. I said that would suit me fine. 'The plice is packed out,' he said. 'Never saw such a hinterest in a contest.' At the moment, I thought this was a dodge to make me buy the two-guinea ticket instead of a cheaper one, but I later discovered that the ticket seller was truthful. The place was sold out.

Near the box office, I saw a number of fellows I had met at other fights. Among them was Phillips – a slender man with a pointed head, an iron-grey moustache, and wavy silvery hair. He introduced me formally to the ticket seller, who turned out to be Grossmith. I remarked that it was too bad Spinks hadn't ridden, since

133

it would have made an unusual sports story, and Grossmith said, 'The fellow oo 'ad the 'orse was very keen to 'ave 'im ride, but I couldn't chance it, what with 'aving already sold out the 'ouse.'

'He couldn't bear to think of refoonding all that lolly,' Phillips said. 'Proper bloody Barnum!'

The glass doors now swung wide to admit Spinks and his faction. The fighter, a blond boy with cropped hair like the down on a duckling, had the face of a malevolent cherub. As Phillips had said, he was tall for his weight – perhaps five feet five inches. The members of his entourage had the air of men who surround a big fighter, although Phillips told me that the lad had had only seven bouts since turning professional. Still, he had won the Olympic title in his class at Melbourne. The English in the last 20 years or so have had such a thin time in international competition that a home boy who beats foreigners at anything is halfway to being a national hero. Spinks, who comes from West Ham, a Labour constituency a couple of miles east of Shoreditch, wore a cap, a long overcoat, and a suit that did not look out of place in the neighbourhood. An English athlete who wishes to remain popular must avoid outward show of the Big Head – or 'Ead – which is a syndrome nearly as fatal locally as Liberty-Tiking, or Miking Free.

Spinks pressed along towards the dressing-rooms, and the fellows who had been standing in front of the Town Hall pushed through the glass doors behind him. They did not wait to see McCready arrive – or maybe he was there already. I had not given much thought to Spinks's opponent, who had been barely mentioned in the thrilling yarn about the two dark horses at Manchester, but now I asked Phillips what sort of boy he was. Phillips said that he was reputed to be tough, and that he had had a good number of bouts as an amateur in Northern Ireland and, like Spinks, seven professional matches.

We all moved up a wide stairway leading to the scene of the evening's entertainment, a large chamber ordinarily devoted to balls, meetings of local associations, big wedding receptions, and amateur theatricals. It had green plaster walls and moulded, gilt-painted decorative motifs, and a balcony and gallery – both full up, I noticed as I made my way to my seat, which was just under one of the two corners to be used by the boxers. There were vacant seats in my row, but they were soon filled with prosperously rounded citizens and their wives, who evidently had bought their tickets well in advance. The hall holds only 900, and 900 spectators in a space designed to hold just that many set up a closed circuit of emotion that you don't get in a bigger cadre. (A cockfight in a fetid, crowded cellar benefits by the same ambience; a cockfight in a high, well-lighted place like Madison Square Garden would be a bore.) The quality of British professional boxing is so rudimentary that it will not bear exposure to more than 999 persons at a time.

I was flanked and backed by a number of chaps who appeared to know one another well. On my right, one of them was relating to a companion the disappointing course of a fight that he had witnessed at some other arena, unspecified.

'"Work awye, Joge," I told 'im,' this fellow was saying. '"Pound awye, Joge," I says."Be the guvnor." But Joge wouldn't use that right 'and – only in a clinch. 'E insisted on reservin' 'issel.' Joge means George, just as a potable typewriter means a portable.

'What price was 'e?' asked the other fellow.

'Five to two on,' said Joge's unheeded adviser, meaning that he was the favourite by a margin of two and a half to one.

'Cor,' said the second man. 'What was 'e reservin' 'issel for?'

'Cost me two fivers, and 'e wuhn't even 'ave a go,' said the first. "E's a bit of a dodger, I fear – our Joge. Don't fancy 'avin' 'is 'andsome fice bashed.'

The programme I had just bought for sixpence informed me that the first bout would be '6 (3 min.) Rounds Feather-weight Contest at 9–4', or nine stone four, or 130 pounds. It listed the participants as 'Terry Brown, West Ham, former ABA champion, first pro fight', v 'Billy Alport, Walsall'. Brown proved to be one of those snub-nosed, good-looking, eupeptic, round-muscled boys who are so frequently adept at sports and too infrequently exceptional. Alport was spindle-limbed, flat-chested, and heron-necked. He looked unhappy – as if he had to live by writing book reviews at *New Statesman* rates. The contrast, considered in conjunction with his modest billing and the international practice of giving an amateur champion an easy professional debut, made it certain he would fall. For this reason, I was offended when the chap on my right, the chap who had been telling the story about Joge, said, in a loud voice, 'Two to one Brown, two to one on!' I wondered if I looked so completely a hick, as the term is defined in the New Canting Dictionary of 1725: 'Any Person of whom any Prey can be made, or Booty taken from; also a silly Country Fellow; a Booby.' It developed, however, that Joge's detractor was seeking to make no Prey of me. He was aiming his offer over my head, howitzer-fashion, at my neighbour on my left – a small, nervous, sharp-faced young man, who wore thick-lensed glasses and had a reddish Groucho Marx moustache, and who was already under the stress of an excitement I did not at once identify. He twisted his hands.

'Three to one, Ginger,' a man in the row behind us said to him.

'Four to one,' the first fellow now bid.

'Mike it five,' Ginger said, in the voice of a member of Alcoholics Anonymous backsliding.

'Five it is,' the tempter behind Ginger said. "Ow many times?'

The boxers, who had been called to the centre of the ring for the paternal spiel from the referee, now returned to their corners to await the bell.

'Wite!' Ginger pleaded. 'I want 11 to two.'

'Eleven it is for two nicker,' the layer in back of us said quickly.

I found all this astonishing, since my programme stated, in clear black letters, 'Betting Strictly Prohibited'.

For a couple of rounds, the ex-amateur pummelled the boy who looked like a book reviewer. The latter was hopeless. The referee stopped what the programme misleadingly referred to as a contest before there was a knockdown. He was quite right. Ginger handed over two limp pound notes to the man in back of him, and

I now recognised Ginger for what he was – an incurable short-end bettor. I wondered how he earned the money that I was sure he sacrificed, night after night, to a vice that can be more expensive than dope. The short-end addict is a man who can never resist a long price, even when he knows it isn't long enough. In the case of the short-endomaniac subjected to daily temptation, the disease takes a galloping, or geometrically progressive, form. When he has lost a hundred short-end bets, he needs a 100–1 shot to bring him even. He never lands the 100–1 shot.

On the motivation of the short-ender there have been many theories. One is that he is too fundamentally greedy to contemplate risking $5 to win one under any circumstances. Another is that he has a craving for distinction that drives him to accept a thousand losing bets in the hope of being able to say in his old age that he made a killing on Jim Dandy or Harry Truman. A third is that he is an anti-social sadist, eager to rejoice in the discomfiture of the majority. I was, of course, unaware of the etiology of Ginger's case, but he had a peach. His false friends knew it, and they went for him like piranhas for a swimmer with a nosebleed.

Before the next bout – 'Johnny Kidd, Glasgow, KO'd Dick McTaggart in One Round, v Roy Hill, Hammersmith, a Tough Two-handed Fighter' – it was pitiful to watch Ginger struggle against his compulsion. Like Spinks, the Dick McTaggart whom Kidd had knocked out had been an Olympic champion. The blurb writer had been able to find nothing comparable to say for Hill; you would hardly expect a fighter to have only one hand. And in addition to the documentary evidence there was the ocular. Kidd looked like a fighter – impassive and confident, with sloping shoulders and loose-moving limbs.

'Five to two on!' the first tormentor cried. 'I'll take Kidd five to one!'

Ginger managed a weak smile and a feeble shrug.

'Six to one on,' the fellow behind said as the fighters came out of their corners.

After the Hammersmith boy had remained upright for the first 30 seconds of the bout, Ginger accepted 7–1 against one pound. A moment later, the Glaswegian hit Hammersmith with a left hook to the body, and the two-handed fighter went down.

'Fifteen to two 'e don't finish the round,' another of Ginger's undoers said, and the short-ender, leaping at the chance to pull out, cried, 'Done!' The Hammersmith boy got up at 'nine', and Ginger came to life as a rooter. 'Box 'im, 'Ammersmith!' he shouted. 'Don't tike no chances!' 'Ammersmith was still shaking his head when Kidd nailed him a second time and knocked him out. Ginger handed over a total of £3.

These first two matches were the votive sacrifices with which the game began. In the next one, at eight rounds, one of the contestants was listed as 'Dennis Booty, Bethnal Green, Challenges the winner of Lazar & Downes', and the other as 'Johnny Woolard, Glasgow, Gave Terry Downes a great fight here'. The fighters were middleweights.

The borough of Bethnal Green adjoins Shoreditch on the east, and Booty had a strong faction of supporters in the house. He is a rarity in contemporary boxing, being a new prospect from a Jewish neighbourhood. One of the plangent laments of British promoters (as of their colleagues in New York and Chicago) is that there are few Jewish fighters nowadays, even though the Jewish fight fan has been a mainstay of the London ring since the days of Daniel Mendoza and Dutch Sam, whose exploits filled the years between 1788 and 1814. Mendoza and Dutch Sam proved that, pound for pound, they had the qualities their age admired, and they did more to establish the Jew on the English scene than any other two historical figures.

Booty, a muscular, balding young man of intellectual appearance, looks more like a college physical education teacher than a prize-fighter. I had seen him fight once before, in another London arena, and had noted that he is easily dazed by a fairly hard punch, although he reacts with courage. In the other corner, Woolard, thick-necked and heavy-muscled, had a well-worn, lustreless fighter's face that reflected more concussion than ambition.

When the sharp shooter on my right said, 'Four to one Booty, Ginger. 'Ow about it?' I thought for once Ginger might have a chance. But Ginger was cautious now, and held out for 9–2.

'All right, you can 'ave it,' the other said magnanimously – and hurriedly – as the bell rang. He sounded like a man buying a ticket for a train that he will have to run for.

Booty, encouraged by his faction – 'Let 'im 'ave it, Dennis. 'E's useless!' – stalked Woolard for ten seconds or so. He then hit a one-two – left to the face and right cross to the left ear – in proper Amateur-Boxing-Association-Playing-Fields-of-Eton style. Woolard retreated, and Booty hit him with an almost professional left hook to the body, dropping his shoulders as he did so.

'I doubt whether Woolward styes a round,' said the fellow who had laid the odds.

'I doubt whether Booty styes a round!' Ginger cried loyally, although his man hadn't struck a blow.

So it went for the first round and the first two minutes of the second, with Booty hitting and Woolard receiving or accidentally and narrowly averting. Booty was that uncomfortable object to contemplate – a visibly thinking boxer. After every punch, he paused to select the next one, and while he usually made the correct choice, each time he paused, he left Woolard an interval for recuperation. Then, towards the end of the second round, Woolard – although I would have laid 50–1 against the possibility – did some thinking on his own account. Just as the Bethnal Green Thinking Machine, after doing the one-two and, completing a run-through of what he knew about simple addition, was starting 'three', Woolard said to himself, 'Two and a half', and threw a right hand to the jaw inside the wide left hook.

Down went Booty, and up jumped Ginger, shouting, "E's 'ad it! Stop that fight, ref! 'E's lible to suffer a permnent injury!'

But Booty, who is game enough, got up on weak legs at the count of nine, and Woolard lost him in the few remaining seconds of the round. In the third, Booty – piqued and a bit out of his head – went in to slug, and so did Woolard. It was a good round, and Ginger, so solicitous of Booty's health a moment before, now shouted to the ref to 'brike 'em' when he thought Booty was hanging on. By the end of the round, the original positions were re-established. Woolard was again resigned to his fate.

At the end of the fourth round, Woolard's seconds summoned the referee to their corner to have him look at their man's left eye, which was apparently bloodshot. The master of ceremonies, who wore a dinner jacket, then entered the ring and announced, 'Woolard retires, hon account hof han hinjured heye!'

Ginger, who by my official, unsolicited count was now seven quid down, was painful for a tender bloke like me to regard. He had seen the near-realisation of the short-ender's dream, which is all that most short-enders ever get to see. This is harder to bear than fiasco, because the short-ender pre-savours a delicious triumph over the forces of conformity, and when his horse fades out in the last 50 yards, he is overwhelmed by a sense that all organised society is against him.

Ginger was discouraged; for the first time that evening, as the main bout came on, he successfully resisted the predatory blandishments. 'Terry Spinks,' my programme read, 'West Ham. Former Amateur Fly-wt champion of Gt Britain v Ivan McCready, Belfast, Ireland's best Fly-wt since Rinty Monaghan.'

To cries of 'Spinks, two to one on!' and even 'Threes, Ginger! Come on, 'ave a go', Ginger replied only with a hurt smile. 'They must take me for a proper mugg,' he said to me. 'Spinks is terrific.'

The jockey-prizefighter – long-legged, long-armed, and short-waisted, but with a wide chest and shoulders – stood a good four inches taller than his opponent, a short, dumpy figure hooded in towels and draped in an oversize maroon bathrobe that touched the floor. Before McCready's handlers peeled these wrappings off him, he suggested a bouncy little peasant woman. When they uncovered him, though, they displayed a big, powerful torso, short, strong arms, and short, thick legs, rounded like birch logs. Present-day Irish boxers, although not remarkable technically, have a tradition of hard physical workouts – running thousands of miles on the road and jumping rope millions of times – and they often win bouts on sheer condition. North and south of the border alike, Ireland is an ascetic country.

The two boys – both had the faces of pre-adolescents – were equal in weight, at eight stone two (114 pounds). Each had the advantages inherent in his particular construction. When the gamblers around me saw the grand shape McCready was in, they offered no more threes on Spinks, and some of them even began taking the odds. "E's trined up in grite shipe,' one of them said. 'Look at the legs on 'im.' But Ginger, suspecting a lure, said scornfully, 'They always pick 'im midgets' – by ''im' meaning Spinks.

The Shoreditchers who had put their stakes on McCready immediately became Irish patriots.

'Up, Paddy!' one of them shouted. 'You can do 'im!' McCready, who has a wide, flat Celtic face with small features, looked distrustful.

In the first round, McCready showed little to encourage the short-enders. He moved towards Spinks, as a man with arms like his must if he is to land at all, but the Cockney boy circled around him easily, flicking a long left jab in his face and immobilising the short arms whenever the Ulsterman got near him. Once or twice, in these close encounters, Spinks utilised the leverage of his longer arms to shoot in uppercuts. There was nothing but confidence in his half-sulky, half-joking street boy's face. McCready went in for solemnity and concentration, and occasionally, growing impatient, he brandished his cocked right hand as if he held a stick in it.

At the end of the round, the gamblers were again chirping threes and fours, and Ginger was smiling proudly because he had not been had.

'The Paddy is 'opeless,' the fellow on my right said. 'The ref is entitled to stop this, yer know. It's no contest.'

The second round was much the same, but the Ulster boy's tirelessness and composure made some impression, as did Spinks's evident eagerness to stay out of his way, except for stabbing him with lefts. "E respects 'im, you know,' a fellow who had taken McCready on the short end of 5–2 said in a faintly hopeful tone, but he refused somebody's proposal that he take fours for another quid. McCready, when he came back to his corner, which was mine, was breathing as normally as if he'd been strolling through a park, and although long years of practice have proved me a complete failure in reading the Irish face, I thought I detected a confident and treacherous expression in his left eye.

Until what will go down in official history as nine seconds before the end of the third round, the match followed the same pattern. At that point, it is possible that the versatile Master Spinks let his thoughts wander to the picking of a long shot for the Autumn Double, which is a parlay on the Cesarewitch and Cambridgeshire Handicaps, the last of the season's important races. At any rate, he got into a position on the rail – as they call the ropes in his other trade – that was hard to back out of, and when McCready threw his ninety-sixth right hand of the evening over the young Arcaro's left, the jockey didn't pull his head back forward enough. Down he went, dreamily rolling, so that the following horses would not step on him.

The referee, bending low over Spinks, shouted the numbers into his ear, but the boy was galloping two horses on Newmarket Downs, like the Roman Riders in the circus. Then a bell, inaudible to me, whispered, or so I was later informed, and Spinks's seconds were in the ring, carrying him to his corner, while McCready came dancing back to mine. 'Nobody 'eard the bell!' the fellow who had bet on McCready shouted. But it seemed at that moment a quibble; I would have laid odds myself that if Spinks came to in time for the next round he wouldn't last it out. The fellow I felt sorry for was Ginger. 'I could 'ave 'ad fours,' he moaned miserably.

It is a grand thing to be 19 years old. In the minute between the third and fourth rounds, Spinks recuperated sufficiently to come out boxing, and within a minute more he was fighting, which he found it necessary to do in order to live. McCready, sure now that he could hurt him, was in after him, Irish-wild, throwing strong lefts to the body as well as rights at the small, artistically swaying head behind the tormenting left hand. The referee gave Spinks a couple of precious seconds by stopping McCready to warn him about roughness, and the crowd howled. But Spinks did the rest himself. In close, he came down on a head-and-shoulder level with the little strong man, pulling his wasp waist back out of the way and pounding from underneath with uppercuts. When McCready smashed into the Cockney's body, he looked as though he might break it, but McCready was not the only boy in good condition. McCready won the round, by a shade, but Spinks survived.

The rest of the fight was a corker, even in the interludes when Spinks went into his jab-and-dance routine, because the crowd now had a sense of the danger he was warding off. I thought it an even thing at the end of the seventh, with McCready much stronger but Spinks doing at least as much damage. Spinks, although he may never be a great fighter, has many of the characteristics that go to make one, and among those is the ability to spurt for a limited period even when tired. The English have a racing term for it; they say that a horse can or cannot 'accelerate'. And in the last round, McCready, though better fitted to go on for another half hour, simply could not fight as fast as Spinks for three minutes, and Spinks won the decision. He had certainly been out for more than a second after the referee heard the inaudible bell. "'E 'ad plenty of 'elp,' the man who had bet on McCready said. Looking at it another way, you might say that a boy who can fight five tough rounds and win after being knocked out is a prime bit of stuff, as the immortal Pierce Egan – the Ibn Khaldun of the London Prize-ring – would have it.

After the master of ceremonies announced the result, a loud jingling noise began, and continued for a couple of minutes, as a great shower of half-crowns and florins – worth 35 cents and 28 cents apiece, respectively – descended upon the ring, shied in from all corners of the hall by spectators appreciative of the battle. This is a custom surviving from a time when fighters met exclusively for side bets, and all the loser got for his work was the silver offering. Nowadays, I am informed, the fighters usually split the silver bonus, if any. On this occasion, though, after the seconds and the referee, the master of ceremonies, and other trustworthy persons had gathered the coins in towels, the MC announced that it was the wish of Spinks that all the silver be handed over to McCready. The papers next day called it a generous gesture, and it certainly was a gracious return for a punch in the jaw.

The happiest man in the hall, perhaps, was Ginger. He felt and articulated the inner satisfaction of an Anonymous Alcoholic who has just turned down a Christmas bottle of distinguished 95 per cent neutral spirits and 5 per cent aged bourbon whiskey. 'Thought I was a muggins, did they?' he said. 'Offerin' me fours on a dead cert like that!' Ginger could take it or leave it alone.

Unfortunately, there was still another fight on the card – '8 (3 min.) rounds Feather-weight Contest at 9–2. George Carroll, Covent Garden, Has Won 21 out of 22 contests, v Johnny Howard, Holloway. KO'd Arthur Devlin.' The two featherweights, muscular fellows of 128 pounds each, looked like heavies to eyes adjusted to the flyweights of the previous fight.

Covent Garden market porters have been considered good prize-ring material since 1746, when Richard Mills, known as the Onion Boy, beat a celebrated pugilist named Edward Hunt. I don't suppose that the Shoreditch punters knew about the Onion Boy, but they seemed to think that a fellow who had lost only one fight in 22 should do. 'Two to one on!' the betting man to the right of me shouted. Somebody cried, 'Done!' but Ginger was adamant, strong in his new power to say no.

The bell sounded, and the two boy huskies moved towards each other. There were more cries of 'Two to one', and I, watching the fighters now, wondered if Ginger had held out.

I had not long to watch. Howard, the short-end fighter, who looked like a Charles Atlas correspondence school strong man, hit the Covent Garden porter a single tremendous punch and knocked him stiff in one minute of the first round. It was the first time that evening that a boxer had upset the odds.

The man at my right was embarrassed. 'I was bettin' two to one on 'im – 'Oward – that won it,' he yelled to the man who had taken his offer. 'It's a crossed bet. I didn't mention no boxers' nymes.'

I turned to Ginger and asked, 'Did you have the winner?' But Ginger had suffered the short-ender's ultimate disaster – to neglect a long shot and see him come in. 'I didn't 'ave 'im,' he said. 'I was greedy. I was witing for five to two.'

I bade Ginger good night, but he was too crushed to respond. The last thing I heard him say was, 'I could of won ite pounds.'

The New Yorker
12 October 1957

Freddie Mills: His Life and Death

Jack Birtley

Within a year of one another in the mid-1960s two ex-British, British Empire (Commonwealth), European and World title-holders – a very rare breed indeed – died violently. The circumstances which led to the untimely deaths of Freddie Mills and Randolph Turpin were explored in two biographies by sports journalist Jack Birtley.

In each case there were personal problems, financial pressures and possible threats and intimidation. But were there also other overriding reasons to ignite such explosive ends?

We pick up the story of the immensely likeable Mills towards the end of his boxing career in 1949, when he was still the holder of four titles at light-heavyweight and about to strive for a fifth and sixth in the heavyweight division.

The meeting at the White City pulled in a crowd of more than 46,000 with Mills giving away 20 pounds in weight in the bid to wrest the British heavyweight, European and Empire titles away from the talented Woodcock. For his night's work Bournemouth's world light-heavyweight champion was getting £15,000, but once again the money was hard earned to say the least and yet another indication of the shortsightedness and obvious dangers in pitting him against big heavyweights.

Once again he turned in a typically courageous never-say-die display, only to absorb tremendous punishment until the accomplished, crisp-hitting Woodcock finally battered him into submission in the fourteenth round. Mills was counted out resting on one knee, holding a glove tightly against his left ear, very much in pain and a totally dejected and beaten fighter. He had taken so much punishment, in fact, that rumours swept Britain and South Africa the following morning that he had died as a result of his injuries.

For the next few months he wisely took things easy, merely taking part in exhibition bouts, attending fêtes and other celebrity-style functions and popping in to keep an eye on the Chinese restaurant. Yet the battering from Woodcock had done nothing to improve the problem of his headaches and dizzy spells. The headaches in particular became much worse and he was frequently seen sitting in a corner away from the crowd, pressing his fingers into the corners of his eyes and grimacing with the excruciating pain. Although there were a few hints about possible retirement, Mills quickly dismissed such negative talk and even before the bruises of the Woodcock battle had disappeared negotiations began for a world title meeting with American Joey Maxim.

The Woodcock fight proved to be Mills's only ring appearance of 1949 and the title defence against Maxim was finally fixed for Earl's Court in January the following year. After the initial preparations had been carried out in London, a training camp was set up at the start of the New Year, again at the Barley Mow in Betchworth, although this time the weather prevented an outdoor camp. Instead, the public bar was transformed into a gymnasium and Mills set about applying the final polish to his preparations, full of confidence and watched by an admiring public who were not to know this would be the last time he would be undertaking the rigours of training for a professional fight.

Freddie Mills, victor and perhaps also victim of 96 fights to date, was nearing the end of a road which, during the past four years particularly, had exposed him to rather too many legalised hidings. His brain and body had absorbed an almost frightening degree of punishment in those two confrontations with Woodcock, the first Lesnevich fight, the mauling by the towering Baksi, the humiliating defeat by Marshall and through the thousands of other punches he had taken so willingly and perhaps so foolishly, in the long line of fights which had started at the Westover ice rink nearly 14 years before.

Yet this obvious pattern and, at that time, hidden repercussions from his much-publicised career were not reflected in the pre-fight sports pages with many of the leading sports writers patriotically forecasting a successful defence. Maxim, a good-looking Italian-American of 27, boasted an impressive boxing pedigree having beaten most of America's leading cruiserweights, including Lesnevich. Although not renowned for his heavy punching, he was an ultra-scientific boxer with a deadly accurate left hand and managed by the famous 'Doc' Kearns who had guided Jack Dempsey to the world heavyweight championship.

With the pro-British crowd roaring encouragement, the champion continued to surge forward nevertheless, but his reflexes were no match for the ringwise American who skilfully shortened his punches to begin catching his much smaller opponent at will. By the sixth round Mills was in a complete daze and already looking battered and weary. At least three of his front teeth had been dislodged by the merciless fusillade of blows raining down on him like a hammer pounding the stationary horseshoe held in the vice-like grip of the blacksmith. There was no escape. Maxim made a complete mockery of the suggestions that he didn't possess a punch of any discernible power. He was the complete master-boxer, virtually picking his blows in the same way an expert snooker player declares his forthcoming shots, and by the start of the tenth round the outcome was obvious. Maxim was not at full throttle, looking for the punch to put the courageous but so battered Britisher out of his misery. A short crisp right hand to the chin finally settled the issue, and Mills sank to the canvas dazed and completely exhausted, to be counted out.

He looked a pathetic figure and immediately after arriving back in his dressing-room he was violently sick. Normally, the loser's dressing-room is a comparatively quiet place with the victor besieged by admirers, hangers-on and the press. But Mills, dazed, battered and bewildered-looking as he lay prostrate and exhausted on a table, was surrounded by an army of people who packed the dressing-room. It was as if the mourners had come to take a final look at the corpse, and as sports writer Peter Wilson forced his way through to the edge of the table Mills looked up wearily. Three front teeth were missing and he lisped, 'I've fooled you all, Peter. I've never been the same since the first Lesnevich fight. Every time I've had a hard punch to the face I've had pains in my head and it's made me go dizzy.' And with an incredible touch of humour at such a time he held his fingers against his battered lips and mumbled, 'Thank heaven for Bevan. Now I can get these put back for nothing.'

A few minutes later Maxim came in to pay his respects and the beaten champion joked to him, 'You're a nice fellow, I must say, knocking out three of my teeth. Look at this mess you made of me.' The American grinned back and replied, 'You're a bit of a hard guy yourself. You've cracked my front bridge, you know.'

'Okay!' quipped Mills. 'So tomorrow it's a race to see who gets to the dentist first. Anyway, you'll be okay because you know you get it free in this country, don't you?'

Back at Denmark Hill there was another crowd of friends waiting to greet him, and while the crestfallen Mills sat in a chair drinking numerous cups of hot tea and glasses of beer to quench a raging thirst brought about by swallowing so much blood, they talked and reminisced over most of his big fights. Gradually, even though his missing teeth made talking difficult, Mills joined in until Broadribb reminded everyone it was 3 a.m. and time to go home. Ten minutes later, with young Donny tucked up in bed, Mills and Chrissie were alone and they talked on for another hour. Instinctively they knew that a big decision had to be made later that day.

The first call that morning was to a Harley Street dentist to see about having false teeth made. Mills was up at 8 a.m. and while he was filling his bath Donny crept into Chrissie's bedroom and whispered, 'How is he, Mummy?'

'He's all right, I think,' she replied. 'But he's lost his front teeth.'

Eleven-year-old Donny's eyes filled with tears. 'Oh, no, Mummy!' he said. 'Not his lovely teeth. Fancy that happening to him when he's never stopped telling me about looking after my teeth. Whatever will he do?'

After Chrissie explained that they were going to see about having some false teeth made, Donny slipped out of the bedroom and tip-toed along the landing to the bathroom door which was wide open. Mills, who never believed in locking the bathroom door and regularly walked about the house naked, was standing in front of the mirror. He had no clothes on and was peering at his reflection and the spaces where his teeth had been.

Suddenly, in the mirror he spotted Donny looking anxiously through the doorway. The boy had a look of extreme sorrow on his face and was near to tears so Mills, pretending he hadn't seen him, began pulling grotesquely funny faces, drawing his lips back wider to expose his teeth. Donny started giggling and as Chrissie walked up to the doorway to see what was happening, Mills began distorting his features even more and the three of them finished up in one another's arms, helpless with laughter.

Broadribb and his wife were waiting for them following the visit to Harley Street. Chrissie set the table for a late breakfast, and after eating in silence for a few minutes her father blurted out, 'Freddie, I think the time has come to hang up the old gloves. When nature begins to give out on you, there's nothing you can do.'

Nothing was said for a couple of minutes. Mills sat looking down at the tablecloth, slowly nodding his head as if in silent agreement. He finally turned to Mrs Broadribb and asked quietly, 'Ma, what would you do if you were me?'

His mother-in-law looked closely at him and replied in a whisper, 'If I were you I would do as Ted says.' Mills nodded again and glanced across the table at Chrissie. His wife was also slowly nodding her head.

Nothing was finally decided. The following Sunday Peter Wilson, perhaps the most graphic and influential sports writer this country has produced, came straight to the point. Recalling Mills's quip about false teeth immediately after his defeat, Wilson wrote:

> *What can you do about a man like that – except applaud him. I do urge him, however, with all the regard I have for him, never to get into the ring again for a serious bout.*
>
> *Mills has come to the end of the trail. An engine can only go on so long. The willing horse must not be over-burdened. Mills is still a champion – he'll always be that in my book. But technically he's still a triple title holder. He won the British, Empire and European crowns.*
>
> *He should surrender them now. He must not risk his reputation – and above all his health – against challengers who weren't fit to lace his ring boots when he was in his prime.*

Even so, Mills was not totally convinced his ring days were over. He mentioned to his manager that he would consider another fight against Maxim. But two days after Wilson's article, Mills picked up his morning paper to learn that Ted had officially announced the retirement. He quickly walked the mile or so to his father-in-law's home to protest, saying again that he felt fit enough to take on Maxim in another fight. Ted shook his head sadly and said, 'Well, it's in the papers now, Fred, perhaps it's just as well.'

By the time he arrived back home, Mills had accepted the situation and, picking up a pair of scissors, carefully cut out the story of his retirement and pasted it in the last of his three big leather-bound scrapbooks containing clippings dating back to the day he had won the final of the novices' competition at the Westover ice rink. He fetched the two other books from his bedroom and spent the rest of the day reading about the former milk roundsman who had battled his way to the light-heavyweight championship of the world. By the time he had finished he knew that Ted had been right to announce the retirement.

For a time after he retired, Freddie maintained a public visibility by skating around the surfaces of the show business world. He then took over a restaurant and nightclub in London's Soho, a place where money can very easily slip through the fingers. We fast forward 15 years.

He arrived at Charing Cross Road just before 10.30, and after parking the car in an alleyway at the rear, walked round to the front entrance of the club where he was greeted by the doorman, a young student named Bob Deacon, a close friend of Andy Ho's son, Tony. He was working there during the summer holidays to raise enough money for a trip to Russia, and had often met Mills at the Hos' home in Bushey Heath.

'Hello, young Bob,' he called out before walking down the steps. 'How many are there in there tonight?' Deacon told him there was only a handful of customers, and about 20 minutes later Mills came out again, stopped at the top of the steps and said, 'I'm feeling a bit tired, Bob. I've just had a couple of drinks and I think I'll have a sleep in the car. It's at the back, so will you wake me in about half an hour in time for me to introduce the cabaret?'

When Mills was awoken at the arranged time he immediately asked Deacon how many customers were in the club by now. On being told there were only seven or eight, he said wearily, 'I'm not going to come in yet, then. Wake me up in another half hour if I am asleep.'

Deacon thought Mills was by now looking rather subdued, but thought nothing of it. After all, he mused, if the boss wanted to sleep in a car at the rear of his club, that was his business. It was just before midnight when the young doorman walked round to the car again to tap on the window to try and rouse his boss. There was no immediate response, so he opened the door and leaned in to shake him gently by the arm. Again there was no response. Deacon felt a little uneasy, so he went into the club to have a word with the head waiter, Henry Grant. 'Leave him for a while. He's had a couple of drinks and just wants to sleep it off,' Grant instructed the young doorman.

The hour was approaching 1 a.m. when Deacon took another walk to the rear of the club. Once again he shook Mills, but there was no reply. The alleyway was poorly lit so Deacon, now becoming concerned, took a closer look and then patted his boss's face. Again there was no response, but this time Deacon noticed saliva around Mills's nostrils and mouth, giving him the appearance of a man who had had too much to drink. Yet Deacon knew this was not the case and dashed back into the club to find the head waiter. Grant came out immediately this time, but he couldn't rouse the still figure either. Andy Ho was then summoned to the scene, and he immediately decided that Mills was ill and dashed to the club telephone to call Chrissie.

But the baby-sitter at Denmark Hill explained that Mrs Mills had left with Donny and his wife only minutes earlier, and when their car eventually arrived at the front of the club, Ho was waiting nervously to take Chrissie by the arm and lead her to one side. Earlier in the week they had had an argument over the telephone, and Chrissie thought initially that he was taking her out of earshot of Donny and his wife to apologise. But with a serious look on his face Ho whispered. 'I want you to come into the yard with me. Freddie is in his car and he is not well. I want you to try and wake him.'

Chrissie, dressed in a white suit, ran quickly to the back of the club and immediately leaned inside the car to start patting her husband's face. She moved what she thought was the car's starting handle so as to get closer, and his head now leaning on her shoulder, she began patting his face again and talking to him, while Donny, Ho, Deacon and the waiters crowded around.

Suddenly she glanced down and, in the dim light, saw a dark stain on her suit. It was blood and she thought to herself, 'Oh, my God! He's cracked his head on the starting handle and hurt himself.' Her eyes focused on what she had thought was the starting handle and to her horror she realised it was a rifle. She looked back at her husband who was still in a sitting position with a hand on each of his knees, his head resting lightly on her shoulder and in a flash, the truth of the situation hit her. She screamed to Donny, 'Get an ambulance, quickly. Freddie's been hurt.'

Within minutes an ambulance was at the scene and it was then discovered that Mills had an ugly wound in the corner of his right eye. He had been shot and as he was being lifted on to a stretcher one of the ambulancemen said quietly, 'I think he's dead.'

At precisely that moment Cissie Jackson was tossing and turning in bed at her home in Bournemouth, having a nightmare in which she saw the dead body of her famous brother. She turned restlessly, trying to blot out the tormenting picture, but the dream carried on with faceless people walking around babbling about arranging a funeral for him. All the time the dream vividly showed the body of Freddie, and when hands lifted him up and began lowering him into an open grave, she woke with a start, feeling cold and damp with sweat. Switching on the table lamp she looked at the comforting sight of Harold lying beside her, fast asleep, and breathed a sigh of relief. Realising then that she had been dreaming she shrugged, and with a quick glance at the bedside clock, put out the light. It was exactly 1.30 a.m.

Meanwhile, Andy Ho, his son Tony, who had been working at the club, Chrissie and Donny took refuge in the tiny office inside as the stretcher was gently placed into the ambulance. The waiters and Bob Deacon stood at a respectful distance, aware now that a sensational drama was being unfolded before their eyes, and only the uncontrolled sobbing of Ho and Chrissie from inside the club broke an almost eerie silence.

The engine of the ambulance was stuttering as the driver attempted to coax it to start, but after about ten seconds he leaned his head out of the window and sighed, 'It's no good, she won't start. Give us a push, boys.'

The waiters and Deacon rushed to the rear of the vehicle and began pushing it out into the main street, and as the wheels gathered speed, the reluctant engine gradually roared to full crescendo to pull away into the night. As the helpers stood panting, watching it disappear, Deacon thought to himself, 'My God, what an inglorious exit for poor Freddie.' The group walked back into the alleyway, each man thinking the same and, after a hurried conversation between themselves, agreed to say nothing about the sorry spectacle. It would have been too much for the already distraught widow.

By this time the police had arrived and they immediately closed the club and escorted everyone to the nearby station for questioning. At 4 a.m. the bewildered assembly was officially told that Freddie Mills was dead.

Charlie Mills, unshaven and wearing his dressing-gown, was busying himself in the kitchen of his Bournemouth home preparing an early morning pot of tea. The time was just after 6 a.m. and his wife Mary was still in bed. Suddenly he was startled by the sound of frantic knocking on his front door. His next-door neighbour, also still in his dressing-gown, was there to say that someone wanted to speak to him urgently on the telephone.

'Hello, Charlie,' said a man's voice. 'This is Donny McCorkingdale. I'm afraid I've got some bad news for you. Freddie's dead. He's been shot.'

'What are you talking about? Was it a car accident?'

'No,' Donny repeated. 'He's been shot. You'll hear all about it on the radio.'

An hour later Charlie had broken the news to Jim and Cissie and he asked his sister to come with him while he told their mother. Lottie was already preparing her breakfast when they arrived at her home, and taking her gently by the shoulders, Charlie guided her to a chair and began explaining what had happened.

While he and Cissie stood close to the radio listening to the latest bulletin on the tragedy, Lottie sat sobbing, quietly murmuring, 'Oh, my God!' Through her tears she could pick out the sideboard on which stood a small rose bowl and her mind flashed back to the scene on the upstairs landing 20 years before when Freddie had proudly given it to her – his first prize for boxing.

Yet as she sat there, the arguments were already raging over the controversial death of her famous son, and by the following morning the newspapers were asking, 'Was it murder?' Incredibly, despite the subsequent inquest verdict of suicide, people are still posing the same question today.

Freddie Mills: His Life and Death
New English Library
1977
Reproduced by permission of Hodder and Stoughton Limited

The Tragedy of Randolph Turpin

Jack Birtley

Whether or not Mills had received a calling card from gentlemen wearing dark suits and with heavy jowls who were looking to provide protection will probably never be known.

If the circumstances which had surrounded Mills's demise were extreme, those that contributed to Randolph Turpin's were even more so. His life had see-sawed between a brilliant career , during which his terrific punching power had enabled him to defeat the incomparable Sugar Ray Robinson, and the traumas of divorce, a rape charge and of being hounded by bankruptcy and the tax man.

Like Mills, Turpin had dabbled in show business (presenting an act in cabarets alongside such stars as the Beverley Sisters) and after finishing with boxing had for a while been a professional wrestler, but mounting debts swallowed all he could earn.

Doing his National Service, Turpin had been a cook in the Royal Navy and he returned to that occupation in his home town of Leamington Spa.

O n the surface the former world champion seemed resigned to his life as cook in the back-street café. He would greet regular customers cheerfully, and acknowledge the hesitant enquiries of newcomers, often overawed at being in the presence of such a famous personality. But he would refuse to be drawn into discussions about his career, excusing himself quickly to return to the kitchen to shift his pots and pans about. Those magnificent days of the early 1950s were a blurred memory; he was more concerned about when the Leamington Council were going to demolish his café, or if the Official Receiver would eventually submit a final demand on his wrestling earnings.

His only outside interest was wrestling, yet even this was dwindling. He would accept the odd engagement where he had to stay overnight in Wales. But an appearance in Ipswich, Tamworth or Liverpool would mean an absence of only a few hours. Despite his dramatic withdrawal from the social scene, he was still pestered to make public appearances, or to present the prizes at amateur tournaments. Usually, he refused.

He made an exception following a tragic car accident which finished the career of his friend Mick Leahy. The Coventry Irishman had lost his British title to Wally Swift some months before, but had been looking forward to a number of lucrative fights against foreign opposition.

But one evening, while motoring from Coventry to see George Middleton in Leamington, Leahy drove into the back of a heavy lorry. The car was a complete write-off and Leahy spent several weeks in hospital hovering between life and death. He recovered, but was blind in one eye and was left partially deaf. So his fighting days were also over.

Councillor Harry Weston, who had been mayor of Coventry when Turpin had won the world championship, formed an appeal fund, and organised several functions to raise money for the stricken Leahy. Turpin agreed to present the prizes at an amateur tournament in Coventry, and the former world champion's advertised presence contributed towards a sell-out crowd which raised over £100 towards the Leahy fund. The souvenir programme contained a photograph of Turpin and he was kept busy during the evening autographing the picture. The name of Turpin still had drawing power, after all.

A few weeks later he travelled over to Coventry again, to pose for a newspaper photograph presenting Leahy with a pair of white gloves which had been autographed by some of the reigning British champions, and a number of other leading fighters. The photograph was the last official one taken of Turpin.

Christmas was approaching, trade at the café was good and with one or two wrestling bouts to supplement his income, Turpin was looking forward to providing his family with a traditional English festivity.

Then out of the blue came a cable from America, which brought memories flooding back. Plans were in hand to hold a farewell gala at Madison Square Garden for his old foe, the incomparable Sugar Ray Robinson. The great Negro had recently hung up his gloves for good, and the promoters of the Emile Griffith–Manuel Gonzales world welterweight title fight were also organising a farewell-to-boxing salute for Robinson. And the old maestro wanted Turpin to be there.

Teddy Brenner, who was still the Garden's matchmaker, sent a cable to Turpin, and said in a press release: 'Everybody in America was so impressed by Turpin's quick title defence against Robinson. He should pack a bag and come over for the gala. We will take care of the cost.' Turpin packed a bag and went.

The Griffith–Gonzales clash proved a dull affair, Griffith retaining his title over 15 dreary rounds. Throughout most of the fight the 12,146 spectators booed and catcalled, obviously displeased with the value they were getting for their money. Yet an interesting comparison comes with the official financial statistics for that fight, and those from the Robinson–Turpin clash some 14 years earlier.

The live gate produced $72,502 compared to the 61,370 people who paid $767,730 to see Robinson win his title back. And whereas Griffith netted less than $20,000 as the defending champion, Turpin had pulled in over $68,000 for his efforts. The former world champion, now dishing up mixed grills to lorry drivers in his Leamington café, must have given this more than a little thought as he climbed into the familiar ring again on the night of 10 December 1965.

Turpin was one of the four former world middleweight champions in the famous Garden to pay homage to the great American Negro. The others were Carl 'Bobo' Olson – whom Turpin had just cause to remember – Gene Fullmer and Carmen Basilio. And, in typical American tradition, the four climbed into the ring prior to the title fight – all dressed in boxing strip.

Sugar Ray, now 45 years old but looking 15 years younger, greeted each of his old opponents like a long-lost brother, and the crowd went delirious as he threw his arms around each of them after shaking hands.

Despite his personal problems, Turpin looked amazingly fit and received a tremendous ovation as he took his turn to greet Robinson. Afterwards, and with all sincerity, Turpin told reporters that Robinson was the best he had ever fought. 'There was no other tactician like him,' he added. Even Cassius Clay who had stopped Floyd Patterson in 12 rounds less than three weeks before in defence of his newly won world heavyweight title, joined in the applause from his ringside seat happy, apparently, to remain in the background for a change.

As Robinson made his way from the ring, someone asked him if he had any regrets, to which he replied, 'Not one. I'd do it all over again the same identical way. I wouldn't change a blessed thing.' Which is more than Turpin could truthfully have said.

A few days later Turpin was back in Russell Street. The brief excursion into the past was a memory he carried with him until his death, less than five months later.

Christmas 1965, however, was a happy time for him. As if to make up for lost time, he played with his daughters and threw his house open for brothers Dick and Jackie and their families.

But 1966 offered no fresh hope. Leamington Council were still pressing ahead with the plans to pull down the café. And the Inland Revenue were regularly demanding a settlement on the wrestling earnings. On 14 May, another official-looking letter dropped through the letterbox, and even before he opened it, Turpin sensed the contents. The final demand. It meant, pay up, or be taken to court.

Even two days before the dreadful finale to his troubled life, the former world champion gave no indication of the way he would end it all. He had never talked of suicide as a solution. One thing which did not come out at the subsequent inquest, though, was that on 16 May he gave his head a fearful knock against the corrugated roof of a shed at the rear of the café. One may wonder whether this may have had some bearing on his actions on that terrible day. Yet even on the morning of the shooting, Turpin seemed his normal self.

Charmaine was ill in bed with a heavy cold, and Turpin busied himself around the café as usual, and spent part of the morning writing a letter. Gwen usually assumed that he was writing to his mother who was on holiday in Woking.

The sun was shining brightly that day and, ironically, Gwen took a photograph of her husband before going shopping. Things even seemed normal when Turpin kissed Gwyneth and Annette goodbye as they left to return to school after dinner. Only afterwards did Gwen Turpin recall the significance when he called the girls back and said, 'Now always watch how you cross the roads on your way to school.' And he emphasised the word always. He usually gave this warning each day as the girls left for school. But this was the first time he had called them back to repeat it. That was the last time the girls saw their father.

After the girls had gone, Turpin went upstairs to look at Charmaine in her first-floor bedroom, and came down a few minutes later saying she was fast asleep. But a few minutes later he went back. Little Carmen followed him. Just after 2.30 p.m. Gwen was overcome by a curious, unexplained uneasiness. After looking at the sleeping Charmaine she climbed the stairs to the attic bedroom to be met with the most terrifying sight of her life.

Turpin was slumped by the side of the bed on which Carmen was sitting – her face covered in blood.

Gwen was terrified and screamed to her husband, 'What have you done to her?' There was no reply. Carmen started to cry and Gwen picked up her distressed and obviously injured daughter and ran all the way with her to nearby Warneford Hospital. It was only when the doctors told her that Carmen had been shot that her thoughts went back to her husband, slumped at the side of the bed.

By then her neighbours had been alerted and when she arrived back home the police were there. An inspector took her gently by the arm and said, 'Your husband is dead. It looks as if he shot himself,' and Gwen was told that, pinned to the bedroom door was a note. The letter he had been writing before her very eyes that morning.

Turpin's tragic death completely stunned his relatives and few close friends. Gwen, however, with the additional anxiety of having to watch young Carmen's desperate fight for life, had little time to grieve publicly, and it was only when her youngest daughter was finally removed from the danger list and allowed to return home 18 days after that dreadful day, that the full impact of the double tragedy hit her.

Carmen, in fact, had been extremely lucky to survive. She had been shot twice, one of the bullets having lodged near her brain and the other piercing her lung after narrowly missing her heart.

The fact that Turpin had tried to kill his 17-month-old daughter was one of the chief talking points of the whole affair. Curiously, any reasons why he should have done this were never raised at the inquest on Turpin, although several theories were put forward by the inevitable gossip which swept the town after the tragedy.

Most widely discussed was the suggestion that Carmen, in fact, was not even Turpin's daughter. It was an avenue of thought that, perhaps, was inevitable – because the gossips also took especial care to point out that Carmen, unlike her three sisters, bore no traces of coloured ancestry.

She was, in fact, a cute little blonde-haired child with dazzling blue eyes and creamy-white skin. The three other Turpin girls were clearly half-castes, and their woolly black hair, deep velvet brown eyes, and *café-au-lait* skin left no guesses as to who their father was. And a significant point, claimed the gossips, was that Turpin made no attempt to injure Charmaine who was in her first-floor bedroom at the time of the shooting.

But a Midlands doctor subsequently dismissed the suggestion that Turpin could not have been Carmen's father. He pointed out that while a white mother could quite often produce a throwback coloured child, it was equally possible for a white woman of a mixed marriage to bear a seemingly non-coloured offspring if the father also came from a mixed marriage. And bearing in mind that Turpin's mother was of white parents this seems quite feasible.

This predicament resulting from mixed marriages, of course, is nothing new and, significantly, has caused much distress in South Africa where apartheid has often forced brothers and sisters to live separate lives.

Turpin's inquest, however, created a stir when it was confirmed that he had left two letters, one dealing with the people whom he claimed had been chiefly responsible for his downfall. This second letter found after his death had actually been written two years before, and made references to threats on his life. It is now thought that Turpin wrote the letter following the threats and after he had been beaten up by four unknown men.

In the letter he also mentioned a gang which could be hired to 'dispose of people', but did not elaborate on a story which circulated two years before his death after he had supposedly enquired about £20,000 which had allegedly been salted away in safe-deposit boxes – to avoid paying income tax – during his career.

The story goes that Turpin, deeply in debt and desperate for money, telephoned a certain person asking for 'my £20,000'.

Shortly after making the telephone call, Turpin is supposed to have been visited by four men who beat him up and left him barely conscious, with the parting words, 'Next time it will be your wife and kids.' That, according to the unfounded rumours, is supposed to have stopped Turpin's interest in 'that £20,000'.

Several people recalled Turpin being badly injured about that time but said that he had explained the cuts and bruises away by saying he had been attacked by a section of the crowd while wrestling in Wales.

With Turpin dead, it is now virtually impossible to confirm this unsavoury incident, although his second letter certainly went to great lengths to name people who allegedly cheated him of money, together with references about a gang of hired killers. Gwen, in fact, asked for this letter to be read out at a resumed inquest on 21 July, but the coroner decided against it.

Gangsters and professional boxing have been linked since the sport became big business at the start of the century. But, the connection is more usually associated with America. A clear example of how boxing sometimes operates in the States was given in the autobiography of Terry Downes, who retired in 1964 after losing a world title fight against Willie Pastrano, the American the British Boxing Board refused to allow Turpin to meet in the ring.

Writing about American Sam Silverman, who promoted 31 of Rocky Marciano's 49 fights, Downes said: '. . . and Sam must be a game guy. A few years ago, because he was operating independently, the powerful promoting combines weren't too pleased about it. So somebody dropped a bomb in the basement of Sam's home. Nice people. Luckily, Sam was out at the time. A few days later his wife was lucky enough to be called to the phone when a bullet whizzed through a kitchen window.

'As if this wasn't enough, poor old Sam, who ain't exactly a Hercules, got nicely beat up in the street . . .'

Silverman, it seemed, was also in trouble with some 'nice people' when he came to watch Paul Pender fight Downes in London. For Downes also said in his book, 'Silverman was apparently at a restaurant nearby and was called outside by a couple of disgruntled gamblers, who planted a right hander on Sam's jaw and gave him a kicking to go with it . . .'

Despite investigations over the years, there has been no proof that gangsters are involved in the running of British boxing, yet Turpin's claims of 'hired gangs' are not so lightly dismissed in some quarters. And even the pathologist's report at the inquest four days after Turpin's death caused some raised eyebrows. At the inquest, Dr D.F. Barrowcliff said that the former champion had died about 2.30 p.m. on that fateful day, but that death was not instantaneous. He said that death was due to a gunshot wound through the heart, although his examinations revealed two bullet wounds – one to the left side of the head, just behind the eye, and the other in the chest.

After stating that death was due to the wound through the heart, the doctor then said, 'As to the head shot, this probably preceded the gunshot wound to the chest, but it is conceivable that it was fired afterwards.' Coupled with Turpin's claim about a gang of hired killers, this invited some speculation.

But such thinking is not only dangerous; it is misleading. It is now accepted that both shots could have been fired almost instantaneously, and it will never be proved if the bullet in the head came from the second shot. One curious feature was it was never publicly disclosed how Turpin managed to get a gun. Gwen told the police she never knew he owned a .22 calibre revolver, and no one subsequently stepped forward to throw any light on the matter.

Dick, who gave evidence of identification, told the inquest that he had spoken to his brother only the evening before his death, and that he had seemed in normal spirits. 'I told him I had just been to the doctor and we were having a good laugh over the fact that I had got to use a throat spray,' said the eldest of the Turpins.

At the resumed inquest, Randolph's previous claims that he had never received much of the ring earnings credited to him were given another airing when 'Mosh' Mancini gave evidence. Mancini said that Turpin had often told him he had never received a lot of his ring earnings. 'He claimed emphatically to me that he never received this money which he was having tax demands for,' he added, and then went on to say that the Inland Revenue recently had been demanding income tax on the money he had earned as a fighter.

This, to a slight degree, was probably a misunderstanding on the part of Turpin's old school pal. For the Inland Revenue had made the final assessment on Turpin's total boxing earnings when they made him bankrupt. The letters sent to Turpin over the few months before his death appertained to the money he had earned as a wrestler.

When he replied to questions, Middleton also mentioned Turpin's finances, but denied that he owed the dead boxer any money. He said that Turpin had earned a 'considerable amount' as a boxer before going bankrupt, but said it all went through accountants, and was then paid into Turpin's bank account.

'Everything was being dealt with straightforwardly by chartered accountants. All purses were dealt with by cheque, and transferred to Turpin's account after paying expenses. It is not correct to say that I owe him a large sum of money, or that I did not give him some of the money,' Turpin's former manager told the coroner.

The coroner read part of the letter that Turpin had left pinned to the attic-bedroom door. In general, it was a farewell note, but Turpin wrote about 'having to carry the can for the money owing to the Inland Revenue'. Turpin also added, 'Naturally, they will say my mind was disturbed, but it is not.' The jury didn't think so either; for they returned a verdict that Turpin had 'taken his own life by shooting himself with a .22 calibre revolver'.

The Warwickshire coroner, Mr S.H. Tibbets, concluded by saying that the theme of the tragedy seemed to be that Turpin had been an extremely generous and friendly man who had given away money when he was well off.

Those remarks must have pricked the conscience of many people who had been only too glad to borrow money from the former world champion, but who had harshly turned their backs when he had been trying to recover debts to clothe and feed his own family, or to pay off his own mounting liabilities.

One can only wonder how many of these so-called friends were at Turpin's funeral. Despite newspaper reports that 2,000 people turned up to pay homage, only a few hundred, in fact, were present at Leamington's Holy Trinity Church for the service.

The crowd did swell later to over double the size. But many of the additional people were curious passers-by and shoppers, and one sad conclusion was how few boxing personalities had braved the rain to pay their last respects. Many of the boxing fraternity present were those who had been associated with Turpin from his early days.

Gwen; Beatrice, his mother; Dick; Jackie; Joan and Kathleen headed the family mourners alongside young Randolph from Turpin's first marriage; and nephew Jackie (son of Jackie). Middleton was also in church, together with Inspector Gibbs, Ron Stefani, Mick Leahy and Peter Price. Old-timer 'Kaiser' Bates had also made the trip and other ex-fighters included Ronnie Vale, Willie Croke, Michael Stack, Johnny Mann, Stan Parkes, 'Mosh' Mancini, Alf Harper and Terry Banning – all from the Midlands.

Representing the British Boxing Board of Control was Dennis Bellman, steward of the Midlands Area Council, but, noticeably, no one had made the trip from the Board's London office. Mr Bellman explained after the funeral service; 'Secretary Teddy Waltham very much wanted to be here to pay his last respects to the memory of a great fighter. But there are still many details to be cleared up in London following the world heavyweight title fight (Cassius Clay had beaten Henry Cooper in London three days before) and he could not get away.' This must have been a bitter pill, indeed, for the Turpin family to swallow.

In a hard-hitting sermon, the Rev. E.J.C. Haselden said, 'His life was marked by tragedy, culminating in the tragic circumstances of his death. The issues of life and death are in the hands of God and it is always wrong to take them into our own hands. However, it is not for us to judge: human judgement is not infallible.' Then he poured out the stinging words which were carried in every national newspaper the following day, and sentiments which must have caused one or two uneasy feelings in some quarters:

> At the height of his career Randolph was surrounded by those who regarded themselves as friends and well-wishers. But he was deserted by many as he lost his position and money. The fickleness of his friends and the incompetent advice must have weighed so heavily upon him that he was forced to desperation. Randolph was a simple man, a naïve man and he needed friends to protect him from the spongers. To our shame he was let down. The tragedy is not his failure alone, but the failure of our whole society.

There is little question the impact these words must have had on those closest to Turpin during not only his career, but his full life-span.

The words of Mr Haselden were wise ones. They were courageous ones as well. But the vital questions still remained unanswered. What, or who, caused Randolph Turpin's downfall?

So much happened during the 12 years he fought as a professional, that it is virtually impossible to pin-point one specific cause. Indeed, the rot, so to speak, could have seeped into his life even before he turned to fighting for a living. A careful study reveals that it was a combination of widely spread circumstances which contributed to the final run of events which disrupted and shattered his life.

It is transparently clear that he did not always receive the best advice; if there had been a stricter watch on his income tax affairs, he may not have fallen into such difficulties, and he may have been able to keep some of the vast fortune which slipped through his fingers. Yet, the onus here also rests with the much-criticised system which allows a person to earn so much money without paying taxes at the same time, for there is little question that the years of persecution by the Inland Revenue proved to be a final pressure which Turpin could not cope with. Or is it merely a coincidence that he took his own life only three days after receiving yet another official demand?

On the other hand, the Leamington boxer was well-known for his free-spending and, regarding his boxing income, didn't he say to Jonah Spencer, 'I fought for it, and I'm a-going to spend it?' The fact that after the second Robinson fight he insisted on handling his own money, instead of manager George Middleton customarily counter-signing the cheques to enable Turpin to draw money, again indicated that he wanted unrestricted access to his cash. This could have been a throwback to the threadbare days of his childhood and youth, when he seldom had money in his pocket and often had to go hungry.

There is no disputing that he never did quite shake off the traces of those bleak, lean days. This was reflected not only in his free spending but the irresponsible ease with which he gave money away. But some of the blame must rest with those hordes of so-called friends – and, perhaps, some relatives – who were quite happy to stand with outstretched hands.

Turpin's relationship with his own relatives had often been a stormy one and, despite Dick's evidence at the inquest that the former champion had seemed in the best of spirits the night before, which gave the impression of no hard feelings, this was far from being true.

In his farewell note the following morning Turpin took his own kin to task in no uncertain manner. And just over two years after his death, Gwen Turpin, then living in Wales and writing to answer a question from this author about a possible misunderstanding between herself and the Turpin family, said:

'You mentioned about ******* being upset over something. Well, to tell you the truth, Jack, I am quite unaware of any trouble or family squabbles. Perhaps ******* is upset because I have not corresponded or visited them since leaving Leamington.

'I can't think of any other reason. You read Randolph's last letter to me, and perhaps you can remember his advice to me, and his wishes.

'Well, I am now fulfilling his wishes and have severed relations with the remainder of the family except, of course, Mrs Manley . . .'

Turpin must indeed have been an embittered man to plead with his wife to stay away from his own family.

On the question of the vast sum of money he earned as a boxer, it is difficult to assess at what stage of his career he became insolvent. But although money – or lack of it – helped to push Turpin to that tragic end, one must also question how many of the defeats towards the end of his career affected him mentally. Few people will dispute that it was right to advise him – and to make him – retire after being stopped by Mitri during 1954.

The following year, it will be remembered, he also suffered another humiliating and damaging defeat when Wallace knocked him out in four rounds, yet another sign that Turpin's best years were behind him, and that perhaps he could have been taking punches which may have affected his thinking ability.

The crushing defeat at the hands of Pompey finally convinced everyone that Turpin had no place in the ring – but did the realisation come over four years too late?

The British Boxing Board of Control will come under the finger of suspicion here. They are delegated with the responsibility of not only advising licensed fighters on general matters, but also to keep a watching brief on the medical standards of the men who throw, and take, punches for a living.

Yet the governing body can safeguard themselves on this score, no doubt, by recalling the medical examination after the Mitri fight which disclosed that he was 'in excellent health and fit to continue his boxing career.' Even so, there was a conflicting difference of opinion on the question of whether Turpin was punch-drunk, or not. There was also criticism over the fact that Turpin's brain was not subjected to a microscopic examination after his death to discover whether there was any damage.

The pathologist who performed the autopsy reported that, 'There was no brain damage apparent to the naked eye that one might have expected in the case of a professional boxer suffering blows in the ring.' The specialist then told the inquest, 'Only a detailed microscopic examination could have revealed such damage. But, in order to do this, the brain would have had to be fixed in preservation for several weeks, and that had proved impossible under the circumstances.'

But the Royal College of Physicians Committee on Boxing consisting of eight leading specialists on the brain, heart and eyes – expressed their disappointment that this test had not been carried out, and subsequently claimed that such an examination would have been a simple matter to arrange.

Turpin's family doctor at that time was convinced that the former world champion had been suffering from brain damage. And he was quoted as saying, 'I do not like using the phrase, but I would say that Turpin was punch-drunk. He was not the sort of man to worry about financial matters or about people he thought had let him down. In my opinion boxing was responsible for his death.'

The doctor, who had attended Turpin for nearly thirty years, countered bitter attacks to this theory from the Turpin family, by adding, 'People close to him constantly may not have noticed the deterioration. But it would hit someone who had not seen him for a long time.' To strengthen this view the doctor went on to say that, during the previous ten years, he had noticed Turpin change from a happy, smiling man to one 'increasingly introspective and worried about his health.'

There is no arguing, however, that Turpin did suffer some injuries during his fighting days. His left eye was out of alignment, his right one had a turn in it and often only the white of his right eye could be seen.

And he once told Pete Price 'I am going blind in my left eye.' Turpin had also complained of double vision after the fights with Mitri and Pompey. After each of the fights he said that he had seen two or three opponents at the same time. If his eye-sight was so poor, of course, this could have left him extremely vulnerable to punches. But the British Boxing Board, it seemed, were quite satisfied that Turpin was in good enough health until that final disastrous fight in 1958.

The question of physical damage in the ring being responsible for Turpin's death was quickly seized upon by a number of anti-boxing extremists, particularly J.L. Manning, then of the *Daily Mail*. Mr Manning posed two questions which he claimed badly needed answering. The first, was Turpin punch-drunk? And what happened to the £585,439 paid to see his four world-title fights?

Mr Manning, who was later banned from the ringside by one British promoter because of his hostile attitude to professional boxing, made an issue of the medical and social consequences of boxing, asking that if these were indeed so harmful, should the sport be abolished?

But the *Daily Mail* columnist weakened his case when he implied that Turpin's partial deafness was a 'tell-tale sign', and also that his irrational behaviour caused the break-up of his first marriage. Turpin, of course, was left partially deaf through a childhood swimming accident, and his first marriage started to break up during the first few months of his professional career.

In fact, Turpin confided to Pete Price that he had decided on marriage only on 'the flick of a coin'. Price later recalled that the former champion had told him: 'Honest Pete, I had some money and didn't know whether to get married or buy an air rifle. So I tossed up, and marriage it was.' An irresponsible approach, maybe. But was it a 19-year-old punch-drunk fighter talking?

Mr Manning also quoted the number of professional boxers who have committed suicide since 1939 (the number was given as five); and then how many amateurs and professionals had died from boxing injuries between 1945 and 1965. These worldwide statistics made a convincing case against boxing. But it would have been perhaps fairer had he published some of the figures released by Lord Newton in the House of Lords in 1962, covering the deaths in British sport between 1955 and 1958.

Lord Newton disclosed that there had been 50 deaths during that period, and gave a detailed breakdown of the tragedies. Cricket, for example, had accounted for 14 of the deaths, soccer 13 and rugby nine. The rest of the official statistics were relatively unimportant, until one arrived at boxing. During that same period only one death had occurred in a British ring.

The ethical case against boxing is a matter of debate. But one would be foolish to attempt to whitewash the dangers in the professional ring. The chief concern is that those delegated with looking after the interests of boxers should know the danger signs. Those who don't, or who choose to ignore them, are risking the health – both physical and mental – of their boxers.

The vital question concerning Turpin, then, is – as Mr Manning put forward – was his mental state such that it contributed not only to his erratic life but, ultimately, to his death? Yet, on the other side of the coin, Turpin was his own worst enemy. He repeatedly turned deaf ears to sound advice and frequently wanted his own way concerning everything from spending money and business investments, to his own training preparations. When his mind was made up, Turpin would not listen to anyone, and it was this stubborn side of his character which caused so much trouble before the Olson fight.

As his one-time business associate, Mr Leslie Salt, said about the former champion after his death, 'He was intelligent in some respects, but childish in others. You can tell people what is the best for them, but they don't always take notice.'

Dick also expressed these sentiments when he arrived back in England from the Olson fight, and probably hit the nail really on the head when he said, 'Randolph's got a lot of friends who can't see him doing anything wrong. But he'll find out who his friends are.' Yet, it was odd that while Dick chose to pontificate about the value of some of Randolph's friends, the eldest Turpin failed to give any reasonable explanation of why he walked out of his brother's corner during that controversial fight in America, a time when Randolph surely needed at least all the moral support he could muster.

But without mincing words, it seemed that Randolph was too easily influenced, and most probably did not have the intelligence to distinguish between genuine and well-meaning friends and hangers-on, the latter being out for just what they could get.

Another sign of weakness in Turpin was his involvement with women. This side of his life again highlighted a lack of responsibility which, coupled with humble upbringing, possibly invited exploitation. Perhaps his one big failing, then, was that Turpin would not listen to constructive advice. Like Lord Chesterfield said in a *Letter to his Son*: 'Advice is seldom welcome; and those who want it most, always like it the least.'

But the causes of Turpin's downfall are still the subject of heated conversations in homes, pubs and gymnasiums across the world. They still talk.

Looking back over his complicated life, one could suggest numerous reasons why this man who had grossed a staggering £300,000 should have ended his comparatively short life in such tragic circumstances.

Talk to his closest friends and the reply unhesitatingly will be, 'He was fleeced.' But there are other possible reasons. Was the cause of his downfall, then, due to: (1) bad advice; (2) mismanagement of money; (3) mismatching (resulting in brain damage and, consequently, irresponsible actions); (4) 'spongers' and so-called friends who helped Turpin spend his fortune; (5) his associations with women; (6) his upbringing; (7) persecution by the Inland Revenue; or (8) boxing in general?

To repeat an earlier theory though, it does seem that Turpin was a victim of a combination of circumstances. And, chiefly, these could be: (1) victim of a humble upbringing which left him totally ill-equipped to face fame and untold wealth; (2) mismanagement of money; (3) the 'spongers' and so-called friends who helped him spend his money and gave bad advice; and (4) the unrelenting persecution by the Inland Revenue.

The blazing build-up of publicity surrounding the world heavyweight title fight between Henry Cooper and Cassius Clay, which eventually took place four days after Turpin's death, also could have played some part in that tragic finale. The bankrupt Turpin, a heartbroken and brooding man at the time, may well have digested the financial statistics from the world heavyweight fight, and then bitterly reflected on his own sorry plight, and the £100,000 net income which had slipped through his fingers.

It is difficult to imagine a man of Turpin's immense courage – then a reasonably happily married man into the bargain – being unable to face up to reality. It is also difficult to interpret the reactions of a man made bankrupt for over £15,000 getting yet another crushing demand (for £800) from that coldly officious body known as the Inland Revenue.

If one had to point a final damning finger in one direction, the temptation would be to accuse the Inland Revenue of being an accomplice to Turpin pulling the trigger on that fateful day. The evidence points to the conclusion that it was that official letter which proved to be the final straw as far as the former world champion was concerned.

It would also be interesting to learn whether the decision to despatch that letter rested entirely on the whim of some indifferent civil servant, or if the act was an automatic procedure of a heartless system. That, in itself, is food for thought. For Turpin is not the only person to possibly have been driven to such desperate measures by this government department. Turpin's controversial life leaves many unanswered questions, indeed. Consequently, it is virtually impossible for anyone to categorically state one specific reason for his downfall. Perhaps only Turpin himself knew the real answer.

His story may well serve as a warning to others. It may also help people to judge for themselves one of the most tragic sporting stories in British history.

One claim which should never be challenged, however, is that Randolph Turpin was Britain's most exciting fighter of the early post-war era, and ranks as one of our greatest pound-for-pound boxers ever.

And even if these claims are contested, no one can ever erase the memory of that glorious night in 1951, when he beat Sugar Ray Robinson to etch one of the greatest achievements on to the history pages of British boxing. To quote:

> *To all the sensual world proclaim,*
> *One crowded hour of glorious life*
> *Is worth an age without a name.*

These words, if nothing else, make a fitting epitaph for Randolph Turpin.

The Tragedy of Randolph Turpin
New English Library
1975
Reproduced by permission of Hodder and Stoughton Limited

Henry Cooper v Cassius Clay

George Whiting

The first Cooper–Clay contest took place at Wembley Stadium on 18 June 1963. George Whiting, whose colourful ringside reports decorated sports pages for half a century, put the most important feature of the fight into context in his introduction to his compilation of Great Fights of the Sixties:

'Henry Cooper was the first (and for at least four years the only) professional to flatten Cassius Clay for a timekeeper's count. The left hook that accomplished it became the most pictured punch for a whole decade.'

What Whiting did not say, because it was still conjecture at the time and only subsequently has been confirmed by Angelo Dundee, was that Clay's glove had been split open deliberately, in order to gain recovery time after his decking by 'Enery's 'ammer.

18 June

Henry Cooper, plasterer-turned-pugilist, heavyweight champion of Britain and the Empire, can have the Crown Jewels, Cliveden and the top of the cake if he spreads America's Cassius Clay all over the Cup final pitch tonight.

Forty thousand people inside Wembley Stadium, and a million or so outside it, will be baying for the Clay-kill . . . urging our 'Enery to turn the lights out for Cas the Gas . . . to hammer this Kentucky Rooster into unrecognisable hash . . . to zip tight the braggart Louisville Lip that has blistered us unmercifully these past few publicity-packed days.

Handsome young Mr Clay came here to boast and to boost tonight's fight to the status of a major war, and the way this slick, 21-year-old stripling has succeeded suggests there is no limit to his horizons. Good fighter or indifferent fighter, Cassius Marcellus Clay has Barnum licked to a cinder.

He could finish up managing the gaggle of millionaires who think they manage him . . . or maybe become President of the United States. Meanwhile, and simply by opening his big mouth, he has shrewdly extracted some £100,000 from British pockets, plastered a melon-wide smile on the face of promoter Jack Solomons and become the guy we all love to hate. If Henry Cooper beats him, Cain v Abel and Turpin v Robinson will begin to look like curtain-raisers.

So much for the showmanship side of this evening's conflict – with sentiment slobbering over for Cooper, but with odds of 4–1 on that referee Tommy Little will be raising the hand of Cassius Clay.

Consider this man Clay! As a gangling cruiserweight of 18, he mopped up the three best amateurs in the world – a Russian, an Australian and a Pole – to win an Olympic gold medal in Rome three years ago.

Professionally, by the devious means of quick fists and careful matchmaking, he has run through 18 heavyweights, from Tommy Hunsaker to Doug Jones – two of the only four opponents to have finished perpendicular against him.

Careful matchmaking? Sure. Some of the alleged opposition stacked against Clay could not beat Winnie the Pooh. But Alonzo Johnson (subsequently hired as Cooper's sparmate), Alex Miteff, Willie Besmanoff, Archie Moore (even at an unenthusiastic 50!) and Doug Jones are nobody's soft soufflés. Cassius dealt with them, and the manner of his fourth-round knockout of a reluctant Moore, which I saw in Los Angeles last year, was not only cocky, but efficient. Clay, to quote his dapper little trainer–coach, Angelo Dundee, is not yet a great heavyweight ready to lick Sonny Liston, and all that malarky. But a sizeable potential is undeniably there.

Clay's punches? More pep than power, I would say – but they keep coming, and their cumulative effect can be seen in the list of 14 quick casualties from Florida to California.

By contrast with the swift improvisations of quicksilver Clay, the ring-moves of Cooper are predictable – the inevitable left jab, the occasional left hook, and the too-rare right. When last did anyone see our 'Enery finish a fight with his right? Old-time pugs, it is true, were so ashamed of missing with their 'dexter' that they kept it under wraps till time and target were unmistakably ripe. But Cooper, on recent evidence, and despite constant practice in training, has become almost a miser with that right hand of his. Is it because our champion is a natural left-hander, a 'converted southpaw'? Whatever the reason, it would be almost tragic to see Cooper's right hand miss an opening through competitive rust.

Fortunately, experience lies with 36-fight Cooper, and his left hand has few superiors – if only he can get it clicking a little earlier than we have seen on some occasions. Dick Richardson, Joe Erskine and Brian London have all assured me that Henry's 'natural' left jab scrambles your grey matter when it arrives on your chin – and they should know.

On the debt side, there are Cooper's vulnerability to eye-cuts, his sometimes fragile knuckles, and the uncomfortable reminder that he can be caught cold in the early rounds. Heaven preserve us (and him) from a repeat performance of that ghastly second-round flop against Zora Folley in 1961.

There is nothing like pugilism to demolish precedent and make a prophet look plain daft. Even with only two starters, we frequently pick the wrong 'un. Yet, on the above assessments, and however much the heart leaps for pale Henry Cooper, the head says tonight's greatest, fastest, most sensational contest (see handbills) will be won by chocolate-coloured Cassius Clay. I just cannot see Cooper's left hand being permitted easy access to Clay's chin, or enough space or freedom of action to score a quick knockout. The Lip goes at too fast a clip.

Indeed, if the quiet man of Bellingham is on his feet, unmarked and with none of his English blood on public parade at the end of the ten listed rounds, I feel he will have earned a substantial bonus on his reputed 20 per cent cut of the Wembley receipts. And manager Jim Wicks, after weeks of anguished and unaccustomed silence, will be able to remind us all of the statesmanlike pronouncement he caused to be issued on battle-eve. "Enery will do 'im!' said Mr Wicks, with natural aplomb, great dignity and almost superhuman restraint.

Fancy a flutter? Bookmakers are looking for business at 4–1 on Clay with the following elaborations. Clay: evens on winning in the first five rounds; 6–4 against a win in rounds six to ten; 2–1 against a win on points. Cooper: 25–1 against winning in the first five rounds; 25–1 against a win in rounds six to ten; 7–1 against a win on points.

Personal note: Last time I reported Britain v America in a heavyweight topliner at Wembley Stadium, their Tommy Gibbons flattened our Jack Bloomfield in round three, nobody got paid, and the promoter disappeared. I do hope things have improved since 1924.

19 June

Britain's Henry Cooper, his left eye a purple mess of bruises, and at least four ugly lacerations from brow to cheekbone, will mend his hurts on holiday in Italy. America's Cassius Clay, the brashest, cockiest, flashiest fighting man ever to mock us with his fists, is already on his way home – talking a million dollars worth of world championship business against Sonny Liston.

Such was today's immediate aftermath of five frenzied rounds at Wembley Stadium, where referee Tommy Little, exercising his prerogative of mercy, rescued a half-blinded, blood-drenched Cooper from Clay's whiplash knuckles when round five was 75 seconds old.

For 13 minutes and 15 seconds we had seen and heard pretty nearly everything – high drama, low comedy, farce, blood, brass bands, back chat, cheers, jeers, wild excitement, feverish apprehension. Above all, we had seen defiant Henry Cooper thrust a brave left hook from under the crimson mist that covered his eyes to dump this young jackanapes Clay in an undignified heap on the floor.

A brief four seconds of bloodshot glory, to be followed all too soon by disaster and eclipse – exactly as forecast by arrogant young Cassius Clay from Kentucky.

Clay wasted no time whipping 30,000 Britons into a state of animosity that was almost comical. He had us on the raw from the moment he clowned his way into the ring like a pantomime king – crimson gown, golden crown, the lot. He gazed loftily upon us, he jigged around in time with the Coldstream Guards trumpeters.

We hated his guts, and we yelled our heads off when Cooper, no longer the hesitant Henry of earlier occasions, pitched headlong into battle with a left-jab fervour that had Clay beating judicious but hasty retreat. Quiet Cooper (13 st 3½ lb) was dishing it out against cocky Clay (14 st 11 lb). We could hardly believe it, and the roars rose to scream pitch when, after less than two minutes, a trickle of blood was seen to ooze from the supercilious Clay nose. Clay held, Cooper hit on the break – but nobody, I suspect, was worrying overmuch about such niceties at this lively stage of the fireworks.

Maybe only those closest to the ring could see a significant reddening under Cooper's left eye at the beginning of round two. Clay, it appeared, was missing badly with mistimed right-handers, but the warning signals were not unnoticed in Cooper's corner. While Henry was going hammer and tongs with his left hand, trainer Danny Holland was already reaching for his lotions and potions.

In round three comedian Clay went into his song and dance act. He dropped his hands, thrust his arms akimbo, pranced around and stuck out an impudent brown chin – inviting and yet defying Cooper to hit it.

'He can't fight! He's an actor!' yelled a Cooper fan.

Yet the same brown chin was nearly always pulled away before Cooper could reach it. And the blood on Clay's disdainful face was coming from another cut on Cooper's eye – a laceration that eventually widened to a two-inch gash across the brow.

Back in his corner Clay brushed aside an admonition from trainer Angelo Dundee that he should quit clowning and get down to business. But not Cassius! He had predicted that he would cut Cooper down in round five and time was not ripe for the Louisville prophet.

Instead, he continued his own private pantomime and even took time out in a clinch to demand 'Who's holding?' when referee Little ordered a break.

But Cassius got careless – and paid for it. Cooper, brushing the blood from his eye, forced his opponent to a neutral corner, unleashed a left hook to the head and had the supreme satisfaction of seeing his tormentor disintegrate on the floor.

For four of the noisiest seconds I can remember in a boxing ring, Cassius was on his pants and out of all commission. The Kentucky Rooster had laid an egg!

But the bell, and a swiftly recovering Clay, cut short our rejoicing. Pushing his man on to the stool, trainer Dundee called referee Little's attention to a split in Clay's left glove and Little ordered a replacement to be brought in time for round six.

Alas, there was no round six. For Henry Cooper there were just 75 seconds more war – 75 seconds in which the fully recovered and supremely confident Clay rained pinpoint punishment on the fountain of blood pouring from the cuts on Cooper's left eye – an ugly flow that no amount of corner repairs could have stemmed.

Tommy Little stepped between them. Courageous Cooper had given all he'd got, come near to upsetting tremendous odds, and now, inevitably, the battle was over.

Backstage, Cooper emerged from a towel to permit himself just one mild cuss word and added: 'The blood was in my eyes and I couldn't see a thing for three rounds. If only I could have caught him with that left hook a little earlier I might have licked him. Clay hurts, but I've been hit harder.'

And Clay? The Louisville Lip reclined at ease, unmarked, and graciously confessed that he had never been hit so hard in all his life. British referees, he pointed out, left something to be desired, but Henry Cooper was the toughest fighter he had ever met.

Great Fights of the Sixties
Leslie Frewin, London
1967

The Final Glory: Ali v Marciano

Everett M. Skehan, with family assistance by Peter, Louis and Mary Anne Marciano

This was the fight that never took place. It represented the ultimate challenge – the undefeated, indestructible Rocky Marciano facing the legendary ring master Muhammad Ali.

Publicity for the film of the computerised clash proudly proclaimed that all those arguments across the generations would finally be settled: 'Who was the greatest of them all?'

Sadly, it was a film that Marciano never saw. On the day before his 46th birthday in 1969, he was killed in a plane crash between Chicago and Des Moines. The pilot of the Cessna had ignored an adverse weather report and was not cleared for instrument flying. His concern was to get Marciano and his friend Frank Farrell to their destination for a public meeting. That was the journey that should never have taken place.

He was an old man for a fighter, with a bad back and 60 pounds of flab to lose as he prepared for what would be his final moment of glory in the ring. He had not fought, nor had he done any serious training, in almost 14 years. And the pain that Rocky experienced – going to the gym ever day, working on the heavy bag, sweating and running in the cool morning breeze – was as intense as any he had ever known.

It was billed as the heavyweight championship fight of the century – a battle of the supreme undefeated heavyweight kings. Muhammad Ali, also known as Cassius Clay, dancing across the giant screen in living colour to test his boxing skill against the sheer power and animal savagery of Rocky Marciano.

The computerised film version of a fight between Marciano and Ali was born in the mind of Murry Woroner, a short, chunky Miami promoter with thinning black hair, horn-rimmed glasses, and a penchant for making the big bucks. Woroner had everything going for him when he hired Ali and Marciano to make a film that summer of 1969.

Ali, who had been stripped of his title and banned from boxing because of his refusal to be drafted into the army in 1967, needed the money.

Marciano had plenty of money, but could always use more, and he truly missed the excitement and charisma of the ring wars. It was something that would enhance his image across the world. It would not be a real fight. But it was an excuse to be a fighter again, and he accepted it eagerly.

And so Rocky sweated and ran and went back into the gym to sharpen his boxing skills, skills he had not used for almost a decade and a half. They remained as imperishable as the instincts of a killer shark. It was pride, more than anything, that forced him to sweat and grunt and give up the rich Italian foods. For he trained as hard as any champion making a serious comeback, and by July 1969, he had shed almost 50 pounds, and his muscles were hard and strong. Five weeks before the crash that claimed Rocky's life, he was eager again and happy in something that just ever so slightly resembled his old stamina and physical condition.

When Rocky went to the dingy gym on the North Side of Miami Beach he was thinking tough, expecting things to go smoothly but prepared for anything. He had been briefed, knew that the punches were to be pulled, and that it would not be a real fight. But Rocky wouldn't go into the ring that way. Even at 46, he had to feel that if something went wrong, if suddenly the punches became real, he would be ready to win.

Ali seemed indifferent. He had not trained and the roll of fat round his midsection appeared larger than Rocky's bulge as they stood face to face in the makeshift ring.

The fights were filmed in secrecy, with only 20 people allowed inside the hot, dirty gym. There was more security than you'd expect to find at the White House. If word of the outcome reached the public before the film's release, Woroner's brainstorm could become a financial disaster for him.

Against a black backdrop, Ali and Rocky sweat for eight hours a day fighting one-minute rounds under the bright lights while cameras grind away miles of film. They pull the punches thrown to the head, and the body blows are like you would expect in a normal sparring session. Nobody is there to hurt or be hurt.

The ring action is filmed like a Hollywood scenario. There are trainers and a referee. The fighters grunt and groan and twist, and the sounds of leather slamming into flesh and bone are dubbed in through a special effects system. Ketchup is substituted for blood and gore, most of it poured on the scar tissue over Rocky's eye and beneath his nose, which must be bloodied by Ali's fast jabs.

Two men work the corners.

Angelo Dundee is a familiar and true figure as Ali's trainer.

Marciano's trainer is a stranger. Mel Ziegler plays the role of Charley Goldman, trainer of The Rock. Little Charley, the man with the derby hat who resembled an older Mickey Rooney, had passed away the previous November at the age of 80. Gone too was Allie Colombo, the loyal pal who had been at Rocky's side for all of his important fights. Al Weill was sick in a Miami nursing home, and died less than two months after Rocky's fatal plane crash.

Every possible situation is filmed, including seven endings, some of which show Rocky winning and others that give Ali the victory. All of this information is supposedly fed into the computer, which makes the ultimate decision.

Ali later claims he chose the ending that was finally used, in which Rocky knocks him out in the thirteenth round. It is an unimaginative carbon copy of the night Rocky, far behind in rounds, KO'd Jersey Joe Walcott in the thirteenth round to win the title.

But while the film is being made, while they punch and tug and dance for the cameras, neither fighter knows the outcome.

Rocky was a good friend of Angelo Dundee, but he had never met Ali. Angelo had often told Rocky that he'd like Ali, but Rocky didn't think so. Before they finally got together in Miami, Rocky had disliked Ali because of his public image.

'This guy likes to shoot his mouth off too much,' Rocky said. 'I know he's just trying to build up the gates, but it's not good for boxing. People don't like that kind of thing. He should do all his talking in the ring with his fists.'

But in Miami they became friends. They spent hours discussing the things that great fighters have in common. Rocky had always had much respect for Ali as a fighter, but now he discovered a different person than he had imagined, a man he could relate to completely and understand as a friend. And Ali wrote that during this filming session he became closer to Rocky than to any other white fighter.

'Muhammad acquired a lot of respect for Rocky,' Angelo Dundee recalled. 'He said Rocky was a lot harder to hit with a jab than he looked. They never really lost their tempers. A few heavy punches got thrown, but it was nothing unusual, and these guys remained friendly. There was no grudge stuff or anything like that involved. They were just trying to do the job, the best they could.'

There was a funny incident that Angelo recalled. Rocky had been fitted with a new toupée for the film. It blended perfectly with his dark hair and made him look years younger. In keeping with the new image of being well groomed and trim he was trying to project, Rocky was very fussy about the wig.

They were exchanging punches when Ali threw a jab that grazed the back of Rocky's head and picked up the toupée.

'Cut! Cut! Cut the camera!' Rocky shouted, his high-pitched voice almost in a panic. 'Watch the piece!'

Some of Rocky's friends who had been allowed to view a few of the sessions remembered Rocky's concern about his hair. 'Guy better stop messing with the piece,' Rocky said. 'You don't think he's doing it on purpose?'

'No, Rock,' his friends assured him. 'It's just an accident.'

'Well, he'd better start aiming those punches better,' Rocky said.

'Rock was really uptight about the toupée,' Dundee said. 'He had this guy in New York that made his toupées. I remember when he got the first one, *Mingia!* It was terrible. It looked like a dead cat. I said, "Rocky, watch out. That thing might get up and run away".

'Rocky was always after me to get a toupée,' Dundee said. 'Every time I saw him he'd say, "Ange, why don't you get yourself a piece?"'

'Excuse me,' Peter Marciano said, interrupting the interview. 'But isn't that a piece you've got there now, Ange?'

'No, this is my God-given,' Angelo said, patting the clump of shiny black hair that covers his crown. 'It's a little thin on top, but I go to the hair stylist once a week, and he combs it down in front for me.'

'No kidding,' Peter said, grinning.

But Rocky seemed very happy during the filming, and even though he pretended to be concerned about the outcome in conversations with Ali, he projected the old confidence of a consistent winner when around his friends.

In his autobiography, Ali suggests the entire fight is a fake, including the computer, and claims that Rocky said he felt the fight would be rigged for the benefit of the promoter and that 'the computer is bullshit'.

One thing is certain, Rocky never thought he would lose. He had refused millions to make a comeback in the ring. There was no way he would risk losing a fight to a computer for a few thousand dollars.

Angelo Dundee figured everything was done fairly. 'The intriguing thing is that nobody knew who the winner was going to be,' Dundee said. 'Muhammad wasn't told, I wasn't told, the referee wasn't told. The only guy who knew was Murry Woroner, and he wasn't telling anybody. It was done strictly by the computer. Nobody set the thing up.'

'To err is a machine,' Dundee said later, when the films showed Marciano to be the winner.

'The guy from Mississippi must have been running that machine,' Ali said jokingly, but he was boiling mad.

Rocky had already won the all-time heavyweight championship in a Woroner-sponsored radio computer tournament. Rocky had KO'd Jack Dempsey in the fifteenth round of the final bout. But Clay had been eliminated in the preliminaries by Jim Jeffries. Ali, then called Cassius Clay, ridiculed the outcome, and criticised both the computer and Jeffries, calling him the slowest, clumsiest heavyweight champ in history.

It is surprising that Ali would have even agreed to the computer fight with Marciano, having so little faith in the computer and the promoter. But he claimed he needed the money. It amounted to $999.99, according to Ali.

Rocky claimed his cut was about $10,000, and he didn't know what Ali was paid.

The fight grossed at least $2.5 million when it was shown the following January at a thousand sites in the United States and 500 in Europe and other areas, according to the *New York Times*.

A few days after the filming was completed, Rocky came into his hotel room and flopped in a chair. He was in obvious pain.

'What's the matter, Rock?' Peter Marciano said.

'My back stiffened up,' Rocky said. 'Guess I hurt it getting ready for Clay. It'll be all right, Pete.'

'How do you think you'll do in that fight?' Peter asked.

'I'm a winner in 13,' Rocky said, grinning.

'You know you won?' Peter said.

'I told you,' Rocky said. 'I take him out in the thirteenth round.'

Peter knew better than to pursue the matter beyond that point. Rocky told people only as much as he wanted them to know.

'Gee, that's great, Rock,' Peter said. 'Clay's a great fighter, but I knew you'd beat him.'

It was August now, and Rocky had tasted the last glory. He was anxious to move again. He planned trips to several cities before going to New York and then on to Brockton to visit his parents.

Following a rigorous training for the Ali fight, he was in the best physical condition he had been in for years, and he was happy.

Rocky Marciano
Rob Books, 1983

My Main Men: Ali v Spinks and Ali v Holmes

Harry Mullan

It was no surprise that Harry Mullan, whose authoritative writing on boxing has illuminated the game for so long, accurately forecast the result of the return encounter between Muhammad Ali and Leon Spinks: 'No doubt Spinks believes that what he did once, he can do again,' he wrote, 'but I'm inclined to disagree. The old master has one good fight left in him. This will be it, and I hope it's his last.'

What a pity Ali did not pay attention to those lines before, in taking on Larry Holmes to try and become world heavyweight champion for the fourth time, 'his pride made an appointment which his body couldn't keep'.

New Orleans, 15 September: Muhammad Ali, heavyweight champion of the world for an unprecedented third time, has two options open: he can quit now, with his place as the greatest of them all secure and unchallenged, or he can name his own price for a confrontation with rival WBC claimant Larry Holmes.

Even before his unanimous points win over defending WBA champion Leon Spinks had been made official, Ali was hedging on his previously declared intention to retire, win, lose or draw. 'I've got six months to think it over, and then I'll make a decision,' he told TV interviewers in the ring as he awaited the formality of the announcement.

But it's hard to see how Ali can refuse the gigantic offers he is certain to receive after a performance which ranks with the most remarkable in the history of sport. At almost 37, the old master is back on top – and as he's done so often in the past, he got there by following a fight plan which defied logic.

In Zaire, he beat George Foreman by allowing one of the hardest-hitting champions of all to punch himself into exhaustion against his arms and sides: in New Orleans, he beat Leon Spinks by doing what the experts said he could no longer do – staying on his toes and dancing his way to victory over a man 12 years his junior.

In many ways, this was his master-work.

It may have lacked the relentless ferocity of the Frazier fights, or the technical perfection of some of the pre-1967 defences, but it's the one for which he deserves to be remembered. He fought as if he wanted it to be so: there was no clowning, no talking or taunting his opponent, no rope-a-dope and no new gimmicks. He won it exactly as he'd said he would, by rolling back the years and dancing his way into legend. Trainer Angelo Dundee promised us before the fight that 'my guy's just going to get in there and do his number', and that's how it was.

He had driven himself into magnificent condition, probably his best since the third Frazier fight in Manila three years ago. The chance to become heavyweight boxing's first and surely last three-time champion provided irresistible motivation for the greatest big-occasion fight of them all.

When he lost the title on a split decision to Spinks in Las Vegas seven months ago he was slow, paunchy, and sluggish. Along with everyone else, he dismissed the unranked outsider as a no-hoper, and paid the penalty. What happened in New Orleans was what should have happened in Las Vegas; an eight-fight novice was comprehensively outboxed and out-thought by a superb ring technician who had had nearly three times as many championship fights as Spinks's total contests.

I gave Ali every one of the 15 rounds, though there were several which Spinks could have been credited with sharing. The three officials were kinder to the champion. Lucein Joubert, a local Louisiana referee who performed adequately in his first championship engagement, scored it ten rounds to Ali, four to Spinks and one even. Judge Herman Dueitriex scored 11–4 Ali, and judge Ernest Cojoe made it unanimous with a 10–4–1 score for Ali.

Scoring was on a straight round basis, with no supplementary points system, a departure from normal WBA procedure. It was the only one of the three WBA title fights on this extraordinary bill to be so scored.

Mr Joubert ordered the judges to take the fifth round away from Ali for 'holding and hitting behind the head'. He said afterwards that he had warned Ali ten times for the same offence, but neither the warnings nor the decision to penalise him the round were apparent from ringside. But Mr Joubert was much more tolerant with Ali than referee Dave Pearl had been in Las Vegas. Pearl's constant cautions to Ali about his holding and spoiling forced him to stand and fight with the younger man, and contributed to the champion's defeat.

Ali, the old con man, fights only 30 seconds of a round these days. The rest of the time he kids, holds, and fiddles, and so it was against Spinks. Whenever Spinks bulled his way inside Ali's jab, Ali denied him room to work by cupping his hand around the back of his head and pulling him close.

Ali's tactics, and Spinks's total inability to devise any effective counter to them, spoiled the fight as a spectacle. In terms of worthwhile blows given and taken, it was probably one of the dullest championships of recent years. The excitement was in the sense of the occasion, of being present at one of the great moments in sporting history.

In previous Ali fights he would dance for at least one or at most two rounds, almost in parody of the boxer he had been in his youth. Against Spinks, you watched in mounting disbelief as round succeeded round and the man was still on his toes, drawing recklessly on his reserve of energy and stamina. Of course the timing wasn't as sharp or precise as it used to be: many of the jabs fell short, and the hooks which used to curve in from impossible angles now often missed by a distance. But for a man of 36 it was a phenomenal display.

Spinks was bemused and bewildered, and couldn't work out what to do about it. He got little help from his corner, either. George Benton, former craftsman middleweight who is credited with devising the strategy which beat Ali in Las Vegas, left the corner, including even Spinks's former trainer in the Marines, who had arrived in town the day before the fight.

Benton wept tears of frustration as he said: 'I had to get out – there's too many amateurs in there.'

The confusion in the corner was another aggravation for a champion whose mind was already overburdened with problems. As predicted, the pressures involved in being the champion proved too much for him, a fact he acknowledged in his post-fight interview.

'I can't let the world bother me anymore,' he said. 'I had a lot of problems and I couldn't deal with them. My head wasn't right. My body was good, but my mind wasn't on the fight. The championship brought me a lot of problems.

'Ali wasn't any tougher than last time. I don't think he ever hurt me. I wasn't tired the whole fight. I didn't fight the way I trained. I tried to follow the plan, but it wasn't in me. But I'm not giving up. You fall down one step, you try to take two steps forward. You never keep going back.'

Spinks's problems were compounded by the arrival on the scene of one of his former Marine friends, who claimed that Spinks had made a verbal agreement with him in 1976 to let him manage him. He applied for a court order to freeze $1.25 million of Spinks's purse, which was the amount he claimed he would have earned as Leon's manager. The court order was granted on the day before the fight.

Ali was, as ever, generous to the man he had just defeated.

'Spinks is a gentleman,' he said. 'I had nothing bad to say about him before the fight, and I'm not going to start now. He could beat Larry Holmes. He's going to be the next to win the title twice.

'Will I retire? Maybe. But this was too hard to get, and I'm not gonna give it up quickly. I'm gonna rest for six, eight months and think about it. If I decide to retire I'll have a big retirement party, if not I'll fight somebody.

'There's $6 million for me to fight Holmes, and an Arab country has offered me $20 million to fight anybody I like. But I want to enjoy my title, and then I'll make a decision. I've already retired twice and unretired the next day. I don't want to hurt my credibility.

'I want to be the first black champion to get out on top. Joe Louis, Sugar Ray Robinson, Ezzard Charles, Jersey Joe Walcott – they all stayed on too long and went out as losers. I'm gonna be different.'

His whole approach to the fight was so different from last time. He looked eager and ready, and even dispensed with his customary pre-fight prayer. Instead it was Spinks who squatted for a long moment of concentration in a neutral corner before the first bell.

The pattern was set in the first 30 seconds, and it rarely varied. Spinks, gumshield bared, charged Ali to the ropes and was immediately grabbed around the back of the neck. Ali moved to the centre of the ring, keeping Spinks off with long, flicking jabs.

At the bell, Ali trudged back to his corner as if he had just completed 14 gruelling rounds, but he was on his toes and dancing again in the second. The jabs were still missing, while Bundini Brown in Ali's corner shouted: 'Get your rhythm together, champ.' Spinks spoke angrily to Ali when he was drawn into yet another clinch, and spoke to him again before the end of the round. Ali leant far over the top rope in the third, much as Jimmy Young had done against him, to deny Spinks a target, but he planted himself solidly to shake the champion with a couple of rights.

Ali was moving beautifully in the fourth and fifth, popping Spinks with jabs and sliding out of range. Spinks plodded after him determinedly, but couldn't get within punching distance. It was noticeable that whereas in Las Vegas Spinks stayed right on top of Ali when they came out of a clinch, pressuring him without let-up, this time he would take one and sometimes two paces back to allow Ali to get on the move again.

Even at this early stage it was becoming apparent that, barring a dramatic change of tactics by the champion or a sudden fold-up by Ali, the title was going to change hands. A great wave of sound swept all round the 70,000 crowd in the Superdome as the chants went up for 'Ah-li! Ah-li!', and the excitement was almost tangible.

Ali, fighting with a wide-eyed intensity, countered with right uppercuts in the sixth as Spinks charged in. Angelo Dundee had a furious verbal exchange with the referee in the corner between rounds, after Mr Joubert had spoken to Ali again about hitting and holding.

Spinks had a better seventh, getting through with thumps to Ali's sides when he pinned him against the ropes, but as always Ali had the last word. Spinks continued punching after the bell, and Ali pulled back to make him miss with a sweeping left hook and then did a cheeky shuffle and mock glower before going to his corner. It underlined what Spinks must have already known and accepted; that Ali's control of the fight was total, and that the shortest-ever tenure of the world heavyweight title, a mere seven months, was about to end.

There was more of the same in the eighth, ninth and tenth. The rounds were becoming repetitive, with nothing new from either man and the fight firmly lodged in a set pattern. Ali got the crowd going again with the shuffle in the tenth, and rocked Spinks repeatedly with rights to the head in the eleventh.

The chants swelled again in the twelfth and thirteenth as Ali jabbed steadily at the ever-advancing Spinks. They quieted briefly in the fourteenth, which all three officials credited to Spinks. For the first time both men's weariness was becoming plain, and trainer Sam Solomon was in the ring soaking Spinks with a cold sponge almost before the sound of the bell had died away. But Ali was totally unconcerned by Spinks's attempted rally, and stood nonchalantly in his corner between rounds cheer-leading the crowd.

Spinks jabbed solidly for the first time in the fifteenth and raised a small lump on Ali's forehead, but at the end the old master was still dancing and popping.

The decision was delayed for almost ten minutes while the usual ring invasion was mounted and repelled, but when it came it merely confirmed the obvious.

The amazing Ali had done it again. He had, as I predicted, got one good fight left in him – but I doubt whether at nearly 37 he could summon up the intense effort needed to whip his ageing body into such superb condition again.

I'd hate to see him go out a loser, but I fear that the multi-million dollar temptation to fight once more may prove too much. There is, too, the incentive to break Joe Louis's record of 25 title defences. For Ali, there's always one more mountain to climb.

Las Vegas, 2 October 1980: after 20 years spent achieving the apparently impossible, Muhammad Ali has finally run out of miracles.

The old maestro, bidding to become world heavyweight champion for an unprecedented and unattainable fourth time, was pounded into a humiliating corner retirement at the end of ten one-sided rounds against his former sparmate Larry Holmes.

The greatest career in the history of sport closed with an undignified scuffle between trainer Angelo Dundee, who wanted to save his man further indignation, and long-time acolyte Bundini Brown, who was pleading for 'just one more round'. Dundee had his way, and boxing owes him for that. It was painful enough to watch the destruction of a legend: it would have been unbearable to have watched him suffer the ultimate degradation of a knockout defeat.

Ali, being Ali, refuses to acknowledge the inevitable and admit that he has reached the end of the long road, but the decay of those once marvellous skills was apparent to the 25,000 crowd in the makeshift arena at Caesar's Palace car park and to the millions of TV and closed-circuit viewers around the world.

All that remained was the courage which had sustained him through three championship reigns and 60 fights against the best heavyweights that a three-decade career span could offer. To paraphrase what he used to say about some of those opponents, his pride made an appointment which his 38-year-old body couldn't keep.

Ali could shed the weight (he reduced by over three stone to 15 st 7½ lbs) but he couldn't shed the years. He was never in contention against a man who might yet emerge as the best of Ali's successors.

The veteran didn't win a single round, or even share one. It was as monotonously one-sided as Holmes's previous defences against Alfredo Evangelista, Ossie Ocasio, Lorenzo Zanon, and the rest. He absorbed a steady beating, until even Holmes himself started to hold off and plead with him to quit. 'I asked him, "Why do you keep taking this?" but he just said "Fight, sucker, fight",' the unmarked champion said afterwards.

It was a sad exit, and Ali of all people deserved better. He used to boast that he would never be forced, like Joe Louis, into an ill-advised comeback, but the temptation of an $8 million payday was too hard to resist. Holmes took the fight for $3 million, and the chance to step up at last out of the shadow of the man against whom all future champions will be compared. It was an emotional victory for the 30-year-old Holmes, who wept in the ring afterwards as he told Ali, 'I love you, man.'

'When you fight a friend and a brother you can't get happiness. All I achieved was money,' he told a packed press conference backstage. 'I fought the best heavyweight fighter in the world. Ali is a hell of a fighter and a hell of a man. He proved that he could go for the title for a fourth time, and that's a great achievement. Of course he shouldn't fight again, but how can I say he was wrong to fight this time? Nobody is wrong for doing what they want to do.

'I thought the referee should have stopped it sooner. I was trying to knock Ali out, but I couldn't. If I could have got rid of him in the first round I would have. He tried to psyche me, but he couldn't. I worked with the guy for years, and I knew everything he could do. Ali fooled some of the writers, but he couldn't fool me.'

Ali, his face bruised and puffy, did not attend the conference but said next morning that he planned to fight on, with Mike Weaver's WBA version of the title as his target. However, it is unlikely to happen. Public opinion will force him into retirement, and in any case another Ali venture would not be a commercial proposition. Boxing's great deceiver has conned the punters once too often, and they will not pay again to watch a once unmatchable talent going through the motions of fighting.

It's such a shame he couldn't have kept his word and stayed retired after that marvellous night in New Orleans two years ago when he outclassed Leon Spinks to become the first and surely last three-time heavyweight champion. I suspected that his decision was not final, and wrote in my report of the Spinks fight that 'When you're Muhammad Ali, there's always one more mountain to climb'.

But now, surely, he had climbed his last mountain. There was concern before the fight about Ali's slurred speech and physical deterioration, and the awful, sustained beating to the head that he took from Holmes will add to that concern. The fierce heat in the open air stadium took its toll on both men, but probably more so on the veteran. It was 104 degrees at ringside during the undercard (the show started at 4 p.m.) and 89 degrees by fight time. The temperature inside the ring, under TV lights, must have been considerably higher.

Ali has fought and won under trying conditions before (in the heat of Zaire, against George Foreman, and the humidity of Malaysia, against Joe Bugner) but he was a younger and fitter man then. He had driven his body into remarkable condition for a man of his age, and in terms of physical appearance he looked like the Ali of old. (He even dyed his hair to hide the grey patches.)

But he couldn't do anything about the lost years and the faded skills. The timing and reflexes were gone, and his movements were ponderous and predictable. Once or twice he tried to dance and run, in a cruel parody of the performer he once was, but Holmes chased him and hit him with jabs that would have been unthinkable in his peak years.

The only moments when it really was like the old days were during the preliminaries, with Ali clowning and conducting the crowd in booing when Holmes was introduced. He made a playful grab for Holmes's WBC championship belt, and went through his old routine of lunging at his opponent during the referee's instructions while Bundini Brown and Angelo Dundee (who, as always, looked rather embarrassed and annoyed by the play-acting) 'restrained' him.

Holmes, in absolutely magnificent condition at 15 st 1½ lbs, stood impass-ively while all this was going on but exploded into action at the first bell. He banged in a solid jab to Ali's face, a left to the body, and then two more jabs and a right to the head. Ali looked startled, and gave ground with, already, a redd-ening patch under his left eye. He kept his gloves high, but Holmes almost contemptuously curved punches around the guard to Ali's head. The crowd roared encouragement as Ali landed his first scoring punch two minutes into the fight, a long right to Holmes's head, but he didn't keep the attack going and Holmes jabbed him steadily for the rest of the round.

The fight pattern was set and it did not vary in the second as Holmes's jab kept Ali on the defensive. Ali taunted the champion, calling to him and slapping his gloves in a 'let's fight' gesture, but Holmes ignored the clowning and hit him with jab after jab. There wasn't a solitary worthwhile punch from Ali, and the round ended with him penned in a corner.

Holmes opened the third with a big right to the head, and followed with three jabs and another right, all on target. Ali tried to rally with a couple of rights and a left hook, but they were cumbersome punches and were easily evaded. Holmes kept him backed up and under pressure, and again the challenger spent the last 30 seconds of the round with his back to the ropes. Ali pulled a face at Holmes as the bell sounded, but he wasn't fooling anyone.

What most of us suspected had already been established: he simply didn't have the tools for the job any more, and even allowing for the man's one-time genius for tactical innovation it was impossible to see what strategy he could devise to save him from a defeat which was looking inevitable. Bundini Brown shouted at him during the interval: 'You've got to land some punches, champ – he's winning the rounds,' but Ali either would not or could not respond with more action when the bell sounded for the fourth.

Holmes snapped off another burst of jabs, and now that red patch under Ali's left eye was looking lumpy and bruised. Ali tried a right which Holmes blocked, and then retreated to a neutral corner. He dropped his guard to taunt Holmes again, and took a heavy right to the head. Ali grabbed the top rope with his right hand, more for clowning effect than support, and hit out at Holmes with his left. Referee Richard Green (who, under Nevada Commission practice, left the scoring to the three WBC-appointed judges) warned Ali for it, but the old veteran stayed in the corner and Holmes was picking his punches as the round ended.

Ali came out for the fifth on his toes, and the crowd whooped with delight as he caught Holmes with a left jab in the face. Holmes mocked him by doing an exaggerated sway from the waist, and then pressured him into the ex-champ's corner as Ali lacked the stamina or the legs to keep the dancing going.

Ali scored with a couple of body punches early in the sixth, but Holmes came back with a four-punch flurry before going back to the jab. The crowd booed the lack of excitement and action, and Ali responded with a fair left hook before retreating yet again into a corner. He jabbed Holmes off and moved along the ropes, but Holmes kept on top of him and the booing resumed. Ali covered up for the remainder of the round.

The seventh was a sad round, with Ali looking heavy-legged, old, and tired. Holmes once more mocked him by dropping his arms and doing a pretend stagger, and when Ali tried to dance and jab on the retreat Holmes went after him and caught him repeatedly with left to the head.

Holmes came out for the eighth looking mean and eager, and pounded heavy rights at Ali as they stood in the challenger's corner. Ali eventually escaped to the centre of the ring, and fully half a minute elapsed without either man attempting a punch. (Holmes claimed afterwards that he deliberately stood off Ali at this point, out of compassion for the man he was beating with such ridiculous ease.) Finally, Holmes moved back on the offensive and caught Ali with right after right, so many that referee Green went over to the corner during the interval to check on Ali's condition.

The ninth was a shocking round, probably the worst of Ali's long career. He was in desperate trouble on at least three occasions as Holmes landed with a whole succession of heavy rights, and by now he was noticeably marked under both eyes. At the bell Ali turned to Holmes and gave him a weary tap of acknowledgement, an admission that the fight and, indeed, his career, had gone beyond recall.

The crowd chanted Ali's name during the interval, as if sensing they were about to watch the man answer the bell for the last time. Ali sat with his eyes closed, and there was obviously anxiety in his corner. He could have pulled out then, and certainly referee Green would have had every justification for stopping it at any time during the painfully one-sided tenth round. Ali moved as if he was in a daze, and Holmes landed with every punch he threw. He seemed reluctant to move in and finish the job, and jabbed him at will throughout the round. At one stage I counted seven in a row, all landing flush on Ali's battered face.

As soon as the bell sounded Angelo Dundee turned towards Green to offer surrender, but Bundini Brown yelled at him and grabbed Dundee's white jacket to pull him away from the referee. There was a brief scuffle, while the defeated fighter sat slumped on his stool, eyes closed, but Green accepted Dundee's decision and walked towards Holmes with his arms spread wide to indicate the end.

It was a chaotic and unseemly finale to a marvellous career, but then I don't think that this is the way Ali will be remembered. As with Louis's knockout by Marciano, posterity will draw a veil over this last sad chapter in the Ali story.

The excitement, the glamour and the skills are gone, but the legend will endure.

Fighting Words
Canterbury, Colebridge Associates
1993

Teofilo Stevenson

Reg Gutteridge

There are only two boxers who have ever won three successive Olympic titles – the Hungarian Laszlo Papp, who eventually turned professional, and Cuban Teofilo Stevenson, who didn't.

On a number of occasions there were murmurs of a possible contest between Stevenson and Ali, but it never happened. When it became clear that capitalist lucre could not tempt Stevenson into the paid ranks, there was talk of an exhibition encounter. Again, it never happened.

In Reg Gutteridge's splendid book The Big Punchers, *Henry Cooper gives his view:*

> If Ali was worth a million to become a pro after the Rome Olympics, Stevenson was worth two million after he won in Munich. The thing he could do better than Ali was knock 'em out with one punch. I say he could do because it seems he's way past it now. Be silly of him to go for the fourth Olympics in Los Angeles. You could never tell if Stevenson had the temperament to become a world champion pro. He was keen to get out of the way of punches, though I couldn't blame him. But had he improved, like Ali, there is no telling how good he could have been. Yeah, terrific one-punch hitter.
>
> I bet old Angelo Dundee would have swum from Miami to Havana if he thought Stevenson would sign with him.

After Gutteridge had written this piece in 1983, Stevenson experienced a surprising renaissance and crowned his outstanding career with a world super-heavyweight gold medal at Reno in 1986.

He made pro promoters eat their hearts out. The picture heavyweight. Height, weight, handsome and, undoubtedly, the hardest punch of all amateur heavyweights. But Teofilo Stevenson preferred to be red than rich. Britain might have called him the one that got away. Had Teo's poor stevedore father followed the customary West Indian emigrant's route to England from St Vincent instead of seeking work in Havana's dockyards, we could have boasted the first 'British' world heavyweight champion since Bob Fitzsimmons left Cornwall in 1897, emigrated to New Zealand, and became champion.

Stevenson's grandfather was English – hence the name. Teo became Fidel Castro's 'pillar of the Revolution' in the western hemisphere's first Communist regime, and was duly voted a seat in the Cuba National Assembly for his home state of Orientes, where the marvellous professional welterweight champion, José Napoles, was born.

Bachelor Stevenson is boxing's best record big fellow. Three times Olympic champion, twice world amateur champion, twice Pan-Am Games champion. At 32, the Belafonte in boxing gloves is being pressured into producing the unthinkable by winning a fourth Olympic crown – a span of 12 years – in Los Angeles in 1984. ('About 28 is the best age for heavyweights,' he says.)

Six feet four inches, nearly 16 stone, upright with a sporting-print stance, slightly knock-kneed, a pose with palms down, Stevenson has the most devastating delayed-action power I have seen. At long range he seemed invincible. He boxed with a patient arrogance, seemingly bored by the proceedings, pawed often with a reconnaissance left and was able to drop a right hand on an opponent's chin with time-bomb effect. Sometimes the shocked receiver would turn away, then collapse as though wondering how the bolt from the blue had landed without warning.

I reported all Stevenson's Olympic bouts, not all epic, but comparable to watching a man weaving his way through a minefield and waiting for the blast. I know a bit about that. In Munich in 1972, the games wrecked by the appalling murder of some Israeli competitors and coaches, Stevenson, at 20, was superb. Inevitable comparisons were made with Muhammad Ali, Olympic champion in Rome 12 years earlier. But Ali weighed inside the light-heavy maximum of 12 st 10 lbs, was 18, and three of his four wins (all against the best opposition) were settled on points.

Stevenson simply poleaxed rivals. Team-mates called him the Doc because he operated with a surgeon's care. Rarely a rash move. He began at 16, coached by a Russian imported for Cuba's ring challenge in the medal-chasing world. Castro had banned professionalism as a decadent West's commercial enterprise, despite the outstanding success in America of Napoles, Kid Gavilan and Sugar Ramos. Stevenson was, and presumably still is, a totally dedicated disciple of the regime which believes in sport, realises its importance and fêtes its champions.

'I don't believe in professionalism,' said Stevenson, 'only in revolution. I tell these men from America, the promoters, that money means nothing to me. What is $8 million against eight million Cubans who love me? All they care about is dollars. The boxer does not matter.' A party line, incidentally, that would not be supported by many champions who climbed out of poverty with the only qualification they had – a punch.

Stevenson paraded around the Olympic village in Munich (it was easier to obtain press visits to Dachau camp than entry into the athletes' pen) reminiscent of Ali in Rome. Ali had lost in his unpaid days, including to Louisville friend Jimmy Ellis, and Stevenson's pride was stunned losing a debatable 3–2 judges' vote to red-haired Duane Bobick, an American sailor, in the Pan-Am Games.

The scene was set for Stevenson's revenge. Big-heart Bobick, who led the US team in training with commendable enthusiasm, began by eliminating a Russian. The Cuban countered, dropping his right-hand anaesthetiser on the chin of a Pole. Regrettably, the big rivals were drawn in the same section. They clashed in the quarter-final. I recall Bobick telling me, 'He couldn't have improved that much. I beat him once, I can do it again.'

Stevenson and his coaching counsel had done their homework well. He speared the US quartermaster with a series of destructive left hands, often ripped weakening blows to the body, and bided his time releasing the right. In the third round, when Stevenson considered Bobick ripe for picking, he fired the deadly weapon. Bobick took two counts and the crowd yelled for a stoppage. He was bruised, bleeding and reduced to a walk. After one minute 40 seconds the referee moved in and the new star was born.

In the semi-final Stevenson clobbered a strong and capable West German, Peter Hussing, breaking his nose with his bolt fists. He then became the first Olympic heavyweight to collect his gold medal with a walkover final. He kissed the medal, gave it to his trainer and was the winner of the Games' Val Barker best-style trophy. Ion Alexe, of Rumania, had broken a thumb winning his semi-final.

Hereby hangs a tale. ABC TV decided to move a commentary position at extra cost from the television row in the first section of the stand (press and television are not normally seated close to the ring at Olympic events). It cut them off from some information. I heard ABC's announcer, Howard Cosell, previewing the appearance of the Cuban wonder boy. There was a surprise when I informed him that Alexe had withdrawn. The Rumanian's hand had a plaster cast. An X-ray of his broken thumb was available for inspection in the medical room. There were ridiculous slurs from the American crew, obviously upset that viewer-puller Stevenson would make only a formal appearance in the ring, that Alexe had faked an injury. Having frequently watched Alexe on the amateur international circuit, I was equally angered by the insinuation. Alexe had certainly not shown fear fighting Herculean George Foreman in the Mexico Games four years earlier.

He who laughs last . . . Alexe went to South America to box Stevenson in a club event. And he won! 'I was not myself for the contest. I am not complaining,' said the golden boy. The result was the biggest turn-up of the time and many newspapers did not publish it because they thought the result had been wrongly wired by the news agencies.

It was defeat by Alexe, Bobick, a clobbering by Cuban compatriot Angel Milan, a novice at the time, plus a KO by Russian Igor Vyssotsky, who did not appear at the Olympics, that created doubts when considering the pro potential of Stevenson. Frankly, I doubted if he could have hit a peak Ali on the backside with a bag of rice. He frequently lacked the desire which gameness demands. He seemed a looking-glass boxer. None the less, he more than matched Frazier, Foreman, Ali and Holmes for lethal hitting. The punch could have overcome deficiencies.

The first world championships were invented for Cuba, 1974. (Britain has not competed.) The sunshine punch-ups were the stage for Stevenson, with television monitors hung on street corners in Havana, the traffic halted when the hero was in action. Alexe, the branded runaway, turned up again. But he was eliminated by German Hussing who, in turn, was duly thrashed in the first round by Stevenson. In the final, America's Marvin Stinson, a solid journeyman later to become a sparmate for Frank Bruno, forced Stevenson to fight a full three rounds.

In Montreal in 1976, maturing Stevenson reached peak. A Sengalese, who did not belong in the same event as the Cuban, was KO'd. Again the right proved might. A Finn could not last a round. Then Stevenson showed the world, via the inquisitive television lens, the power that proved him the amateur game's greatest. Big John Tate, from Tennessee, staggered like a bull taking a few seconds to feel the pain of the matador's sword as he reeled back to a corner, slumping slowly to the canvas, when the Cuban clobbered him with one punch. Tate's chin subsequently proved susceptible to big hitters, like Mike Weaver and Trevor Berbick, but he also won the WBA heavyweight title. It showed that Stevenson had the form to become a king in the commercial world.

In Belgrade, Yugoslavia, in 1978, Stevenson yawned his way to a second world series gold with three of four bouts failing to finish. Then Moscow, in 1980, and cracks finally appearing in the Cuban's make-up. He had been injured when a stove blew up. Training had always been a chore, but the double medallist had sufficient skill from memory, backed by the reliable chiller punch, to come good again.

The Games that propagandists tried to convince us were designed to display Soviet mastery were certainly wrong at the boxing arena. The Cubans were the stars and Stevenson was virtually a bit player among them. Russia won only one gold medal, at light-flyweight, and that by a 3–2 verdict. We sadly missed the competition of the Americans in Moscow. (The refusal to compete by many countries because of the Russian invasion of Afghanistan is an issue of personal opinion. I disagree with politics influencing sport; Games have taken place when other nations, including Britain and America, were 'in conflict' – the modern soft-pedal words for war. The protest made no visible mark on Russia's conflict with her neighbours and while sport was barred there was no stoppage of commercial trading. Total hypocrisy. Perhaps actor Peter Ustinov is right when he says Russia is always regarded as the enemy of the West, but history has never shown it.)

Stevenson, as expected, starred in the final bout of a well-organised event when, for a change, there were few controversial decisions. I witnessed every blow of 262 bouts. It was left to a Nicaraguan judge, now probably holding a ticket to obscurity, to vote against Stevenson in his bid for a third gold against rolypoly Zaev, of Russia, chosen for his strength and awkwardness to compete against the Cuban. The Soviet squad surely had sharper boxers, but Zaev was designed to give the Cuban a hard workout. He did. Three judges marked the Cuban a winner by only one point. Much of his golden glory was tarnished. But you can't knock success.

It was time for Stevenson to retire. I was convinced Moscow was his last stand. Instead, they wheeled the great man out for the world championships in Munich in 1982, and he was humbled by so-so Italian Francesco Damiani, outpointed 5–0. The bout, expected to be shown in continual rerun on British television was, in fact, blacked out because the ring was plastered with advertising. So a limited world audience saw the downfall of Stevenson. It was a face-saver. If Stevenson is pushed to compete in Los Angeles he can genuinely be compared with Ali, who was sadly encouraged to fight when he became an embarrassing shadow of himself. The slide continued on June 1983, losing in Santiago, Cuba, to the Soviet's Alex Krupkin.

The Big Punchers
Stanley Paul Co. Ltd.
1983

Laszlo Papp

Norman Giller

In this case, the ideological hang-up lay with the state rather than the individual. Laszlo Papp was a professional boxer until he was stopped from continuing his trade.

As he looks out from his house on the hill in Buda, across the flowing Danube and over the symmetrical skyline of Pest, he must wonder what might have been. The goal was within his sights, a world championship challenge in the offing, only for the cruel curtain to come down. Were they afraid he might lose?

Laszlo Papp is a legendary figure in boxing because of his feat of becoming the first man to win three successive Olympic titles. He then became the first 'Iron Curtain' boxer to be allowed officially to turn professional, and was undefeated and ready to challenge for the world middleweight title when the Hungarian government suddenly barred him on the grounds that his newly won wealth was not compatible with his country's socialist principles. How Laszlo must wish that glasnost had come 25 years earlier!

Papp, a stocky, compact southpaw with a lethal left hook, started boxing as an amateur in Budapest in the last year of the Second World War and was coached by national team trainer Zsiga Adler – 'Uncle' Zsiga, Laszlo used to call him. He came to London in 1948 to capture his first Olympic Games gold medal at middleweight, outpointing Britain's Johnny Wright in the final. I took part in the 1952 Olympics in Helsinki and saw Papp boxing beautifully to win the light-middleweight title. This was a newly introduced division. If he had defended his middleweight championship he would have come up against a young American called Floyd Patterson. What impressed me most about Papp was the accuracy of his punches. He was happiest when counter-punching but could also be the aggressor when it suited him, and he rarely wasted a single punch.

Dissatisfied with his token job as a librarian, Laszlo already had the taste to become a professional, and when he approached the Hungarian authorities he was told they would consider his request only if he won a third gold medal in the 1956 Olympics in Melbourne. Papp duly did his duty, outpointing future world light-heavyweight champion José Torres for his record hat-trick.

The Hungarian authorities, picking up the pieces after the 1956 uprising, dragged their heels when Laszlo pressed for his right to become a professional. They finally gave in on the understanding that his wife, Erszebet, and 11-year-old son remained in Budapest while he based himself in Vienna, starting a paid career at the age of 31.

For many years Papp had suffered from brittle bones in his hands, but this did not stop him punching his weight and in eight years as a professional he stopped 15 of his 29 opponents. He won the European championship in 1962 by stopping Dane Chris Christensen in seven rounds, and over the next three years only British champion Mick Leahy managed to stay the course with him.

Papp, a handsome man with a distinctive moustache and crinkly black hair, was being lined up for a shot at the world title held by Brooklyn's Joey Giardello when the Hungarian government suddenly lowered the iron curtain on him. They played on his national pride and pointed out that it was bad for the morale of his countrymen to see him flaunting his riches while they were working conscientiously for the good of Hungary.

Knowing that he could not get his wife and son out of Budapest, Papp reluctantly retired at the age of 38 and became the national team coach. He had never been beaten as a professional and lost just 12 of 230 amateur contests. In another time and another place, I am convinced he would have become an outstanding world professional champion.

Henry Cooper's 100 Greatest Boxers
Macdonald Queen Anne Press
1990

Mighty Man with a Mean Streak: Carlos Monzon

Bob Mee

Even with the satellite technology of today, with few exceptions the heroes of the fight game in Central and South America tend to be remote figures. One who broke through that invisible barrier with his unbreakable force in the ring and his flagrancy out of it was the master middleweight from Argentina, Carlos Monzon.

That most knowledgeable writer on the fight game, Bob Mee, gives a typically comprehensive summary of Monzon's life at the time of his death in 1995.

Ray Robinson, Marvin Hagler, Carlos Monzon . . . rate them where you will. Old-timers may have added Harry Greb or Stanley Ketchel, but these men were the élite middleweights in history.

After last Sunday's car crash that killed Monzon at the age of 52, only Hagler is left. Greb and Ketchel died young, Robinson's last years were spent as a prisoner to Alzheimer's. This could be said to be the most tragic division of all.

Monzon, a hard, occasionally violent man from a poor background, was demonstrably the best middleweight in the world from 1970 until 1977, yet was more than that. Partly because he could never be accused of a monastic attitude to his craft, he was also one of the most popular boxers South America has ever produced.

'Monzon was always Monzon,' said Argentine boxing writer Carlos Irusta in 1990, after the great champion was jailed for the murder of his lover Alicia Muniz. 'Living in the fast lane, attending parties, driving a Mercedes, always the centre of attention in magazines and on television programmes.'

Truly, he was an extraordinary athlete, one of the leading sporting heroes of his generation. In the ring he was grim, expressionless, cold, his personality understated. Out of it, he was usually jovial, readily quotable, every inch the 'machismo' hero. Maybe it was his ruthless, almost mechanical, efficiency that appealed to the rest of us.

He was deceptive and cunning. He appeared to do nothing exceptionally well and yet dealt with every world-class opponent who was put in front of him until his retirement after the second Rodrigo Valdes fight in 1977. He lost only three points decisions, all before the end of 1964, and was unbeaten in the last 82 of his 101 professional fights.

Yet for all his greatness as a fighter, history will always remember the tragedy of a man who spent the last five years of his life serving a jail sentence for the murder of Alicia Muniz, the woman who bore him his son Maximillano and whose ultimate reward was to fall to her death from the balcony of Monzon's Mar del Plata home on Valentine's Day, 1988.

Monzon, who also toppled over as a result of whatever struggle took place and suffered minor arm injuries, said it was an accident. However, medical evidence revealed that before she fell to the concrete below Muniz had received substantial pressure injuries to her neck and was unconscious before she hit the ground.

While Monzon never admitted murder, he did acknowledge: 'Me and my bad temper are the ones really responsible. Yes, my bad temper.'

The case made sensational reading in South America. A thousand people crammed into the courtroom to hear three judges hand down a unanimous guilty verdict on 3 July 1989. A thousand more milled around outside.

Monzon was jailed for 11 years, but at the time of his death was on a permitted home visit, pending parole, and was driving on a country road near Santa Fe, the teeming city on the banks of the Panama river where he spent his childhood. Nobody really knows what happened.

He was driving back to the Las Flores prison when the car left the road and overturned near the town of Santa Rosa de Clachines, 25 miles out of Santa Fe. His friend, Geronimo Motura, also died and a woman survivor, Alicia Guadalupe Sesia, was driven to hospital by a local farmer.

It was a sudden end to a strong, remarkable life. There was time as a boy spent selling newspapers, shining shoes and delivering milk, but his youth was wild, undisciplined and sometimes beyond the law.

Once he was jailed for starting a riot at a football match; another time for brawling on a bus. He ran a string of whores.

Eventually, police interest persuaded him to flee to Brazil until the heat died.

At a Christmas party in 1967, he allegedly hit a photographer and damaged the man's eye. At other times he was accused of beating up men at his mother-in-law's house, a discotheque and a casino.

His first wife, Beatriz Mercedes Garcia, by whom he had three children, signalled the end of their volatile relationship by shooting him. One of the bullets stayed in his back for the rest of his days.

After the long-suffering Beatriz came the actress Susana Gimenez, with whom he made a film. Their parting more or less coincided with his relinquishing of his world title in 1977. Then at an airport in 1979, he met the ill-fated Alicia Muniz, a Uruguayan model. Their relationship was always stormy and, in the end, tragic.

Monzon had been playing host to six-year-old Maximillano when Muniz came from Buenos Aires to collect him. Although she had a hotel room booked, she decided to stay with Monzon for the night. They went out to a nightclub, returning in a taxi at 5 a.m., apparently kissing like young lovers in the cab. By 5.30 a.m. the passion had boiled over into the incident which left Muniz dead and Monzon disgraced and deprived of his freedom.

And yet during his peak years, somehow, out of all this chaos, came a truly legendary fighter who held the world middleweight title for seven long years and through 15 championship contests.

It took the boxing world a long time to catch on to him: 81 professional fights, to be precise. It seems crazy now that when he travelled to Rome in November 1970 to challenge the Italian, Nino Benvenuti, he was given little chance. Of course, this was the age before video, before satellite.

Monzon was upset at the weigh-in, when he claimed Benvenuti 'touched my ass . . . I looked at him and thought "Tonight, I will kill you". When the referee stopped the fight he was correct. That night I would have killed Benvenuti.'

In a chilling rematch on a soccer pitch in Monte Carlo in May 1971, Benvenuti lasted only three rounds. 'I wanted to die,' he said.

This week Benvenuti paid tribute: 'As a boxer his strength was unstoppable . . . he was a real champion and always defended with honour the title he had taken from me. We had become friends following my retirement. I'm upset. It's terrible. It's a piece of my life, a piece of sport history that ended with him.'

He accumulated his reputation, as great champions generally do, by systematically proving he was better than the rest of his generation.

Emile Griffith, Benvenuti's predecessor, was tipped to beat him. In Buenos Aires in September 1971, Monzon stopped Griffith in the fourteenth round.

Denny Moyer furiously protested his fifth-round defeat in Rome in March 1972 and then Jean-Claude Bouttier fought out a classic with Monzon in Paris in June. The champion won in the thirteenth.

The Dane Tom Bogs was overpowered easily in Copenhagen and then Monzon earned $100,000 as Bennie Briscoe, the fearless, ferociously tough Philadelphian was cleverly outpointed in Luna Park, Buenos Aires, in November 1972.

Emile Griffith bitterly disputed the verdict when he was unanimously outpointed in Monte Carlo in June 1973, but Monzon, who had weighed in first at 11 st 9 lbs and then run three miles to shift the excess, won the fight with his strength over the last five rounds. Officially it was by two-, three- and four-point margins. And it was another $100,000 payday.

Even then Monzon was talking about retirement, but he plugged on, outlasting Bouttier in a rematch that went the distance in Paris in September 1973. A crowd of 13,000 went to see it.

José Napoles was one of the finest welterweights in history, but his step up to meet Monzon, although lucrative, was ill-advised. In February 1974, Monzon manhandled him. After six rounds a bloodied Napoles was pulled out by Angelo Dundee, who described Monzon as 'the complete fighter . . . he can box, he can hit, he can think, and he is game all the way'.

After the fight Monzon was fined $10,000 by the WBC for refusing to give a urine sample. Then they stripped him for failing to meet number one contender Rodrigo Valdes within 90 days of the Napoles fight. They matched Valdes and Briscoe for the vacant title. Valdes won, but was never considered a viable alternative to Monzon who, by now, had the total respect of the trade.

Tony Mundine, the big-hitting but fragile-chinned Australian, was next to try to dethrone him in front of 25,000 adoring Argentine fans in Luna Park in

October 1974. He lasted into the seventh round, it seemed because Monzon carried him for six of them.

Monzon fulfilled an ambition by boxing in Madison Square Garden in June 1975, stopping American challenger Tony Licata in ten rounds. And then in a final trip to Paris, he blew away Gratien Tonna in five.

Before he retired, he knew he had to meet the only real threat to his supremacy – Valdes. In the Louis II football ground and for a payday of $250,000 in June 1976, Monzon used his experience to outwit and outlast the WBA champion. The 15-rounds decision was unanimous.

After making a film with Susana Gimenez in Rome, in which he played a violent lawman, Monzon closed his career by meeting Valdes again, in Monte Carlo in July 1977. Again he won on points, but this time he had to get off the floor to do it.

He knew that at almost 35 he was fading rapidly. And after 101 fights, he walked away to a life of ease.

In retirement, daytime usually found him in a card school with old men in a Buenos Aires bar. He spent his nights in clubs. Business deals didn't work out, and his drinking increased as time went by, but he was by no means broke or down on his luck.

Then came that terrible few minutes that led to Alicia Muniz's tragic death and the incarceration of a great athlete and a flawed man.

French movie star Alain Delon, his friend since the great years in Paris in the middle '70s, said: 'Carlos was always an honourable man, exceptionally strong as a boxer, a kind of a beast in a pure, savage state. All his friends knew his final days would be tragic. I am upset. It's like I lost a part of my life.'

Argentine President Carlos Menem and Diego Maradona also paid their respects.

Osvaldo Bisbal, president of the Argentine Boxing Federation, called him 'one of the most extraordinary boxing champions of all times . . . he will be sorely missed'.

Perhaps the most eloquent statements were expressed by the silent line of mourners who waited for hours in fierce heat to file past his open coffin at Santa Fe Town Hall and catch a last glimpse of one of the greatest fighters in history.

Boxing News
13 January 1995

Lord of the Ring: Julio Cesar Chavez

Greg Logan

In a way, Julio Cesar Chavez had been Monzon's lower-weight successor during the 1980s and early 1990s. One of four boxing brothers, he learned his craft the hard way with eight bouts in his first year and 14 in the second, all of which he won by knockouts.

Chavez is a prowling, pressure fighter and has won world championships at three weights and been involved in more battles at that level than anyone else. Subsequent to Greg Logan's report Chavez has reached 100 bouts, although his immaculate record has been slightly tarnished by a couple of defeats.

Julio is coming.

Word goes out through the narrow streets of the meat-packing district, where the air is pungent with the aroma from just-butchered sides of beef and dripping wet bushel baskets of freshly plucked chickens being loaded into delivery trucks under the noonday sun. In no time at all, parents carrying toddlers, labourers in dusty work clothes and teenaged street peddlers find their way to Gimnasio Nuevo Jordan, where they climb five flights of stairs to the boxing gym to await the arrival of Julio Cesar Chavez, the man who fights for all of Mexico.

Ordinarily, Chavez trains in the small village of Temoaya, which is 11,800 feet above sea level on the side of a rugged mountain called Xinantecatl, where the Otomi Indians worship a huge monument to the weather gods that rule the harvest. Or, he works out in nearby Toluca, an industrial centre south of Mexico City, where American corporations – including Chrysler, DuPont, Nestlé and Pfizer – have relocated to take advantage of the low wage scale for Mexican workers.

But on this early August day, Chavez is coming down from the mountains to touch base with the people and to promote his fight with American Parnell Whitaker, 10 September, in San Antonio. At stake is Whitaker's World Boxing Council welterweight championship and the undisputed title of best pound-for-pound fighter in the world. Without question, the latter designation currently belongs to the 31-year-old Chavez, whose 87–0 record and 13-year undefeated span is unmatched in boxing history. In that time, Chavez has scored 75 knockouts and never been knocked off his feet.

That is why Chavez is the most worshipped sports icon in a land that treats its gods with great reverence. At Gimnasio Nuevo Jordan (pronounced new-wave-o hoar-don), there are two shrines, though on a much more humble scale than the ancient structure at Temoaya. One is the photo gallery, featuring Salvador Sanchez, the world featherweight champion who died in an alcohol-related auto accident in 1982, and Chavez, who succeeded Sanchez in the hearts of the Mexican people.

The other equally traditional shrine is a picture of the Virgin Mary located directly above the mirror boxers face while choreographing their ring ballet. The Madonna is framed in blue neon with a red neon crown glowing above her bowed head. Three small potted cactus plants are mounted on the wall to each side and below the picture. Believing they can reach greater heights if blessed by the Virgin, Mexican boxers sometimes make offerings to the shrine in this temple of sweat.

As Chavez batters his sparring partners for six rounds, he is watched closely by the other young boxers, many of whom don't have enough money to purchase proper boxing shoes and instead wear simple tennis shoes and hiking boots to train. To these hopefuls, Chavez is the living embodiment of their dreams and prayers, the boxer who escaped the poverty that shapes the Mexican landscape.

Finishing his workout with a shadow-boxing session under the neon Madonna, Chavez answers a few questions from television reporters and then goes back to the seclusion of the mountains. The next day in Toluca, while watching TV coverage of the Pope's visit to Merida, he explains through an interpreter why boxers are so important in Latin cultures as symbols of both hope and suffering.

'Most people in my country come from humble homes,' Chavez said. 'They see boxing as the great escape to fame and fortune. In reality, few attain it because it is a very difficult sport.'

Chavez is the blessed one who climbed over all the bodies in the notoriously macho Mexican boxing wars to reach the top of the pyramid. He will make $5 million for the Whitaker fight, which is his largest purse and is $2 million more than welterweight champ Whitaker will receive. There was a time when Chavez was grateful for a plate of rice and beans. Now, his favourite food is sushi, but he hasn't lost touch with the essential hunger that drove him to such heights.

'No matter how much I triumph, I will continue to be the same person. I can't change my roots because of fame and fortune,' he said. Although he is aware that he always carries the hopes of the Mexican people, Chavez added; 'When I enter the ring, I am fighting for myself. At times I think of Mexico and pictures of my children come up in my mind, but basically, I'm thinking of myself. There's pressure, but I try to relax and concentrate so I will not lose what I've gained.'

It is only in the past three years that Chavez's purses for major fights have reached seven figures, but over the course of his long career, he has maintained an average of one fight every two months. In the beginning, his only goal was to take care of a family that included six other brothers and three sisters. With his first significant pay cheque he bought his mother, Isabel, a washing machine. As his wealth grew, he was able to subsidise small business interests and to buy houses and cars for everyone in his family and to eventually provide jobs for many of his cousins, friends and relatives of his wife, Amalia.

Chavez himself owns 19 cars, including three limousines, a Jaguar and a Lamborghini, and he has gotten into real estate development, constructing two major office buildings, four gas stations (with another four to come) and about 15 homes, as well as buying property in the United States. Each of his three sons, Julio Jr. (seven), Omar (three) and Christian (one), is set for life as a millionaire with homes, stocks and college funds.

In recent years, Chavez has expanded the boundaries of his generosity to include his native town of Culiacan and several Mexican charities. He has plans to build a 3,000-unit, low-income project in Culiacan, where he has established a food programme that provides bags of rice, beans, flour and corn to poor families. In between title fights, Chavez fights benefit bouts against lesser opponents in towns throughout Mexico and turns the entire purse over to charity. He has contributed approximately $5 million to charity in the past two years, according to a close associate.

'You have to be able to give when God has given you so much,' said Chavez, who describes his religious faith as meaning 'everything' to him.

As a youth, his family was not so blessed. His father, Rodolfo, was a railroad worker, and the family lived in an old caboose until they could afford to move into a small two-bedroom flat in Culiacan, a place widely viewed as a *bandido* town because the major industry seems to be illegal drugs and murder. Chavez's mother did ironing for others, which pained little Julio, who was the closest of all to his mother. He worked selling gum and newspapers on the streets and gave the money to his mother for food. She called him 'little father' because of his determination to help provide for the family.

'I told my mother, as long as we had rice and beans, I would be happy,' Chavez recalled.

When he wasn't working, Chavez played constantly at soccer, baseball, running and boxing. Some thought his future was in soccer, but he displayed a special passion for boxing at an early age. His older brothers, Rodolfo Jr. and Rafael, were top amateur boxers, but whenever they lost, little Julio would be furious with them.

'I got very angry and said I would never let anyone beat me,' Chavez said. 'I told them I would be one to be undefeated.'

Chavez was 16 years old when he quit school to train full time. For two years he fought in local matches where the winner got maybe $5. After turning professional, it took Chavez four and a half years and 44 fights to win the vacant WBC super-featherweight title over Mario Martinez with the fortieth knockout of his career in 1984.

Although he followed the footsteps of his older brothers to the ring, Chavez relied on natural ability and heart once he got there. He's not the product of a great mentor. There's no Eddie Futch or Ray Arcel in his corner. Cristobal Rosas, a squat man barely taller than a ring-post, is Chavez's nominal trainer. Daniel Castro supervises Chavez's aerobic conditioning and has no boxing expertise.

In short, Chavez is the sum product of everything he has learned in his 87 fights. He combines the courage and vicious body-punching ability of a Roberto Duran with the intuitive intellect and relentless pursuit of an Alexis Arguello. He never goes into the ring with a specific fight plan, preferring instead to analyse his opponent on the spot and react.

A granite chin and an unusually thick skull are the secret to his ability to withstand the punishment of 87 fights. For that, he thanks the genes he inherited from his father, Rodolfo, who left the family when Chavez was 16.

'It's a gift from my dad,' Chavez said. 'He was a very strong man. My talent is natural. I have never studied boxing. I can't explain it, but God has blessed me. No one has been able to hurt me yet.'

Chavez has won some close, even disputed, decisions, but he has been in grave danger of losing only once in 87 fights – against Meldrick Taylor on St Patrick's Day in 1990. And then he dug down and produced a miracle that stands as his defining moment.

Trailing on two of three judges' cards entering the twelfth round of a slugfest that had raged from pillar to post, and knowing he needed a knockout, Chavez nailed Taylor with a short right that came from the depths of his soul with 12 seconds left in the fight. Taylor collapsed in a corner of the ring but, using the ropes, pulled himself up. Unaware of the time remaining but seeing a man out on his feet, referee Richard Steele stopped the bout with two seconds left.

One of Chavez's sisters, Perla, told one interviewer Julio once said to her that, in his moment of need, he thought of his dead brother, Omar, who was run over at the age of four by a drunk driver 14 years ago. Chavez named his second son after Omar, but the scar never has healed and he now refuses to talk about the source of his inspiration against Taylor.

Admitting he was bothered by Taylor's hand speed, Chavez said, 'I was aware I was behind, but once I knocked him down, I knew I had won. Taylor was severely injured during the fight and at the end. If you looked at our faces, it was Taylor who was swollen. He was completely knocked out. If not for the ropes, he would have stayed down. It was the most spectacular fight of my career, a great fight. I don't think Taylor has been the same since.'

Like so many of Chavez's opponents, Taylor was the victim of a body attack that left him hospitalised after the fight. Former heavyweight champion Mike Tyson once boasted of how he tried to drive an opponent's nose into his brain. Chavez is more succinct, describing his target in one word: 'liver'.

His approach won't change against Whitaker (32–1, 15 knockouts). Chavez expects Whitaker's footwork, speed and awkward southpaw style to present problems, and the Taylor fight taught him not to take winning for granted.

'I know that I could lose at any time,' Chavez said. 'I'm a human being. But I prepare with great conscience.'

While he respects Whitaker's talent, Chavez doesn't believe Whitaker could be the one to beat him. He said Whitaker's punch isn't as strong as Taylor's, and he doesn't see how Whitaker can win by dancing away from him.

'For this fight, I have to be the controlling factor,' Chavez said. 'All southpaws are difficult, but I'm preparing like it's a crossword puzzle. Don't worry. I'll find him in the ring. No matter what, I will force him to fight with me.'

Whitaker has said he plans to 'play to the crowd' and to 'frustrate' Chavez by using his slick, showboating moves, his trademark deep squats and sideways spins that leave opponents jabbing air. Whitaker's tactics may resemble Sugar Ray Leonard's taunting antics that caused Roberto Duran to quit in their second fight and the tap-dancing style Leonard used to dazzle the judges in his victory over Marvellous Marvin Hagler.

Upon learning of Whitaker's statements, Chavez permitted himself a belly laugh. He understood Duran's frustration in the '*no mas*' fight, but Chavez vowed not to chase Whitaker 'like a crazy man'. He said Whitaker can't do what Leonard did to Hagler because he lacks Leonard's reach and power.

'I'm a man with a great deal of experience,' Chavez said. 'Whitaker's not getting hold of a small child. He can't spank me, as he expects. He's going to have to fight. I'll be throwing punches from the point of his toes to the top of his head. He can't play with Julio.

'What he must remember is that he's fighting a man with an 87–0 record. I'm not to be taken lightly.'

When he said it, Julio Cesar Chavez, a fighter blessed by the Virgin Mary and worshipped by a nation, made it sound like a threat. Julio is coming. Watch out.

Sports, NY
New York Newsday
22 August 1993

Fire and Fear: Mike Tyson

José Torres

Nobody is better placed to give this short perceptive assessment of the once impregnable and turbulent Mike Tyson than José Torres. Torres has known Tyson since the latter was 12 and he was also trained by Cus D'Amato on his way to becoming world light-heavyweight champion.

Now an acclaimed author, Torres wrote these words as a kind of codicil to his definitive study of Tyson in 1989. Much has happened since, as all who follow boxing are aware, but the tenor of Torres's remarks remains as true today as when it was written.

Every now and then, pictures of Tyson and his life run uncontrollably through my head. The savage childhood, the perverse boyhood, the spoiled adolescence, the crazy adulthood. The deaths of his mother, his mentor, his manager, and his marriage. He didn't have a fighting chance.

When Cus D'Amato first saw Tyson in action, his heart pounded with euphoria. He saw the raw anger, the determination to inflict pain, the will to win, the lack of grace and tolerance, the meanness and the so-called killer instinct. No true boxing man could've asked for more. Cus took this kid's ghetto instincts and honed them. He didn't take Tyson away from his blood family; he took him away from the street, reform school, and a possible premature death.

But when Cus and Jimmy Jacobs died, Tyson became an orphan. His civilising influences were no longer around. People trying to survive in the street often say they have no friends, just acquaintances. If Tyson was not the undisputed heavyweight champion of the world, worth untold millions of dollars, would 1989 have found Don King constantly at his side?

In Tyson's last fight as of this writing, a scheduled 12-rounder against Great Britain's Frank Bruno on 25 February 1989, the champion had Aaron Snowell as his trainer, Jay Bright as his second, and an anonymous cut man picked off a list. In the first round, Bruno attempted to make a fight of it, even though he went down in the first half-minute of boxing. He hit Tyson with two left hooks that Tyson later admitted were the hardest he'd taken in the ring. I was broadcasting the fight for HBO's Spanish language feed. I saw Tyson wobble, and I was worried. But then in the second round, although Tyson was missing with wild, badly timed strokes, strangely, I noticed Bruno's discouragement and knew it was a matter of time. Between rounds, Snowell and Bright shouted instructions at

Tyson, which the champion brilliantly ignored. It was as if no one was in his corner. Matt Baransky was in Albany, Kevin Rooney was in an HBO studio in Schenectady, Steve Lott (who bet Tyson before four – and of course lost) rooted for Mike from the fiftieth row.

In the fifth round, Tyson put Bruno away with a barrage of unsynchronised punches. Jim Jacobs's widow, Loraine, watched from the fourth ringside row as Tyson's natural power and speed concealed his inadequacies. That night Mike was a great puncher, but not the great fighter he could be. Not even close. The complex championship skills Cus D'Amato had drilled into him, the timing, the patience, the lightning combination punches, the side-to-side moves, and even the basic left jab, were missing – and so were Tyson's real cornermen, Mike's last link to the old man of boxing.

A man from Queens recently told me to leave Mike Tyson alone, to forget him. 'I was in the concentration camp and I know what it is to survive,' the man told me. 'You should only know what I did in order to pull through. I cheated and I lied and I robbed; I became a master of deception and I wounded and killed people. I had six nice, non-violent, decent brothers and sisters, and they all went straight to the ovens. I was the only one to survive. But I have never recovered.' The man had Tyson figured out, he said. Bedford-Stuyvesant and Brownsville were Tyson's concentration camps, he insisted. 'Only a very few ever recover, and Tyson is not one of them.'

The realist in me suspects the man may be right. But the young, starry-eyed fighter from a Puerto Rican ghetto who still has a place in my being – that part of me that still yearns for those 'special moments' in the ring – says it cannot be. Fight fans have waited too long, Mike Tyson has struggled too hard, for him not to get up off the canvas.

Fire and Fear
Warner Brothers
1989

Hamed Not Big Enough To Fill Ali's Boots

Kevin Mitchell

Naseem Hamed is one of the most exciting performers in boxing. Throwing darting punches from unexpected angles while seemingly off balance, this bewilderingly unorthodox showman has so far done everything that has been asked of him – just. Not all the performing is confined to the ring and the hype; extrovert behaviour and over-the-top laser-beam first-night preliminaries (which have, on occasions, taken longer than the actual contest) dismay many fighting aficionados.

Hamed already holds the WBO and IBF world featherweight titles and his laudable ambition is to capture the WBA and WBC belts to unify the division. Whether or not the politics of boxing will allow the chances for him to succeed remains to be seen. Only then will we know if the Yemeni Prince is really King of the Ring.

Naseem Hamed, supernova, claimed recently never to have heard of Tiger Woods, a mere moon, apparently, in the sporting galaxy. Youthful flippancy? Probably. But the impression was strengthened that the semi-detached fighter is often out of touch with reality and cares little for matters that do not involve sparring all day, dancing all night or crashing one of his 13 cars on a Yorkshire roundabout he ought to know as well as spit-bucket. Indeed, he talks like he drives: with his eyes in the skies and the accelerator flat to the floor.

Last week Naz was at it again. Before leaving for New York to fight the tough American Kevin Kelley this Friday at Madison Square Garden, a venue that demands respect for its richly storied past, he was asked to confirm that he had claimed, 'I'm a young Ali coming to town'. He had, he said, and he was. Even so, he looked uncomfortable as he shifted ever so slightly under the deceptively gentle television inquisition, head lolloping boyishly on to his designer-labelled shoulder as he sought to justify his impertinence, compounding his blasphemy with each verbal ricket. He might even be better than his idol, he said. If not yet, soon. Ali had one way of boxing; he, the prince who would be king before Christmas, had five ways. It was an unsophisticated declaration of his credentials, bringing more gasps of dudgeon than disbelief from those old boxing hands still unconvinced about either Hamed's substance or his presentation.

Is he even halfway entitled to such bombast? On the face of it, Naz is as absurdly absent-minded an historian of boxing as he is of golf. He ought to be sat down in front of a few old videos for a day or so and watch the magic of Ali flicker in front of him, not one way or five but a thousand. He should observe how a man of 15 stone could pirouette on his left toe in front of an oncoming juggernaut such as Joe Frazier and, defying all laws of physics and boxing, snake a right hand into Joe's fearsome mush, pull back, shift under the retaliatory left hook that could wreck a phone box, and flit to safety. He should watch him make Sonny Liston, the bona fide monster, miss all but one punch in the first round they ever boxed. He should witness the punch-perfect dismantling of Cleveland Williams. He should draw lines on his television screen, charting the bewildering combinations – if he can slow the film. He should marvel at the balance and poise, the presence and beauty. He should soak up the monumental courage of the Rumble in the Jungle. Or the Thrilla in Manila. Or a score of other nights that it seems inconceivable will ever be bettered, or forgotten, yet which somehow are now regarded as merely on a par with the achievements of an outrageously gifted youth who has never fought further away from his home than Dublin and several of whose opponents have been fistic pensioners.

Finally, with pencil and paper, Naz should list all the times he has missed his target by a foot or more, sometimes almost throwing himself out of the ring. He should wonder why he no longer attempts combinations of more than a couple of punches. And he should ask himself how long he can survive at the highest level, chin in the air, with KO-crazy head-hunting that has become seriously predictable.

Most of all, Naz should get a life outside his little world, stop listening to the cacophony of sycophancy that inevitably attends someone capable of generating such huge amounts of money. And he should pay heed to his snow-haired Irish mentor Brendan Ingle occasionally, when he tells him that Ali was as big a man out of the ring as in it, that Ali's greatness was not in his fists but in his heart.

There is a case for the defence, of course. Naz is not such a bad kid as some might imagine. He can be rude, certainly, and I have seen him talk to Ingle as if he were the hired help. There was even a recent whisper that they had fallen out to the point where one of the longest and soundest manager–fighter relationships in boxing was in danger of disintegrating. But they are umbilically close, having known each other since Hamed was a spindly urchin scrapping on the streets of Wincobank, and they have survived many knockabout rows, in and out of the ring. Ingle, not so soppily Blarney-stone romantic as sometimes painted, recognised in the kid's sassiness from the outset the sort of mental strength needed for boxing. It has put steel in Hamed's mind that he translates to the very bones of his business, and from there to his opponents, all 28 of whom have suffered terribly because of it.

I would not expect Kelley to go more effectively where fighters of roughly similar pedigree – Johnson, Manuel Medina, Freddy Cruz and Vincenzo Belcastro – have fallen before, although it does not serve the promoter's purposes to downgrade the 30-year-old challenger in his own town, and he is formidably hard, with a string of good stoppages listed among the 32 on his 50-fight log. Still, as they optimistically expect to double a claimed 7,000 ticket sales before the off and fill this grand old place to near its 15,000 capacity, it might also be convenient to overlook a significant blot on his CV. In January 1995, Kelley, who was then billed as 'boxing's next little giant' and had not lost in 42 bouts, was comprehensively beaten up by the Mexican Alejandro 'Cobrito' Gonzalez. Kelley was knocked down and nearly out in the tenth, having absorbed an unhealthy amount of punishment for most of the contest, and could not come out for the eleventh, surrendering his World Boxing Council nine-stone title and subsequently being marginalised in the division.

Kelley's one-punch power remains a significant threat after nine years, and he will be well paid for his pains, lasting maybe half a dozen career-threatening rounds before resuming his reign as featherweight title-holder of the World Boxing Union, whose paltry bauble is not for sale here, but Hamed will go on to establish a reputation in America as the villain/magician Arab from Yorkshire, thundering over pundits and opponents with equal insouciance. And whatever the quality of the performance, you would bet he will accomplish his task with all the zestful showmanship befitting a 23-year-old teenager.

The ring is Naz's *Palais de Danse*; inside it, he is as mean as the old hoofer-pug-mobster George Raft, on the way to and from it, he is about as threatening as Prince. As a wildly unconventional practitioner of an art that historically demands strict adherence to proven principles, he has always carried irreverence to extremes, and with few bruises to show for it so far. Now he seeks to graft his ego on to boxing history.

Madison Square Garden – where Ali fought nine main events, where Joe Louis defended his title seven times, the spiritual home of Sugar Ray Robinson, Jack Dempsey, Willie Pep, Rocky Marciano, Henry Armstrong and a supporting cast of thousands – has already got a grip on Hamed. 'This is where Pep walked,' he said last week, while waiting for the multitudes to roll up and buy tickets. He'd heard of Pep; Mickey Duff reckoned Naz was better than him. He could be right. But who will possibly know until the Prince has proved himself against the very best? There are few better places to start that journey.

The Observer
14 December 1997

Acknowledgements

The man who really got this book underway was Bob Mee, whose remarkable knowledge of boxing enabled him to answer every query with practised ease. For his patient assistance and a well-stocked library, special thanks.

Immediately supportive also were those fight-game luminaries Norman Giller, Reg Gutteridge and Harry Mullan, and for their respective and readily-given permissions, much gratitude.

Others who helped in all sorts of ways were Bill Campbell; John Beaton; Sarah Edwards; John Pawsey; John Rawling and Janet Reeve. And a special cheer too for Linda Duncan who zealously sought the after-life of several defunct publishing houses on the copyright trail.

A compilation of this kind involves many people, not all of them in a position to realise they have been involved. A departure from earthly ways is, to some extent, arbitrary, but that seems no good reason not to thank retrospectively, or should it be posthumously, those now inhabiting other arenas.

And so, in spirit and in person, acknowledgements are due to: Nellie Bly, *New York World*; James J. Corbett, Curtis Publishers, G.P. Puttnam Publishing Group; the anonymous reporter from *The Sportsman*; Jack London, *New York World – Telegram and Sun*; The Society of Authors on behalf of the Bernard Shaw Estate, *The Nation*; Frank G. Menke, *The Sporting News*; James R. Fair, Smith and Durrell; Gene Tunney, British Publishers' Guild, Jonathan Cape, Random House; Jimmy Cannon, *Sports Magazine*; Dr Laurence F. McNamee, International Sports Limited; Rocky Graziano, Rowland Barber, Simon and Schuster, New York; Jake La Motta, Joseph Carter, Peter Savage, United Artists Corporation; Dominique Grimault, Patrick Mahé, Barbara Mitchell, W.H. Allen & Co., Editions Robert Laffont; Willie Pep, Robert Sacchi, Friday's Heroes Inc., Frederick Fell Publishers Inc.; Jack Birtley, New English Library, Hodder and Stoughton Publishers, Adam Sofianos; George Whiting, Leslie Frewin Publishers Ltd; Everett M. Skehan, Peter, Louise and Mary Anne Marciano, Robson Books Ltd; Harry Mullan, Canterbury, Colebridge Associates; Reg Gutteridge, Stanley Paul & Co. Ltd; Norman Giller, Henry Cooper, Macdonald, Queen Anne Press; Bob Mee, *Boxing News*; Greg Logan, *Sports N.Y.*, New York Newsday; José Torres, Warner Books; Kevin Mitchell, *The Observer*.

Thanks also for 'They Must Tike Me for a Proper Mugg' by A.J. Liebling originally published in *The New Yorker*, 12 October 1957, which is reprinted by the permission of Russell and Volkening as agents for the author (Copyright © A.J. Liebling, 1957, renewed 1985 by Norma Liebling Stonehill).

Finally, the publishers wish to point out that every effort has been made to trace all copyright holders for permission to include their pieces in this anthology. They apologise for any errors that may have occurred in the form of acknowledgement.